THE IDEA OF COMMUNISM VOLUME 3

THE IDEA OF COMMUNISM VOLUME 3

The Seoul Conference

EDITED BY ALEX TAEK-GWANG LEE
AND SLAVOJ ŽIŽEK

VERSO

London • New York

First published by Verso 2016
The collection © Verso 2016
Individual contributions © the contributors 2016

1 3 5 7 9 10 8 6 4 2

Verso
UK: 6 Meard Street, London W1F 0EG
US: 20 Jay Street, Suite 1010, Brooklyn, NY 11201
www.versobooks.com

Verso is the imprint of New Left Books

ISBN-13: 978-1-78478-394-5 (PB)
ISBN-13: 978-1-78478-393-8 (HB)
ISBN-13: 978-1-78478-396-9 (US EBK)
ISBN-13: 978-1-78478-395-2 (UK EBK)

British Library Cataloguing in Publication Data
A catalogue record for this book is available from the British Library

Library of Congress Cataloging-in-Publication Data
A catalog record for this book is available from the Library of Congress

Typeset in Cochin by Hewer Text UK Ltd, Edinburgh
Printed in the US by Maple Press

Contents

Editors' Note

This book is a collection of speeches and interventions that were presented at the Idea of Communism Conference in Seoul, 24 September–2 October 2013. The pursuit of communism has a long history throughout the Asian region. For countries like North and South Korea, Vietnam, Cambodia and China, the passage to a form of 'modernity' is even unthinkable without this history. The struggle between communism and anti-communism still defines the region's politics. The anti-communism once employed during the Cold War era, especially in South Korea, has not yet faded away, and is still used for attacking the left in many Asian countries. In this sense, Asia is a lively location for discussing the idea of communism from a non-Western perspective and evaluating whether the idea is universal; or, instead, whether it is to be defined by its regional situation, or by its historical or temporal moment or movement(s). The idea of communism, as Alain Badiou and Slavoj Žižek conceive it, involves the global struggle towards absolute equality. Seoul, the capital of South Korea, was chosen as the conference venue because here the idea of communism is once again in the air, re-insinuating the excluded passion for the real into the struggle for independence, justice and rights, into the seamless reality of global capitalism. The Korean peninsula is divided into two regimes, the North being an 'actually existing' communist country and the South, on the contrary, a highly developed capitalist country. But a conference such as this could never take place in the North, any more than in China. How should we read this apparent paradox? Here, in summary form, we have the history of communism's development: the negation of communism = anti-communism, and then the liberal negation of anti-communism (negation of the negation) = anti-anti-communism. But what of communism itself? As the authors in this collection all agree, today one should face up squarely to the legacy of anti-communism, and also to its future, and to the political and intellectual oppression of the idea of communism. Crucially, however, the alternative to such oppression is nothing so negative as anti-anti-communism in the Asian context. The contributors to this volume intervene on many issues relating to the reassessment or reaffirmation of the idea of communism in light of the various political experiments found across Asia and elsewhere.

Foreword: Why Communism Today?

Slavoj Žižek

Towards the end of September 2014, after declaring war on Islamic State, President Obama gave an interview to *60 Minutes* in which he tried to explain the rules of the US engagement: 'When trouble comes up anywhere in the world, they don't call Beijing, they don't call Moscow. They call us. That's always the case. America leads. We are the indispensable nation.' This holds also for environmental and humanitarian disasters: 'When there's a typhoon in the Philippines, take a look at who's helping the Philippines deal with that situation. When there's an earthquake in Haiti, take a look at who's leading the charge helping Haiti rebuild. That's how we roll. That's what makes us Americans.'

In mid October, however, Obama himself made a call to Tehran, sending a secret letter to Ayatollah Ali Khamenei in which he suggested a broader rapprochement between the United States and Iran based on their shared interest in combating Islamic State militants. Not only did Iran reject the offer, but when the news of the letter reached the wider public, the US Republicans denounced it as a ridiculous gesture of self-humiliation that can only strengthen Iran's arrogant view of the United States as a superpower in decline. That is how the United States rolls, effectively: acting alone in a multi-centric world, they more and more accumulate wars and lose the peace, doing the dirty job for others: for China and Russia, who have their own problems with Islamists, and even for Iran – the final result of the invasion of Iraq was to deliver Iraq to the political control of Iran. (The United States got caught in this process already in Afghanistan where their help to the fighters against the Soviet occupations gave birth to the Taliban.)

The ultimate source of these problems is the changed role of the United States in the global economy. An economic cycle is coming to an end, a cycle which began in the early 1970s, the time that saw the birth of what Yanis Varoufakis calls the 'Global Minotaur' – the monstrous engine that was running the world economy from the early 1980s to 2008. The late

1960s and the early 1970s were not just times of oil crisis and stagflation; Nixon's decision to abandon the gold standard for the US dollar was the sign of a much more radical shift in the basic functioning of the capitalist system. By the end of the 1960s, the US economy was no longer able to continue the recycling of its surpluses to Europe and Asia: its surpluses had turned into deficits. In 1971, the US government responded to this decline with an audacious strategic move: instead of tackling the nation's burgeoning deficits, it decided to do the opposite, to *boost deficits*. And who would pay for them? The rest of the world! How? By means of a permanent transfer of capital that rushed ceaselessly across the two great oceans to finance America's deficits: the United States has to suck up $1 billion each day flowing in from other nations to finance its domestic consumption, and is thereby the universal Keynesian consumer that keeps the world economy running. This influx relies on a complex economic mechanism: the United States is 'trusted' as the safe and stable centre, so that all others, from the oil-producing Arab countries to Western Europe and Japan, and now even the Chinese, invest their surplus profits in the United States. Since this 'trust' is primarily ideological and military, not economic, the problem for the United States is how to justify its imperial role – it requires a permanent state of war, in which it can offer itself as the universal protector of all other 'normal' (not 'rogue') states.

However, even before it has fully established itself, this world-system based on the primacy of the US dollar as the universal currency is breaking down and is being replaced by . . . what? This is what the ongoing tensions are about. The 'American century' is over, and we are witnessing the gradual formation of multiple centres of global capitalism – the United States, Europe, China, maybe Latin America, each of them standing for capitalism with a specific twist: the United States for neoliberal capitalism; Europe for what remains of the welfare state; China for 'Asian Values' (authoritarian) capitalism; Latin America for populist capitalism. In this world, the old and new superpowers are testing each other, trying to impose their own version of global rules, experimenting with them through proxies – which, of course, are other small nations and states.

The present situation thus bears an uncanny resemblance to that around 1900, when the hegemony of the British Empire was questioned by new rising powers, especially Germany, which wanted their piece of the colonial cake, and the Balkans was one of the locations of their confrontation. Today, the role of the British Empire is played by the United States, the new rising superpowers are Russia and China, and our Balkans is the Middle East. It is the same old battle for geopolitical influence: Moscow hears calls not only from the United States, but also from Georgia and Ukraine; maybe it will start hearing voices from the Baltic states.

There is another unexpected parallel with the situation before the outbreak of World War I: in recent months, the media have continually warned of the threat of World War III. Headlines such as 'The Russian Air Force's Super Weapon: Beware the PAK-FA Stealth Fighter' or 'Russia Is Ready for Shooting War, Will Likely Win Looming Nuclear Showdown with US' have abounded; at least once a week, Putin makes a statement seen as a provocation to the West, and a notable Western statesman or Nato figure warns against Russian imperialist ambitions; Russia expresses concerns about being contained by Nato, while Russia's neighbours fear Russian invasion – and so on. The very worried tone of these warnings seems to heighten the tension, exactly as in the decades before 1914. And in both cases the same superstitious mechanism is at work: that talking about it will prevent it from happening. We know about the danger, but we don't believe it can really happen – and that is why it can happen. That is to say, even if we don't really believe it can happen, we are all getting ready for it – and these actual preparations, largely ignored by the mainstream media, are mostly reported in marginal media:

> America is on a war footing. While [a] World War Three Scenario has been on the drawing board of the Pentagon for more than ten years, military action against Russia is now contemplated at an 'operational level' . . . We are not dealing with a 'Cold War'. None of the safeguards of the Cold War era prevail . . . The adoption of a major piece of legislation by the US House of Representatives on December 4 [2014] (H. Res. 758) would provide (pending a vote in the Senate) a de facto green light to the US president and commander in chief to initiate – without congressional approval – a process of military confrontation with Russia. Global security is at stake. This historic vote – which potentially could affect the lives of hundreds of millions of people worldwide – has received virtually no media coverage. A total media blackout prevails . . . On December 3, the Ministry of Defence of the Russian Federation announced the inauguration of a new military–political entity which would take over in the case of war. Russia is

launching a new national defense facility, which is meant to monitor threats to national security in peacetime, but would take control of the entire country in case of war.[1]

What further complicates matters is that the competing new and old superpowers are joined by a third factor: the radicalized fundamentalist movements in the Third World which oppose all of them but are prone to make strategic pacts with some of them. No wonder our predicament is getting more and more obscure: Who is who in the ongoing conflicts? How to choose between Assad and ISIS in Syria? Between ISIS and Iran? Such obscurity – not to mention the rise of drones and other arms systems that promise a clean, high-tech war without casualties (on our side) – gives a boost to military spending and makes the prospect of war more appealing.

If the basic underlying axiom of the Cold War was the axiom of MAD (Mutually Assured Destruction), the axiom of today's War on Terror seems to be the opposite one, that of NUTS (Nuclear Utilization Target Selection): the idea that, by means of a surgical strike, one can destroy the enemy's nuclear capacities while an anti-missile shield protects us from a counter-strike. More precisely, the United States adopts a differential strategy: it acts as if it continues to trust the MAD logic in its relations with Russia and China, while it is tempted to practice NUTS with Iran and North Korea. The paradoxical mechanism of MAD inverts the logic of the 'self-realizing prophecy' into a 'self-stultifying intention': the very fact that each side can be sure that, should it decide to launch a nuclear attack on the other side, the other side will respond with full destructive force, guarantees that no side will start a war. The logic of NUTS is, on the contrary, that the enemy can be forced to disarm if it is assured that we can strike at him without risking a counter-attack. The very fact that two directly contradictory strategies are mobilized simultaneously by the same superpower bears witness to the phantasmatic character of this entire reasoning.

How to stop our slide into this vortex? The first step is to leave behind all the pseudo-rational talk of the 'strategic risks' that we have to assume, as well as the notion of historical time as a linear process of evolution in which, at each moment, we have to choose between different options of action. We have to accept the threat as our fate: it is not just a question of

---

1   Michael Chossudovsky, 'War on Russia: House Declares War on Putin', 6 December 2014, at veteransnewsnow.com.

avoiding risks and making the right choices within the global situation; the true threat resides in the situation in its entirety, in our 'fate'. If we continue to 'roll on' the way we are now, we are doomed, no matter how carefully we proceed. So the solution is not to be very careful and avoid risky acts – in acting like this, we fully participate in the logic that leads to catastrophe. The solution is to become fully aware of the explosive set of interconnections that makes the entire situation dangerous. Once we have achieved this, we should be able to embark on the long and difficult work of changing the coordinates of the entire situation. Nothing less will do.

Nothing less than a new communist project.

General Introduction to the Seoul Conference

Alain Badiou

After London, Berlin and New York, I am pleased to be in Seoul to open the fourth international conference on the word 'communism'.

First I want convey to Alex Taek-Gwang Lee, Yong Soon Seo and all their friends my personal gratitude, and the gratitude of my great philosophical comrade Slavoj Žižek, for their magnificent work. Without them, this conference would have been absolutely impossible. And this work was not easy – not easy in general, and specifically not easy in Korea, for evident historical reasons. So, my friends, thank you!

We are here to discuss whether it is possible to use the word 'communism' after the disasters or the last century.

Certainly, this discussion is also about the tension, maybe the contradiction, between the classical use of this word, by Marx, Lenin and many other thinkers and activists on one side; and, on the other side, the necessity of a new meaning and a new use of this word.

We are here in Korea, a country that was destroyed and divided since World War II by the effects of the Cold War between the socialist states and the capitalist Western world. We have the duty to affirm that this conference has no relation at all with this historical disaster. We have nothing to do with the nationalist and military state of North Korea. We have, more generally, nothing to do with the communist parties that here and there continue the old fashion of the last century. Under the beautiful word 'communism', in its original meaning, we seek a new strategic vision for the collective destiny of humanity as such.

For almost thirty years, the present, our historical present, has been a disoriented time: a time that does not offer its youth, especially the youth of the popular classes, any principle to orient their existence. The continuation of globalized capitalism provides no sense at all of collective and individual existence. This is why we can, and probably must, return to the old discussions, during the nineteenth century, concerning progress, historical becoming, and the great contradiction between the huge power of private property and the idea of a collective organization of productive energy. All of this was in fact a discussion concerning the word 'communism' as a unique alternative to the violent birth and success of modern capitalism.

So what can the principle and the name of a genuine orientation be today? I propose that, in keeping with the history of the politics of emancipation, we call it *the communist hypothesis*.

Let us note in passing that our critics want to scrap the word 'communism' under the pretext of the tragic failure of an experience with socialist states, also named 'popular democracies', that lasted for seventy years. What a joke! When it is a question of overthrowing the domination of the rich and the inheritance of power, which have lasted millennia, their objections rest on seventy years of stumbling steps, violence and impasses! Truth be told, the communist idea has only traversed an infinitesimal portion of the time of its verification, of its effectuation.

What is this hypothesis? It can be summed up in three axioms.

First, the idea of equality. The prevalent pessimistic idea, which once again dominates our time, is that human nature is destined to inequality; that it is of course a shame that this is so, but that once we have shed a few tears about this, it is crucial to grasp it and accept it. To this view, the communist idea responds not exactly with the proposal of equality as a plan, but by declaring that the egalitarian principle allows us to distinguish, in every collective action, that which is in keeping with the communist hypothesis, and therefore possesses a real value, from that which contradicts it, and thus throws us back to an animal vision of humanity.

Second, we have the conviction that the existence of a separate coercive state is not necessary. This is the thesis, shared by anarchists and communists, of the withering away of the state. There have existed societies without the state, and it is rational to postulate that there may be others in the future. But above all, it is possible to organize popular political action without subordinating it to the idea of power, representation within the state, elections, and so on. The liberating constraint of organized action can be exercised outside the state. There are many examples of this, including some recent ones.

Third, a final axiom: the organization of work does not imply its division, the specialization of tasks, and in particular the oppressive differentiation between intellectual and manual labour. It is necessary and possible to aim for the essential polymorphousness of human labour.

This is the material basis of the disappearance of classes and social hierarchies.

These three principles are *maxims of orientation*, which anyone can use as a yardstick to evaluate what he or she says and does, personally or collectively, in its relation to the communist hypothesis.

After the clear explanation of the communist hypothesis by Marx and Engels during the nineteenth century, after the attempts to create a new society by the pure strength of some states during the last century, we are in a third stage of the possible existence of a strategic communist vision of our future.

What we need, in these early days of this third sequence, is a *provisional morality* for a disoriented time. It is a matter of maintaining a minimally consistent subjective figure, without being able to rely on the communist hypothesis, which has yet to be re-established on a grand scale. It is necessary to find *a real point* to hold, whatever the cost, an 'impossible' point that cannot be inscribed in the law of the situation. We must hold a real point of this type and organize its consequences.

For example, in practically all the European countries today, the living proof that our societies are obviously inhuman is the foreign undocumented worker, and more generally the status of strangers coming from Asia or Africa. All these strangers, who are the new workers in our cities, are the sign, immanent to our situation, that *there is only one world*. To treat the foreign proletarian as though he or she came from *another world*, this is indeed the specific task of the police vision of the world. This idea that there exists a good and human world and an other world, neither good nor really human, has its own police force (the 'border police'). To affirm, against this apparatus of the state, that any worker, even undocumented, belongs to the same world as us, and to draw the practical, egalitarian and militant consequences of this – this is an example of a type of provisional morality, a local orientation in keeping with the communist hypothesis, amid the global disorientation which only its re-establishment will be able to counter.

The principal virtue that we need is *courage*. This is not always the case: in other circumstances, other virtues may have priority. For instance, during the revolutionary war in China, Mao promoted *patience* as the cardinal virtue. But today, it is undeniably courage. Courage is the virtue that manifests itself, without regard for the laws of the world, in the endurance of the impossible. It is a question of holding the impossible point without needing to account for the whole of the situation: courage, to the extent that it is a matter of treating the point as such, *is a local virtue*. It partakes of a morality of place, and its horizon is the slow re-establishment of the communist hypothesis.

Our conference is also a conference dedicated to the new courage – the courage to affirm that we can clarify the world and its future in terms of the practical new meaning of this old word: communism. So I can only conclude: 'Courage!'

1 The Crisis of Representativeness and Post-Party Politics

Wang Hui

The Decline of Representation in Global Politics

The decline of representation in contemporary politics is the result of a unique, multilayered political crisis.[1] First of all, its core aspect, a crisis of party politics, is a fracture of representativeness, a discursive failure of established political values in actual political processes, and consequently a crisis of legitimacy. Party politics took its modern shape in nineteenth-century Europe. In China, it was the most important political innovation of the twentieth century. The party politics of the Xinhai Revolution period, especially between 1911 and 1915, attempted to emulate the multiparty parliamentary system developed in the framework of European constitutional politics. Faced with the challenges of secessionism, monarchical restoration, and the crisis of republicanism, the revolutionaries and many political elites began to shift away from their original political objectives.

The leading party as vanguard

There were three prerequisites for the formation of the uniquely Chinese modern party politics. First, after the establishment of the Republic of China, regional secessionism, military separatism and partisanship interlocked with one another, leading to the formation of a new national politics crucial in early Republican-period political thinking. Second, during World War I, many political parties in the West participated in nationalist war mobilization and supplied a political impetus for the war. Consequently, reflection on traditional modes of party politics peaked among European intellectuals after World War I. The reconstruction of

---

1   An earlier version of this article was published, in Chinese, in *Beijing Cultural Review* 文化纵横, January 2013. This version was published in *Modern China*, the author has expanded and revised some parts of the article.

Chinese party politics occurred in this intellectual atmosphere. Lastly, when the Russian Revolution erupted during World War I, some Chinese revolutionaries believed that Bolshevism as a political model could overcome the limits of bourgeois party politics. (Debates and reflections on Bolshevism and its party structure also began in this period, but I do not have enough space to elaborate on this issue.) In other words, the crisis and failure of party politics gave birth to the party system that was the political nucleus of this revolutionary century. In contrast to the parties in crisis, this new model of political parties, influenced by the Russian Revolution and the Comintern, bore the dual features of a super-political party (超级政党) and a 'supra party' (超政党). The term 'super-political party' indicates that both competing parties, the Guomindang (GMD) and the Chinese Communist Party (CCP), were obliged to adopt some of the elements or forms of party politics and claim themselves to be political parties, but neither of them intended to form a competitive party politics within the structure of a parliamentary system. Instead, both aimed to become a hegemonic party, or 'leading party'. The term 'supra party' implies that the political representation of both parties was different from the multi- or dual-party structure of a parliamentary system, and was much more similar to the Gramscian concept of a 'modern prince' who represents the people and the future. In the case of the CCP, the role of party is that of the vanguard of the proletariat. The theory and praxis of 'people's war' that was developed in the late 1920s and expanded during the war against the Japanese invasion (1931–45) and the civil war (1945–49) generated a new form of party politics. It consolidated military struggle, land revolution, base-area building, and the construction of a revolutionary constitutional state into an unprecedented practice, the core of which was political strategies – namely, military struggle, the mass line, and the united front. With its class politics based on the proletariat, the union of workers and peasants, and the united front for national liberation, the CCP eventually overtook the GMD, which gradually deviated from the peasant movement and mass politics towards state politics.

The detachment of the political system from social forms

In both the multiparty system in the West and the system of multiparty cooperation under one-party rule in China, the representativeness of political parties has become increasingly obscure. In the case of China, the representativeness and the politics of the party have mutated drastically as categories such as the proletariat, the union of workers and peasants, and the united front have lost their clarity.[2] After the PRC was established, the Communist Party searched for a new path for its own renovation under the conditions following people's war. The failure of the Cultural Revolution signified the end of this search, as well as the beginning of the full integration of the party into the framework of the state. In my view, the decline or rupturing of representation is the consequence of depoliticization, the most severe symptom of which is the statification of the party: the party has submitted itself increasingly to the logic of the state, depriving itself of its essence, which should be a form of political organization and political movement, as both its function and form of organization have been assimilated to the state apparatus. This process implies the end of the mass line that had engendered the political dynamism of the CCP. Two interrelated forms of the statification of the party can be identified: first, the bureaucratization of the party in the early days before the economic reform, which became one of the pivotal reasons why the Cultural Revolution was launched; second, the marriage between the party and capital in the process of the corporationalization of government during the market reforms. For the party, the rupture of representativeness manifests itself most intensely in the incongruity between the party's claim to general representativeness as it transcends previous class categories and its increasing distance from the people, especially those from lower social strata. There are of course policies protective of workers and peasants; however, we can barely find any organic connection between party politics and the politics of workers and peasants.

The detachment of the political system from social forms happens not only in socialist or post-socialist countries, but also in European and American parliamentary party systems, as well as in other political systems based on them. In China, the relationship between the party and its class base has become ever more vague, just as among Western political parties the distinction between the left and the right has blurred. In the contemporary world, the fracture of representativeness has so intensified that it leads to the belief that the type of party politics that flourished

---

2   The 'decline of representation', which suggests a detachment between the political system and social forms, is an issue that I have discussed on various occasions. In Wang Hui, 'Depoliticized Politics, the Multiple Components of Hegemony, and the Eclipse of the Sixties', *Inter-Asia Cultural Studies* 7: 4 (December 2006), I discuss the question of depoliticized politics, and in Wang Hui, 汪晖 '再问'什么的平等' ('The Decline of Representation: Another Inquiry on "Equality of What"'), *Beijing Cultural Review* 5 (October 2011) and 6 (December 2011), I explore the different types of equality crisis and their relationship with the crisis of representativeness.

in the nineteenth and the twentieth centuries has already disappeared, or persists merely in confined areas; it is transforming or has already transformed into a state-party politics – that is, one that serves as a structure of state power. Unlike in the nineteenth and early twentieth centuries, it is hard to find in contemporary party politics political movements with a clear agenda. The growing scale of the political party and its monopoly of state power are normally interpreted as the expansion of party politics. However, if we investigate whether it is political parties that control the state, or the converse – the logic of the state that controls parties – the latter may be the proper answer. The boundary between party and state is vanishing, the outcome of their assimilation being precisely the dissolution of political representativeness, which in turn renders power relations in the political sphere no longer capable of balancing or reducing the inequality in the socioeconomic sphere, but instead only of providing institutional support for such inequality. Under the conditions of the fracture of representativeness, the political rhetoric of politicians degrades into a performance aimed at grabbing power, while technocratic bureaucrats inevitably gain higher political positions. In the Western multiparty or dual-party structure, the role of political parties is fundamentally that of voter mobilization, pivoting on elections that take place every four or five years. This is more like a state apparatus for the rotation of leaders.

In the twentieth century, the super-political party in China originally possessed an intense politicalness sustained by rigorous organization, a straightforward value orientation, and mass movements mobilized through the vigorous interaction between theory and political practice. However, under the contemporary mode of political parties, party organization almost equals administrative organization. The party has become a component of the management apparatus, its function of mobilization and supervision increasingly identical with the state mechanism as its bureaucratic features intensify and its politicalness diminishes. The crisis of representativeness in party politics is a crisis for ruling parties as well as for non-ruling parties. In China nowadays, the representativeness of the democratic parties has become unprecedentedly elusive.

The waning of the representativeness of public institutions that mediate between state and society (parliaments in the West; in China, the National People's Congress and the Chinese People's Political Consultative Conference) echoes the above-mentioned process. In parliamentary democracy, seats in the parliament usually centre on political parties. There are theoretical debates regarding whether parliament functions as part of the state or as an institutionalization that includes certain public spheres. But with the statification of political parties, the connection between parliament and society is gradually being severed. During a visit to India, I noted that grassroots social movements prospered there. Even the most active types of social movement, however, could not play a parallel role in the making of public policy, because political parties monopolized parliamentary power. In contrast, in terms of theoretical orientation, the social representation system used by the People's Congress of China seems more removed from party politics than does party-centred parliamentary politics. In practice, this social representation model needs to be buttressed by politics centred on the so-called mass line, the decline or the transformation of which will undermine the process of selecting people's representatives and the role of the People's Congress in the political life of China. The ratio of representatives in the People's Congress – for instance, the percentage of workers and peasants whose numbers in the People's Congress are disproportionate to their contribution to Chinese society – has often been criticized in the past. The homology between a system of representation and social power relations is a symptom of the crisis of representative politics, and a consequence of depoliticization.

The second aspect of the decline of representation relates to the fact that typical public spheres, such as the media, are experiencing a crisis of publicity. The large-scale expansion of the media entails the contraction of the public sphere: freedom of the media industry has replaced the freedom of speech of citizens; the media are not only unprecedentedly allied with capital, power and the media's own interests, but in some cases even attempt to take over the role of political organizations, the party among them. In Italy, Silvio Berlusconi's media group propagates values that enabled him, a criminal suspect, to be elected prime minister repeatedly. The media, especially massive media groups – regardless of whether they are private or state-owned – cannot be simplistically reckoned as an independent vehicle for citizen and public opinion. They should rather be seen as a network of interests disguised as a public vehicle. The permeation of media influence in political and other public spaces cannot be considered as part of a process of democratization either; rather, it is the colonization of these spheres. On the surface, we can say that the media are controlled by politics. But, in reality, the political sphere is also being gradually colonized by the media – political figures cajole the public with claptrap, and it is not unusual that they adopt discourses structured by the logic of the Eastern and Western media. The Chinese media have been industrialized and corporational-ized since the 1990s because of the new political and economic strategies of the party aimed at adapting to marketization and globalization. But with the statification of the political party, the corporatization of the government, and the partification of the media, the relationship between the media and the party has turned into a contest between two entangled sets of interests that, in their games of strategic conflict or cooperation, resort to pretensions either to democracy and liberty, or to stability, rule of law and situation awareness. The confrontation between the editorial department of *South Weekend* and the Guangdong Provincial Party Committee in the early spring of 2013, for example, was absolutely not a struggle between public opinion and the state, but an entanglement that arose as both sides hijacked public demands – in other words, a confron-tation that emerged in the process of the contemporary redistribution of power. The two sides had different interests, but their political discourses were nearly identical.

In China today, censorship is a deep-rooted problem. The realm of public speech is crying out for true reform. But any reform based on the established structure will become merely a struggle for power that disguises itself as a demand for a free press. Today, the methods used to suppress public opinion have changed: the media have often served as one of the mechanisms to muzzle public opinion. Such a power struggle evinces the political competition between partified media and the tradi-tional political party that generated them. The former possess more political energy and features; the latter resembles an entrapped power apparatus deprived of its ideological function, no longer a political organization in the classical sense. Ironically, these two sides are none-theless parabiotic. They replace and conceal the problems of political debates and freedom of speech with games of strategic conflict and cooperation.

The third aspect of the decline of representation is the crisis of law. Under depoliticization, legal procedures are often manipulated by inter-est groups. This manipulation is seen not only in general legal procedures, but also permeates the process of legislation. Hence, instead of simply asserting proceduralist opinions, it is an urgent and unavoidable necessity for the legal reforms of our day to reconsider the relationship between law and politics.

The problems in the three above-mentioned areas constitute the essence of today's political transformation.

Hence, I raise the following questions: As party politics has degenerated into the politics of a state-party or state-parties, is a post-party politics possible? While modern political parties are still widespread around the world, the post-party politics alluded to here refers not to politics after political parties disappear, but to the fact that the political party has already taken up new features in the context of depoliticization. The political party was established in nineteenth-century Europe on the basis of a political movement. In twentieth-century China, party politics – especially Communist Party politics – was largely reshaped by people's war and its political aftermath. On the one hand, the term 'post-political party' indicates that, although parties still act as leading political entities, in reality they have lost the representativeness held by parties in the nineteenth and twentieth centuries, and have parted from their original logic. At the same time, political forms have stabilized – major political institutions were built upon the principle of the representativeness of party politics. Consequently, the fracture of representativeness has become the main symptom of today's political crisis. On the other hand, the term 'post-party politics' indicates the necessity of devising a new form, and corresponding practice, beyond the framework of party politics. The key issues for post-party politics are how and on what level to reconstruct representativeness, or even whether we should think differently about representativeness itself. In the political practice of twentieth-century China, elements of post-party politics were active, but only as the practice of a super-political party – namely, as people's war, the mass line, and the united front. All these practices of representativeness attempted to move beyond conventional relations of representation. Although it partly evolved from such super-party politics, present-day party politics in China has also been generated by the degradation of a super-party into a state-party system. In order to overcome the crisis of representation, we need to reconstruct representativeness and explore new avenues of post-party politics.

Today, representativeness cannot be reconstructed by repeating old slogans or praxis. We have to face the problems of representative politics and the detachment of social structure from the political system. From this perspective, two dimensions of post-party politics need to be tackled: we should re-examine the principles of representative politics in twentieth-century China, and explore the conditions and possibilities of post-party politics.

Rethinking the Principles of Representative Politics of Twentieth-Century China

The problems of representativeness, as well as the related problem of a system of representation, were the core issues facing modern political systems. In the nineteenth and twentieth centuries, the content of representative politics consisted of categories such as political party and social class, as well as their actual application in the framework of state politics. After monarchy declined, representative politics became connected with problems of democracy. Political principles of representative politics in China differ from those in the West, which pivot on a parliamentary multiparty system and principles of universal suffrage. This difference has been fundamentally misunderstood and neglected. We need to clarify the problems related to the forms of democracy: Western democracy based on general elections is not the only model of democracy; nor is democracy a mere abstract form. It has to be based on political momentum, without which none of the democratic forms can survive.

The meaning of 'the working class as the leading class'
In analyzing the principles of Chinese representative politics, we could start with the constitution of the PRC. The Chinese constitution is seldom quoted by constitutional scholars in discussing the meaning of constitutionalism. Its Article 1 states: 'The People's Republic of China is a socialist state under people's democratic dictatorship led by the working class and based on the alliance of workers and peasants'; and Article 2 declares: 'All power in the People's Republic of China belongs to the people.' These two articles illustrate the principles of representative politics during the socialist period, which were constituted by many fundamental political categories. But these political categories cannot be reduced to common-sense categories: they cannot be verified by simple a priori principles, or understood as general empirical facts. They emerged in twentieth-century China in the political praxis of revolution.

For example, what does 'the working class as the leading class' mean? In the first half of the twentieth century, the Chinese working class was weak. The Chinese Revolution, judged by the composition of its participants, was mainly a peasant revolution. How can the working class become the leading class? In empirical terms, it is also disputable whether the bourgeoisie, as opposed to the working class, could be regarded as a class in itself. For most of the twentieth century, the working class made up only a small fraction of the Chinese population, but it nonetheless generated class revolution and class politics. Today China has the largest working class in the world, but there is no class politics of a commensurate magnitude.

The concepts of class and class politics are interconnected, but need to be treated separately. Modern Chinese class politics certainly had its objective reality and material basis, which can only be grasped from the perspective of a universal connection. Without theoretical analysis, political mobilization could not have existed. Without people's war from the late 1920s to the late 1940s, the practice of class politics, with the peasants as its major participants and representing the proletariat, would have been impossible; without Third World countries' efforts to industrialize through a socialist approach, the subjectivity of the working class could not have been created. The working class as an objective reality cannot spontaneously spark working-class politics. Without the building of political organizations for the working class, without movements fighting for it and its liberation, there cannot be a working-class politics.

The identification of the working class as the leading class is a political statement rather than a positivist conclusion. It was generated in the political and economic analysis of the conditions of China and of other oppressed nations in the context of global capitalist development, and emerged only with people's war and the campaign for the construction of a socialist state. Thus we can say that working-class politics emerged from theoretical analysis of the internal contradictions in so-called 'backward areas' (rural societies) due to the imbalances of capitalism, and the socialist movements within them. It is in this context that 'class' is not a general, positivist category of analysis, but one of political economy rooted in the analysis of capitalist production and expansion. As capitalism and imperialism expanded, all the non-Western areas, including China, were woven into the structure of the global capitalist division of labour. Industrial capitalism centred on the West subjugated all the social classes and social domains. Consequently, in every society, struggles against one's own unequal condition and governance all aimed at abolishing class exploitation. Capitalist class exploitation is the final stage of class exploitation. This is why, although China in the early twentieth century did not have a large working class, it witnessed the rapid growth of working-class politics within large-scale political and military struggles initiated by peasants, students and urban citizens. The genesis and reality of working-class politics cannot be denied by reference to the small number of working-class participants. In other words, class politics refers to movements against the contradictions created by the logic of capitalism and its derivative class inequality. Hence, the political concept of class, and with it the concept of a leading class, cannot be equated with class in the sense of social stratification or occupational division. The essence of leadership is located in the fact that it constitutes the momentum – which has different manifestations in different historical periods – to change this capitalist logic.

Two crucial social realities formed the basis for the working class to become the leading class representing the people's general interests. First, China was an agricultural society, and 90 per cent of its population were peasants. Hence, the representativeness of the working class had to connect with the problems of the peasants and include the peasants in order to construct the political category of 'the people'. Second, the working class was not only an appurtenance of capitalist production, but also a political identity constructed as the opponent of the capitalist class, and reflected the general interests and the future of the people. The existence of the working class as an appurtenance of capitalist production – as reified forms of labour – is not equivalent to the existence of class politics. Class politics, manifested as a general impetus liberated from the capitalist logic of production, originated from the analysis of the capitalist global division of labour, of the dynamic of its internal contradiction, and of its political practice in many areas, including those without industrialization. As the characteristics of national oppression under capitalism differed from those in the pre-capitalist period, class politics also represented the interests of the oppressed nations, and the liberation of the working class included national liberation. The concept of 'leadership' signified the political momentum for comprehensive social movements: although in different periods it can be represented by particular dominant political forces, this concept does not refer to a political bureaucratic system. The logic of modern political transformation was generated not according to established social structures, but by theoretically analyzing capitalist development. This theoretical analysis and its political praxis directly shaped a new political subjectivity. It is for this reason that, even when the structure of social classes changes, political momentum that has emerged in response to inequality can still remain vigorous by means of diversified political participation, theoretical debates and social experiments.

The depoliticization of the category of class

Today, however, the political logic of the twentieth century has weakened. Most intellectuals investigate social stratification and its politics in China from a positivist perspective. Right-wing, and even some left-wing, intellectuals believe that in twentieth-century China, because the working class, compared with the peasant and other social classes, has occupied a very limited space in political life, and because the capitalist class was immature, the nature of China's modern revolution could not be socialist, and the working class could not truly become the leading class. This positivist opinion, to some extent, deconstructs the foundational principles of the Chinese Revolution and modern Chinese politics. It prevailed when the flow of historical theoretical analysis, the main element of twentieth-century politics, receded. Intellectuals taking this approach share the view that 'class' is a structural and essentialist concept, and refuse to recognize its political character based on a politico-economic analysis of capitalism.

In the context of depoliticization, the concept of 'class' begins to follow a formalistic logic, and slips towards a structural concept of 'class division'. Currently, the connotation of class barely differs from the notion of stratification in contemporary sociology, which pivots around the state and regards social strata as objective structures without any impetus for the political. In contrast, the twentieth-century concept of class is political. Its connection with the state – in, for example, the concepts of the workers' state or the socialist state – was represented formally by the pioneer party and its class alliance. Without the background of people's war and the campaign for the construction of a socialist state, there would have been no class politics in praxis. Based on the concept of class as a structural stratification, a structural system of representation could accordingly be established in the socialist state. The system of social representation used in political parties and the People's Congress is an example. On the contrary, although in the twentieth century it contained elements of social stratification and its politics consequently included elements such as proportional representation, the concept of class was fundamentally political. It was closely associated with political representativeness or political leadership, of which the so-called 'mass line' policy was its actualization. Hence today's social sciences can neither explain the crisis of representativeness nor provide an understanding of the origin of twentieth-century representative politics. Under depoliticization, the dilemma caused by the fracture of representativeness cannot be resolved by the nonetheless necessary and positive steps of increasing seats for certain classes, such as workers or peasants, in the political party or in the People's Congress. Reconstructing representativeness and repoliticization are actually two different expressions of the same problem, the latter referring to the need to re-analyze the internal contradictions and imbalances within contemporary capitalism in order to discover its driving force and change its logic.

The Conditions for Post-Political Party Politics

To return to the topic of the formation of class politics in the early twentieth century, Chinese class politics at that time already had elements of supra-representative politics, since the political parties that played the central role in such politics had features like those of a supra-political or super-political party. If we use the classical Chinese political concepts 'rites and music' (礼乐) and 'institutions' (制度) as a basis for comparison, so-called supra-representativeness can be compared to the logic of 'rites and music', and representativeness to the logic of 'system'. Just as 'rites and music' refer to systems that are to be formed and forming, supra-representativeness indicates a political process that allows people to participate and leads to the formation of order (秩序). This process emphasized by supra-representativeness functions also within the framework of a representative system, but is not its equivalent.

After World War I, prolonged debates on parliamentary politics broke out between different political schools, and even between communists from different countries. A key issue in the debates was the redefinition of the political party. In the struggle between the GMD and the CCP and in the war against the Japanese invasion, armed struggle, the mass line and the united front – as well as party construction in the practice of these principles – became political assets for the CCP. The mass line, summarized as 'all for the masses; all rely on the masses; from the masses and to the masses', was the guideline by which this supra- or super-political party politics was consolidated. First applied to the construction of the base areas, and later to the governing of the whole country, the mass line was a political praxis that inherited or borrowed from some forms and principles of the Western representational system that originated in the nineteenth and twentieth centuries, such as the election of representatives and the narrative of representativeness. This was true not only of the CCP, but of all the other democratic parties as well. It remains clear that this political praxis contains supra- or post-political party elements that embody the endeavours to establish organic and political connections between the political party and society.

In the political heritage of twentieth-century China, the supra-repre-sentativeness of Chinese representative politics bears two essential features: the importance of culture and theory, and the sustaining of the political dynamics of the party through the practice of the mass line.

Theoretical debates and 'self-revolution'

A recurring phenomenon in modern Chinese history was that cultural movements established the foundation for new politics, while political parties in turn attempted to discipline cultural movements. The emer-gence of political representativeness and political subjectivity was closely linked with cultural movements and theoretical struggles, to which histor-ical research was often subordinate. I do not have enough space here for a thorough discussion of these cultural movements and what we might learn from them, and will instead focus on one point: I believe political dynamics always come from the interaction between culture and politics. They will be lost if the political party overly interferes with or disciplines cultural movements, thereby destroying the interaction between politics and culture. Today, culture is generally categorized as a sphere independ-ent from politics and economy. It is no longer a space for the continuous creation of new political subjectivity. The term 'culture industry' encap-sulates the position of culture in an economic society. In his *On Contradiction*, Mao Zedong writes that, in backward countries, theory normally occu-pies the primary position; it is impossible to establish a new politics without theoretical development. Founding a theory does not mean draw-ing up plans behind closed doors. The relation between theory and its praxis determines the results of theoretical struggle: Is it a relation between theory removed from reality and its dogmatic politics, or between theory that comes from and resorts to praxis and its application? To emphasize the importance of praxis is not to deny the importance of debates on ideas, theories and lines (路线), but to oppose dogmatism in order to prevent a separation between the policy orientation of the politi-cal party and the demands of society.

The Chinese state system is characterized by the symbiosis between the party and the government, which generates energy as well as crisis. Simply praising or criticizing this union cannot resolve any problems. Rather, we should try to understand why this system can, under certain conditions, generate political energy, and, under others, weaken the political energy of the party to an unprecedented degree, and force it to prostrate itself before the logic of power and capital. In other words, it is not productive simplistically to denounce the union between the political party and the state in general; instead, we should analyze its various forms and connotations. The formation of the structure of Chinese party politics is closely associated with the Chinese revolutionaries' exploration of the socialist path. State ownership that aimed at resolving the contradiction inherent in capitalist private ownership provided a historical prerequisite for the direct union of the state and capital in the days of reform. That the state was in control of a large amount of capital had the benefit of enabling the state to be free from manipulation by a single capitalist or oligarch, and to maintain its strong regulatory capacity. But in the circumstances of depoliticization, political energy is mainly manifested through state power – especially administrative power, rather than political power. With the weakening of political power, state power is also gradually surrendering to the control of interest networks centred around capital. Accordingly, like privately owned capital, state-owned capital also faces the same problems of corruption, monopoly, and, as a result, inefficiency. Hence, the crucial problem is not the privatization of state-owned property, but how to free state-owned property in China from interest networks centred around capital. The dissolution of subjective initiative due to the alliance between power and capital is a consequence of depoliticization. Since the positive and negative elements of the system are entangled with each other, we will inevitably face a political crisis if there is no continuous 'self-revolution' to create new political energy.

During the Chinese Revolution and the ensuing socialist period, theoretical debates within the party were one of the methods of accumulating political energy and adjusting the direction of development: the elevation of practical problems to the level of theoretical discussions and debates on lines can generate a new political momentum; it is also the best approach for helping people understand that the best way to correct mistakes is through debate based on praxis and the implementation of appropriate institutional adjustments. Even during that time, such debates were not confined to the intra-party sphere, but were enriched by the mass line and by the reciprocal relations between theory and praxis. After thoroughgoing reform, such theoretical debates ineluctably extended to the social sphere. There are several prerequisites for post-political party politics – namely, citizens' freedom of speech, space for debate in the political sphere, citizens' political participation supported by modern technology, and the reinstallation of labourers to the centre of Chinese political life. The healthy development of political debates and citizens' political participation will not be achieved without reforming the political sphere, the essence of which is to set ourselves free from the logic of media capital as it conglomerates and functions in the role of a party, in order to create a space of true tolerance and freedom. Only on this premise can positive interaction between social debates and public policy adjustments be accomplished. Today, the forces suppressing citizens' freedom of speech come not only from the traditional political sphere, but also from media power that has been corporatized and partified. The tasks of expanding the public sphere and opposing a media monopoly do not contradict one another.

Theoretical debates cannot be treated as abstract discussions removed from political practice; rather, they are a recapitulation of practice, also using the outcome of practice and new practice to examine previous theories and practice. The experience of the Chinese Revolution is based on praxis, correcting its mistakes through theoretical debates and political struggle, and consequently creating premises for new strategies and new practice. In *On Practice*, Mao Zedong argues that the Chinese Revolution had no pre-existing model, and that it was always learning and exploring. So too for reform. In the twentieth century, whenever theoretical debates and the struggle over the political line were relatively active, the political realm was also more lively and the innovations in political structure more dynamic. The current practice of 'decentralizing power and transferring benefits' (放权让利) has increased the importance of local experiments; theoretical orientations should accordingly be more diverse. The dynamic of reform in China largely derives from different local experiments and their competition, and from the constructive dialectical interaction between central and local governments, termed 'initiative from two sources' (两个积极性).

Struggles over the line in the Chinese Revolution, through which new political paths were created, are closely associated with theoretical debates. The process of reform has also witnessed such line struggles. Theoretical and political struggles have the ability to correct mistakes during revolutionary politics. Emphasizing the rectifying capacity of theoretical and political struggles does not conflict with criticizing the tendency of violence and despotism in the process of struggle. The result of cruel struggle and unmerciful punishment in line struggles has taught us a heavy lesson: the CCP must resolve problems on the basis of democracy and law. Still, we should not simply regard theoretical debate and line struggle, simply because of the existence of violence within them, as cases of mere power competition and political repression. Political repression marks the end of theoretical debate, of line struggle, and of the practice of competition within the party. Today, the oppression against intellectual debates implemented by political and media power also marks the end of politics. A large quantity of writings claiming to summarize and reflect on violence in history actually focuses on discrediting necessary theoretical debate and line struggle, leading to the dysfunction of the self-rectifying mechanism of the political party and to the self-enclosure of the political sphere. This type of research is a product of the politics of depoliticization. An urgently relevant question here is: Why were theoretical debates, especially those having reached the level of debate over the political line, more likely to be transformed into violent oppression? The consideration of this issue cannot exclude the process of the statization of political parties, through which the necessary boundary between the party and the state disappeared and the political party no longer had a relatively independent theoretical space. In addition, this issue cannot be understood without considering the partification of the media, whereby media power tries to become a sort of political agent for the state or for capital, and begins to colonize the public sphere. Criticism and self-criticism used to be key elements of political life in China, but they were eliminated after Deng Xiaoping promoted the dictum of 'don't argue' (不争论) in the 1980s. Without debates, struggles and challenges, how can the practice of criticism and self-criticism be carried on? How can political innovation be achieved?

The mass line
The close connection between party politics and the power structure is a contemporary condition. It is now almost impossible to depend on the self-transformation of the political party to formulate a new politics. The level of bureaucratization in state and party structures is unprecedentedly high in the current situation of statized party politics. It is impractical to rely on the power of the political party alone to diminish bureaucracy. Hence, the mass line not only serves as a channel for the political party to maintain its political vigour, but also needs to acquire a new dimension – namely, political openness, or greatly increased political participation.

The mass line policy was first put forward by the Central Committee of the Communist Party of China in 1929, in a letter to the Fourth Route Army. However, 'all for the masses; all rely on the masses; from the masses and to the masses' is not just a political and military strategy, but also a description of an organic revolutionary politics. Like 'the people' (人民), 'the masses' (群众) is also a political category containing a new political subjectivity produced by uniting the political party and the common people (大众), especially peasants. The mass line policy reveals the underlying affinity between the politics of the political party and the politics of public society. This is a unique element in Chinese politics. The party was said to be the political representative of the masses, but in reality it embodied the process of shaping the masses into a political subjectivity, and was a way for the masses to represent themselves in people's war or the campaign for the construction of their own state. We can hardly find explanations for this element in the nineteenth- and twentieth-century party politics of Europe, or in its equivalents elsewhere.

People's war
How was the connection between the CCP and mass politics formed? The mass line was proposed in 1929 after the Northern Expedition failed, and the CCP shifted from a struggle focused on cities to a people's war based in the countryside. People's war – a political category, and not war in general – was a process that created a political subject as well as its political structure and form of self-expression. In people's war, relations of representation in traditional politics were fundamentally transformed: the subject – the people (人民群众) – was born in war, and all forms and aspects of politics, such as the political party and the border region government, were either produced or transformed according to the people's needs. Without people's war, the transition of the CCP would have been unthinkable. In terms of membership composition, social basis, party work methodology, and the interpretation of revolutionary politics, the CCP born in 1921, which was composed of a few intellectuals and had no substantial connection with the working and peasant classes, differed greatly from its counterpart during the period of the Jiangxi Soviet. The failed urban revolts and workers' struggles led by Li Lisan, Wang Ming and Qu Qiubai after the Great Revolution (大革命, 1924–27) also differed from people's war, which unfolded through the strategy of encircling the cities from the countryside. The union of the party with the army, the red government and the masses, with peasants as the majority

during the people's war, along with its changed relations with other parties and social strata and their political representatives, reminds us that the people's war created not only a political party that differed thoroughly from its predecessors, but a class subject that featured the peasants as its main component and differed thoroughly from historical proletarian classes. I call this political party a super-party containing supra-party elements.

When it was founded, the CCP was mainly composed of intellectuals whom the Comintern representative 'Maring' (Henk Sneevliet) regarded as petit bourgeois, and whose connection with the working and peasant classes was even looser than the GMD's. In 1925 and 1926, as the GMD adopted a policy of alliance with Russia and the CCP, the two parties allied to promote the peasant movement, the fruits of which included the Peasant Movement Training Institute at Guangzhou. The GMD made some political innovations: first, it established a party-army instead of relying on the old warlords; second, it cooperated with the CCP to advance the peasant movement and to use the mass line to assist the Northern Expedition – a policy gradually abandoned after 1927. The concept of party-army and the resistance to armed anti-revolution by armed revolution were not inventions of the CCP, but of the GMD, which was still in its revolutionary stage and influenced by the international communist movement.

People's war was the outcome of the failure of the Great Revolution, but its elements first emerged as early as during the Northern Expedition. The armed forces that participated in the Autumn Harvest Uprising and the Nanchang Uprising joined forces at Jinggangshan, and established the Jiangxi Soviet base area – a milestone marking the unfolding of the people's war. In the base area, land reform and military struggle served as the basic method of transforming party politics into a mass movement. The pivotal issues of the Jinggangshan period hence became land reform and regime construction under the revolutionary war. The union of the political party with the army, and with the peasant movement and land reform mediated by the army, not only changed the content and major task of the revolution, but created a brand-new revolutionary political subject through the quadruple union of the party, the army, the construction of a new regime, and the peasant movement – that is, the political foundation of people's war. Unlike the political party, party politics, and other political phenomena that originated in nineteenth-century Europe and twentieth-century Russia, people's war in the revolution of China was a new and original invention.

Mao Zedong said that the army and the people were the basis of success. His words deserve explication: first, the war depended on mobilization and the masses; second, there must be local armed forces and guerrillas in addition to a strong regular army; third, the categories of military and civilian were established in the land reform and the construction of a new regime. These historical prerequisites brought forth the so-called mass line. The mass line advocated first of all that both the starting point and the ultimate end of party work should be to benefit the largest number of people.

The Soviet council system in people's war

In addition, the Soviet Council was the organizer of the lives of the masses. Only when the Soviet had done its utmost to solve the problems facing the masses and to improve their lives concretely could it establish the faith of the masses in the Soviet and mobilize them to join the Red Army, help fight the war, and defeat the GMD's encirclements.

How should we understand the Soviet as the organizer of the lives of the masses? On the surface it seemed to emphasize the organizing function of the Soviet, but in praxis, it above all required the CCP members to immerse themselves among the masses and to learn from them. Without the organization, the subjectivity of the masses could not come into being. Without the process of becoming one with and learning from the masses, the organization would lose its energy and become a mere structure that dominated the masses. The Soviet was a form through which the masses came into being, and the CCP was a political organization through which the proletariat was enabled to express itself. In the vast and unindustrialized countryside, the proletariat acquired the ability of self-expression in movements coordinated by the political party. In this sense, it was the political party that created the self-expression of classes, and therefore created political classes. But it is important to note that this party was not the one that existed before people's war, but the one reconstructed through land revolution and the making of the Soviet. The former could not create a proletariat with peasants as its major component; only a political party engaged in people's war and base-area building could accomplish this mission.

Since it was the organizational form of daily life, the Soviet equalled a political regime. Although a political regime in this sense also needs to learn from the experiences of the state in Chinese and world history, it was not a capitalist state in general but a political form that produced classes with self-awareness. Under people's war, the Soviet handled not simply military issues but also the organization of daily life. Issues concerning land, labour, daily necessities, women, schools, and so on, all formed major parts of people's war. The mass line was the basic strategy of people's war, and changed or reconstructed the significance of the political party. This is one of the unique creations of the twentieth-century Chinese Revolution.

The mass line, 'from the masses and to the masses', as well as the cultural politics of 'for whom' (为了谁) and 'how to serve' (怎么为), are all questions about the relationship of the political party with the masses and society. Since the crust of modern politics is the state, political movements cannot operate by themselves, detached from political power. The problem of a representative system actually emerged when the party and the state became affiliated. That is to say, a political system depends on a certain type of representation for its construction. In the Jiangxi Soviet and the other base areas for the war against the Japanese invasion, there was political regime construction under people's war. The issue of a representative system arose in this process of regime construction, but the representative system of this period was closely associated with the praxis of supra-representativeness – 'from the people and to the people'. After 1949, as people's war ended, the formalization of the state system required the formalization of the representative system as well, and consequently the relationship between the party and the masses gradually transformed from one of supra-representation to a representative system pivoting on the state system. The system of representation can function in the form of general elections, local elections, elections within political parties, recommendation, rotation, or election by lot. The merits or disadvantages of these forms are not absolute. Instead, they should be determined by analyzing the concrete circumstances – that is, according to whether active politics of the people and for the people exists.

Supra-Representativeness in the Politics of Representativeness

When we are discussing the problems of the system of representation, however, we often neglect the element of supra-representativeness in the politics of representativeness. In fact, the mass line policy contains such an element. The concept of 'the masses' in the mass line, a political process, contains the connotation of a political subjectivity that is about to germinate and take shape. 'The masses' is political energy in formation. Its relationship with the political party also changes in this process – the duality gradually integrates into a relative unity. This relationship is not completely one of representation; in other words, it often transcends the relationship of representation. The two sides mould each other in such a relationship in the struggle to accomplish their purposes, so that the mass line becomes the process of creating a new political subjectivity. In this process, the masses become a political category, and the political party, part of mass politics; the two define each other and intermingle. Hence, the question of how to respond to a changing era and to the different compositions of the masses in new social conditions becomes a major one for political organizations seeking to reconstruct political representativeness. Without this process, political representativeness, regardless of its form of application, will face the danger of becoming empty, as a consequence of which the political system will become detached from public life. The aspect of supra-representativeness in representative politics is often neglected when discussing the problem of representative systems.

As class politics has ebbed, party politics has shifted to post-political party politics. Contemporary China is undergoing an historical process of class reconstruction and of the suppression of class politics, which contrasts sharply with the situation in the twentieth century, when class politics was extremely active despite the relatively small size of the working class. What are the political connotations of the 'mass line policy' under post-party politics? In the Chinese Revolution, especially in the people's war, the mass line can be roughly described as a political process through which a mature and highly disciplined political party, according to its clear political orientation and mission, mobilized the masses and recruited members active among the masses in order to strengthen and reform itself while fully guaranteeing the freedom and legal rights of mass organizations and mass movements, and respecting their independence. For instance, after the war against the Japanese invasion broke out, the CCP Central Committee issued, on 16 October 1937, the 'Policy on Mass Movements'. It emphasized the need to 'establish organizations that truly belong to the masses, including labour unions, peasants' unions, student unions, merchants' unions, and other organizations for youth, for women and for children, based on the political, economic and cultural needs of the masses' and asserted that it was 'necessary to organize as many workers and hired farm hands as possible into labour unions and as many peasants as possible into peasants' unions'. These mass organizations practised 'extensive democracy' internally, and participated in government work as autonomous groups, while promoting the economic and political interests and cultural activities of the masses.

The State-Party System and Its Overcoming

In today's state-party system (国党体制), we can use the mass line policy concept, but we should not and cannot re-create the previous political mode. One of the results of the statification of the political party is that the relationship of the political party, as the end point of a political movement, with the masses gradually transforms into one between the state and society. Nowadays, a meticulously organized and highly disciplined political party with a clear agenda – that is, a political party in the twentieth-century sense – no longer exists, and the politics of the masses (大众政治) created by the mass line policy has also vanished: politics has degenerated into the category of management, a politics of depoliticization. The statification of the party signals the end of the era of the mass line. In a context completely different from that of the twentieth century, what does it mean to broach the topic of the mass line once again? Do we talk about the masses in the relationship between the state and the citizens, or in the relationship between the political party and classes? The birth of the masses, as a political subject coming into existence, proclaimed the birth of a new political form. Under globalization and marketization, what does the mass line – the outcome of people's war – signify? What political power does the reference to the mass line today intend to create? What political subject does it intend to cultivate? And what future does the mass line actually point to?

The mass line is not simply rhetoric, and as a political thesis it is not as self-evident as the words in this phrase are. Hence, to bring up this issue again is not to return to a particular historical period, but to pursue a probable and uncertain future. Relying on the masses does not simply imply social supervision or participation, but requires a certain form of social organization. When we say there is no class politics in the twentieth-century sense today, it does not mean there are no active class movements or citizen politics. Among contemporary social organizations, NGOs receive more media attention than working-class and peasant movements, which are seldom covered. These two groups engage in political, social, ecological and cultural issues in different ways. Currently, many social organizations and movements have political potential, but they might not all lead to more positive politics. Under the conditions of financial capitalism, even social movements are penetrated by the capitalist system. Hence, no matter whether we discuss civil society or analyze class politics in the contemporary world, we cannot avoid examining new forms of contemporary capitalism.

Financial capitalism is a global problem. Under financial capitalism, just as the accumulation of capital and its internal contradictions have reached an unprecedented scale, so too has the gap between the fictitious economy and the real economy become extraordinary. This distorted process of accumulation continues to disrupt social relations. Compared with Western countries, China has a larger real economy and a correspondingly larger labour population; the economic regulatory capability of its state is also stronger than in many developed countries. Financial capital, highly mobile and transnational, has escaped from the traditional restrictions of industry, guild, and even the state. What significance do these new developments have for the political dilemma discussed here? How are the state, political parties, class and social organization changing? These are problems that remain to be discussed. What we can be sure about is that we need to redefine and re-analyze a series of fundamental concepts that constitute the modern state system and power structure, including sovereignty, citizen, class, labour, and so on. In the Chinese context, the way in which we understand these issues is directly linked with the issue of political practice.

For example, in the Chinese context, reconstructing representativeness is one of the methods of overcoming the crisis of representativeness. The question is what type of representativeness should be adopted. Is it necessary to re-emphasize the importance of the working class or the alliance of workers and peasants? Under financial capitalism, Western countries experienced and are still experiencing deindustrialization. Many intellectuals have noted the radical shrinking or even disappearance of the working class as a revolutionary class, and have begun to challenge the idea of class and class politics theoretically. The other side of this social process, however, is industrialization and the formation of a working class on a grand scale in China and in many other non-Western countries. Under globalization, this structure of class formation is not stable. An important phenomenon in contemporary China is the restructuring of class society (重新阶级化). Here, a return to the concept of class is unavoidable. But the expansion and reorganization of the working class and the decline of working-class politics took place almost simultaneously. The newly emerged working-class politics has not been able to

reach the depth and scale of the preceding one. We can immediately identify its two features: first, it is detached from party politics; and second,
the new working class is unstable, due to the mobility of the contemporary system of production. This instability renders the new working class
different from its equivalents in the era of socialist industrialization, and
in the early stage of their formation.

We can roughly identify four types of workers' struggles. First, strikes
and attempts at self-organization (unionization) in order to protect workers' own personal rights and interests, of which the workers' strike at the
Guangzhou Honda factory is an example. This is typical working-class
politics. Second, attempts to shorten the contract period, in which workers refuse to work in a factory or for a company for longer than a certain
period, instead staying in one position for a year or two before taking
another job. From a classic perspective of class politics, this tactic will
jeopardize the solidarity of workers; but as a means of demanding a higher
salary from the state and from capitalists, it is a most effective strategy.
Third, in addition to traditional forms of organization such as unions, new
forms have appeared. The so-called 'foreman system' (领工制), which
used to be seen as a way of enabling double exploitation, has become a
new organizational form for workers' struggle. It protects some of the
interests of workers through informal contracts. There are also associations for people coming from the same province, town or village, and for
ethnic minorities, all of which have the same function. Lastly, civil rights
protection (维权) movements have emerged that focus on the protection
of the legal rights of individuals. In addition to these four types, rural
reconstruction (乡村建设) also provides an alternative form of support
for the labour movement. Discussions on these issues are myriad, but are
mainly conducted within the framework of social stratification, barely
exploring the political potential of these forms of organization or their
overlap with and differences from traditional class politics.

If the fracture of representativeness is manifested as the detachment of
political forms from social forms, what is the political form that can
organically connect with social forms? Class and class politics exist in
contemporary China. The reconstruction of representativeness is inevitably linked with the need to restructure class society. But as the statification
of the political party intensifies, instead of reconstructing a political party
of a certain class, post-party politics will probably take the approach of
formulating a more independent social politics (including political organizations in a broader sense, such as workers' unions, peasant associations,

and other social organizations) and shifting to an active labour politics that focuses on reforming relations within the production system. In fact, urban–rural conflict and its repercussions, regional imbalances and their reverberations, and class relationships and their transformation, as well as the ecological damage caused by contemporary modes of production and consumption, all constitute the most intense manifestations of the contradictions in modern capitalism. Thus, rural reconstruction, environmental protection, transformation of the development model, the protection of ethnic equality and cultural diversity, and improvement of the social status of the working class, should all come to provide the impetus for a contemporary politics of equality.

Why raise the issue of post-party politics? The answer lies in the understanding that two conflicting proposals for contemporary political reform share the same premise of returning to party politics. For the right wing, the basic political model is the classic multiparty system based on the framework of parliamentary politics. For the left wing, it is important to recuperate or reconstruct the political representativeness of the party, and consequently to raise a series of questions concerning class and its political forms. Chinese reality reveals that the latter poses the more urgent question. But it is very likely that contemporary political reform will not necessarily return to the political model of the nineteenth or twentieth century, but will instead rely on the new political and economic reality. Reconstructing representativeness through the mass line policy, theoretical debates, and organizational reconstruction is an inescapable political process, but its purpose is very probably not to return to the old political party model. Today, although the political organization called 'political party' still exists, its political meaning has changed significantly. In the early twentieth century, this change was undertaken deliberately, and was accomplished by establishing a super-political party to overcome the crisis in multiparty politics. In the late twentieth century, however, this change was more passive, as it was completed in the shift from a partified state to a statified party. Under the new conditions, working out how social power can engage in political processes on a larger scale and in a more direct fashion becomes a necessary project in the exploration of a new political framework. It is also the precondition for the party to practise the mass line to some extent. Hence, the process of rebuilding political representativeness cannot simply rely on traditional party politics; it must include the practice of post-party politics, for which current technological developments also provide more possibilities. So-called post-party politics does not negate the function of political organizations, but rather highlights their characteristics of being open, unfinished, and non-bureaucratic. The mass line and mass politics are the source of political vigour and the foundation for resisting right-wing populism.

Post-political party politics

Today, social structures are undergoing drastic change. The design of their course of development and reconstruction should be everyone's concern. A new political agency needs to be established based on the interests of most of the Chinese people, which in the past demonstrated its political implications and social significance through the category of 'the people'. Since the concept of 'the people' is generally shifting towards the meaning of 'population', its political connotation has evaporated to such as degree that we can no longer find any political expression for general interests aside from the concept of 'citizen'. The disdain for the concept of the people manifests the fragmentation of society in ideology. In modern Chinese history, 'the people' was a disputed concept constantly appropriated by different political powers. But it was not always empty. In the period when mass politics and the mass line were active, it was a vibrant political category. Its rich connotations were drained as the result of depoliticization, as mass politics and the mass line were replaced by bureaucratic state politics. I bring up the concept of 'the people' here again not to oppose it to the more popular concept of citizen. On the contrary, I argue that it is essential to re-establish the political connection between these two categories. The politics of the citizen is not equal to a politics with the individual as its main subject; it should also embrace the politics of the masses and society, and thus the politics of the people. In ethnic minority areas, it should also include the politics of ethnic equality. In the twentieth century, progressive parties that proposed a political role for the proletarian class were not prompted by the interests of the working class or workers' groups alone. They believed the mission of the proletariat had a universal significance that surpassed the limits of its own interests. It would necessarily become the people's politics – the politics of every citizen. In the system of state power, people's politics is manifested as the politics of true equality. The politics of equality is defined neither by the policy of providing relief for the poor nor that of meeting the national target of eliminating poverty. It includes reflections on the premises and motivations of politics. I analyzed the various connotations of the politics of equality in an earlier article,[3] and will not repeat myself here.

Current research on social stratification can quickly identify the interests of particular social classes, but it fails to identify a general interest. This is a problem that positivist methodology cannot resolve. Whether or not our politics in the future can develop in a positive direction will be determined by whether or not the latent power that represents the future can be discovered within social transitions. This latent power is universal, and what is dormant now will become manifest in the future. To discuss a 'reconstruction of representativeness' is to unearth the universality of this suppressed potential. This discussion is essentially a battle for the future. For any type of political system, only when it can create universality – when it can represent universal interests – will it possess representativeness. Hence, the process of reconstructing representativeness is the process of creating universality. I have no interest in the widely celebrated official slogan of 'great cultural development and prosperity'. My inquiry is more concerned by the problem of the relationship between culture and politics. Can we still, as happened in the twentieth century, study the transition of social structures, analyze their possible direction, redefine the boundaries of politics, and discover a universality that can represent the future in today's development in China and the rest of the world through the domain of culture? This is a question that must be raised. It is also a challenge we must overcome.

The twentieth century was in a sense a prophecy – one that was embroiled in crisis soon after its articulation. But it was also a suppressed potential. Re-examining the cultural and political legacy of the twentieth century does not mean simply returning to outdated praxis. Rather, the object must be to discover its untapped power that contains universality and potential for the future. This suppressed potential reminds us that returning to the old politics of the nineteenth century is not our objective. Our attention should be on the establishment of a constitutional politics in the context of post-political party politics, based on the historical legacy of the twentieth century.

---

3   Wang, 'Decline of Representation'.

2 Chinese Communism Revisited: Still a Class Perspective, but Why?

Pun Ngai

The Failure

The spectre of the 1960s haunts the world and calls us to revisit the concepts of 'revolution' and 'communism' for today's emancipatory politics. My proposition is simple and direct: the ideal of communism cannot be salvaged in its metaphysical form as seen through the first world's lens; but from the third world class perspective, a real dialectic of revolution exists among the angels of communism's ideal and the devils of its failures. The angels are gone, while the devils assume the shape and form of revolutions.

Today global capitalism has triumphed over the world, defeating all the attempts at communist revolution of the twentieth century. It has destroyed the fruits of socialist goals including economic equality, human emancipation and people's democracy, which the vanguard of revolution shed its blood to achieve. This destruction has continued until the arrival of a neoliberal world – a point at which Fukuyama claimed that humanity has finally reached the 'end of history', and thus the word 'revolution', not to mention 'communism', has become taboo in intellectual circles in both the West and the East.

Blood was shed in vain when true revolutions were hysterically denounced. Communism has become the symbol of 'dictatorship', 'irrationality' and 'repression of democracy and freedom', which has scared away the young generation growing up in the neoliberal age. The defeat was not simply a result of failure on the ideological battlefield in the post-1960s era, but also of the fact that in the last decade of the twentieth century the USSR dissolved, and China reformed and opened its doors to international capital.

The study of this defeat is pending. A Western narrative of failure is repetitive, and at times both simple and naive. The failure is portrayed as a defeat due to an authoritarian party-state, an inevitability of bureau-cracy and ossified state organs, stagnancy of economic development, suppression of personal freedom, and, especially in China, the chaos of the Cultural Revolution. The narrative that accounts for the failures of both the Russian and Chinese revolutions has engendered a *common sense* of the failure of communist revolutions shared by both right and left. Nothing needs to be explained. The failure is self-explanatory. What is needed are new and inventive political forms, in order to move beyond party-state politics.

The collapse of the socialist world, however, is not complete. China's reform created a 'miracle'. China stands as one of the exceptions in which the party-state has been able to maintain its survival for another three decades and more. China is now not only the rising star on the global economic platform, but also occupies second place in the world economy.

No current literature on communist revolutions is more inspiring than Perry Anderson's 'Two Revolutions' and 'Modernity and Revolution'. In 'Two Revolutions', Anderson charts the different trajectories of the revo-lutions in the USSR and China, and provides an interpretation of the diverse outcomes of the two great transformations. On top of the 'common sense' that is said to characterize the nature of both revolutions, Perry Anderson adds that China's revolution, as compared to the Russian Revolution, was of a longer duration, and has thus contributed to a stronger power base for the Chinese communists from which to enact their sovereignty over the decades. Chinese communism has brought both national independence and internal peace, he says.[1]

Anderson is absolutely correct when he writes: 'If the twentieth century was dominated, more than by any other single event, by the trajectory of the Russian Revolution, the twenty-first will be shaped by the outcome of the Chinese Revolution.'[2] But he is probably wrong when he adopts 'common sense' to frame the Chinese Revolution. He states: 'The Chinese Party inherited the Soviet model as it took shape under Stalin, developing much the same monolithic discipline, authoritarian structure, and habits of command.'[3]

To a few Western leftists and many Chinese nationalists, China is nevertheless an exception to the history of the failure of communism. The

---

1   Perry Anderson, 'Two Revolutions', *New Left Review* II:61 (January–February 2010), p. 65.
2   Ibid., p. 59.
3   Ibid., p. 66.

perceived 'authoritarian state' or 'bureaucratic organ' that contributed to the breakdown of the Russian regime did not do the same in China. Instead, the 'authoritarian state' contributed to rapid 'capitalist develop-ment' in China, and it squarely fitted itself into the international division of labour by helping to speed up global capital accumulation. China has become a paradise for the final reproduction of global capitalism.

The 'common sense' that led to the fall of communism in the USSR, ironically, contributed to the continuity of the 'communist' state in China. As Anderson puts it, 'The PRC of the twenty-first century is a world-historical *novum*: the combination of what is now, by any conventional measure, a predominantly capitalist economy with what is still, by any conventional measure, unquestionably a communist state.'[4]

Here the concepts of 'capitalist economy' and 'communist state' seize my attention. Several questions arise. First, is it correct to say that the perceived 'common sense' could lead to two diverse outcomes in Russia and China? Are those outcomes really different? If we adopt a perspec-tive of political economy, are Russia and China not both predominantly varied forms of capitalism, creating similar capitalist relations of produc-tion, one relying largely upon an energy economy and the other upon export-oriented industries? Second, what does 'common sense' mean? Do we really understand it? Third, what is the nature of a 'communist state'? Could a capitalist economy coexist with a communist state in theory and in practice? What do revolution, communism and class really mean?

The Form

Understanding 'common sense' is a matter of controversy. The contro-versy is subsumed in public and academic circles, however, simply because both the collapse of the USSR and the rise of China serve the logic of global capital accumulation and the globalized reproduction of capitalism. Common sense now stands as a common factor in the Chinese context – an 'authoritarian party-state' and its subsequent 'devils' contrib-ute to the logic of accelerated capital accumulation on a global scale, and also provides inventive forms capable of transgressing human limits to create wealth and development. The logic of global capital accumulation wins. Who cares about common sense now?

---

4   Ibid., p. 95.

A few progressive European theorists care. Among them, the leading ones are Alain Badiou and Alessandro Russo. No theory, no revolution. In order to ignite the revolutionary imagination for a future communist movement, they attempt to revitalize communism from its 'scientific history' towards 'affirmations of its singular innovations and truths' by seriously revisiting the 1960s in general and the Chinese Cultural Revolution specifically. They engage in a 'project of muse' in which they put forward the slogan, 'Today's research, tomorrow's inspiration', with the aim of re-theorizing the revolutions in the 1960s, and hence disclosing the 'common sense' that led to their failures.[5]

In a 1998 interview with Peter Hallward, Alan Badiou clearly states: 'Today we are developing a completely different idea, which we call "politics without party". This doesn't mean "unorganized politics". All politics is collective, and so organized one way or another. "Politics without party" means that politics does not spring from or originate in the party.'[6] Badiou's politics is to denounce the party-state that dominated the politics of the communist movement of the twentieth century, and in his view the Leninist party stands out as an offensive devil to emancipatory politics. According to him, the logic of the party originates from the logic of classism, and the ideas of Marx's class politics and of the category of the proletariat have to be questioned and transgressed. He writes,

> For a long time we were faithful to the idea of a class politics, a class state, and so on . . . There is no going back on this; there is no need for a revision of Marxism itself. It is a matter of going beyond the idea that politics *represents* objective groups that can be designated as classes. This idea has had its power and importance. But in our opinion, we cannot today begin from or set out from this idea. We can begin from political processes, from political oppositions, from conflicts and contradictions, obviously.[7]

He further claims, 'This time has come to an end, and so we can say, if you like, that the category of the proletariat, as a political category, can no longer play much of a role.'[8]

---

5   See Alain Badiou, 'The Cultural Revolution: The Last Revolution', *Positions* 13: 3 (2005), p. 503.
6   See Alan Badiou, *Ethics: An Essay on the Understanding of Evil* (London/New York: Verso, 2001), pp. 95–6.
7   Ibid., p. 97.
8   Ibid., p. 114.

While Badiou tries to save the figure of workers in his politics of truth, the representation of the workers, the proletariat, and its organizational form, the party, has to be eliminated. He repeatedly denounces it. In 'The Cultural Revolution: The Last Revolution', Badiou writes: 'We know today that all emancipatory politics must put an end to the model of party, or of multiple parties, in order to affirm a politics "without party."'[9]

The Chinese Cultural Revolution never fails to arrest Badiou and his colleagues' attention, because it embodies a paradox of revolution that profoundly engages human emancipatory politics and 'great exchanges of experience' among the masses through an attempt to crash the party-state machine by means of a violent force comprising student youth, workers and social forces external to the party.

The Cultural Revolution was seen as the 'last revolution' of communism, as it embodied a great political experiment to move beyond the 'party'; but it ultimately failed. The failure, according to Badiou, was because 'Mao is also a man of the party-state. He wants its renovation, even a violent one, but not its destruction.'[10] For Badiou, Mao was the recognized leader of the Cultural Revolution. In this position, Mao held out no alternative to the existence of the party-state, and hence concluded with a conservative project of party reconstruction at the end of the 1960s.

'Mao' is thus the name of a paradox: the rebel in power, the dialectician put to the test by challenging the authorities of the party. But 'Mao' is also the name of the party that was unable to allow a complete collapse of the state's bureaucracy.[11] Badiou concludes: 'In the end, the Cultural Revolution, even in its very impasse, bears witness to the impossibility truly and globally to free politics from the framework of the party-state that imprisons it.'[12]

In 'The Sixties and Us', Alessandro Russo helps further define the problematic of common sense: 'The sixties were a worldwide political mass laboratory composed of an unprecedented range of themes and experimental grounds: experimental politics had never previously involved so many disparate fields of collective life. That multifarious political moment had a singular center of gravity: *the question of the political value of the "class party"*.'[13] Russo describes the class party as the 'despotic

---

9   See Badiou, 'Cultural Revolution', p. 507.
10   Ibid., p. 503.
11   Ibid., p. 506.
12   Ibid., p. 507.
13   Alessandro Russo, 'The Sixties and Us', Chapter 7 in this volume, p. 138. Russo places the word 'class' before party, which is a redundancy, because all parties are a product of class relations. (Emphasis added.)

government of industrial labour' that 'moulds the hierarchies that govern the entire collective life of the modern world'.[14]

The questioning of the value of 'party' was the defining spirit of the 1960s revolutions in both capitalist and socialist societies. A belief in 'common sense' led to the common problematizing of 'party' – a universal form that stands out among those who organized revolutions in the twentieth century. Russo recognizes that the party made a decisive contribution to twentieth-century state formations, derived from the existence of the workers' parties from the second half of the nineteenth century. However, the party became the target of insurgency in the 1960s, as it proved one of the most pervasive variants of the modern forms of government. As Russo points out, 'Mao's last political statement in 1975 was that "the bourgeoisie is in the Communist Party".'[15] He prefers to turn the phrase upside down by arguing that 'the Communist Party is in the bourgeoisie.'[16] He states further that the 'thesis of "the bourgeoisie is in the class party", or the "class party is in the bourgeoisie", summarizes the main experimental result of the sixties.'[17]

Though the common problematic of 'party' singled out by Badiou and Russo adds no new knowledge to the 'common sense' of the failure of communism, Russo's thesis that the 'class party is in the bourgeoisie' is particularly pertinent in describing China in the reform period, if not yet in the 1960s. The party was hence in the hands of the bourgeoisie. This was a true problem.

In his later analysis, however, Russo shifts the problem from 'the class party in the bourgeoisie' to 'the dictatorship of the proletariat' – the party:[18] 'The issue of the "dictatorship of theproletariat" had to be declared "obscure" as a necessary precondition so that it could "be clarified": the political events of the preceding decade required a radical reopening of that basic theoretical concept.'[19]

What Mao viewed as the real enemy – the bourgeoisie hidden in the party – becomes the *form* of party organization in the eyes of Badiou and Russo. There is almost no distinction between 'class party in the

---

14   Ibid., p.141.
15   'Bourgeoisie' refers to the class of modern capitalists, owners of the means of social production and employers of wage labour. 'Proletariat' refers to the class of modern wage labourers who, having no means of production of their own, are reduced to selling their labour-power in order to live.
16   This saying is echoed by Claudia Pozzana.
17   Russo, 'The Sixties and Us', p. 139.
18   Ibid., p. 143.
19   Alessandro Russo, 'How Did the Cultural Revolution End? The Last Dispute between Mao Zedong and Deng Xiaoping, 1975', *Modern China* 39: 3 (2012), p. 245.

bourgeoisie' and the dictatorship of the proletariat, because in both cases the historical subjects use the same organizational form, the party, to organize and to accomplish the seizure of power.

The form matters; the form is the devil in the detail.

To Mao, the bourgeoisie is the real historical subject that holds power over the party and turns it into a 'class party'. This was the reason to call upon the Cultural Revolution to smash the party with the power of the masses. The class party was the product or the result of class struggle, and Mao tirelessly sought a 'permanent revolution' or 'continuous revolution' to resolve it. This included education campaigns and thought reform inside the party, and mass movements outside it.

Mao said that the enemies with guns were easy to identify in the pre-Liberation period, but that those hidden in the party without guns were more difficult to recognize. Unless we agree with vulgar political scientists who take Mao's paranoid personality as a factor contributing to his preoccupation with securing personal power in order to act as a modern emperor, we can hardly dismiss the complexity of class relations that existed and re-emerged in the socialist construction period. I will return to this issue below.

However, Badiou and Russo dismiss the real problems of class and the existence of class enemies by regarding these real historical elements as inherently part of the abstract *form* of political organizing. By dislocating the problem of 'class', they replace the party (which is actually a bourgeois party or a party under the control of the bourgeoisie) with the *form* of 'party' instead.

Badiou and Russo seem unable to provide an answer for developments at the closure of the 1960s, even though they call for in-depth analysis. But obviously they take the closure as a setback for the multiple forms of self-organization of the 1960s, and the suppression of experimental egalitarian mass politics. The closure, to them, was characterized by the return to the traditional 'class party' politics in the post-1960s period.

The main obstacle, Russo claims, to the theoretical description and periodization of the 1960s is that the categories of 'class' and 'class struggle' are not only inadequate but also obscure the singularity of the political configuration.[20] Russo argues that, 'Since the entire "encyclopedia" of classist political culture together with the class party "did not pass the test", new categories must be found in order to reflect on all modern

---

20   Ibid., p. 20.

egalitarian policies.'[21] Instead of an outdated 'class politics', Badiou refers to singular 'political processes, oppositions, conflicts and contradictions' that could open up new emancipatory politics. But what is the nature of these events? And what are the alternatives for emancipatory politics in terms of political agenda, mass mobilization and political organizing? I find this prescription equally obscure.

Inventive forms, new categories and 'politics moving beyond party' are what a few European leftist theorists are calling for in envisaging a future communism, which would incarnate itself as an 'ideal' and not an 'historical' communism. Inventive forms of organization are the priority in the emancipatory movement, and by all means, these forms should be achieved.

Within this model, the perspective of class is not missing, but dismissed. Instead of a call for more in-depth analysis of the power struggles between different classes that were inherently embodied over the course of the 1960s, Russo asks for research that 'should certainly be carried out on the specific weaknesses of organizational experimentations among Chinese, Italian, French or Polish workers as well as the obstacles that they had in common'.[22] This prescription precludes the possibility of a true class analysis of party, state and ideology, resulting in an urge for a *form* of utopia devoid of the concrete, daily struggles among different social and class forces, and hence distances itself from real struggles and historical materialism.

In short, the real enemy – the bourgeois class – escapes unobserved through the back door, and the 'pseudo enemies' now emerge as the form of party or form of state. 'Common sense' hitherto becomes the 'form'.

What Is a Communist Revolution?

'Common sense' can be better revealed if we return to the very basic question: What is a communist revolution? Who are its enemies? What are its goals? What are the methods for achieving revolutionary goals? In the opening of *Manifesto of the Communist Party*, Marx and Engels define the enemies of the revolution: 'A spectre is haunting Europe – the spectre of communism. All the powers of old Europe have entered into a holy alliance to exorcise this spectre: Pope and Tsar, Metternich and Guizot,

---

21   Ibid., pp. 20–1.
22   Ibid., p. 11.

French Radicals and German police-spies.'[23] In short, the enemies are the ruling classes representing the interests of the bourgeoisie and other oppressive classes. Marx and Engels explain: 'The immediate aim of the Communists is the same as that of all other proletarian parties: formation of the proletariat into a class, overthrow of the bourgeois supremacy, conquest of political power by the proletariat.'[24]

The more specific goal is to abolish the bourgeois property system, which is the foundation for building a communist society and the groundwork of all personal freedom, activity and independence. They further explain that 'modern bourgeois private property is the final and most complete expression of the system of producing and appropriating products, that is based on class antagonisms, on the exploitation of the many by the few . . . In this sense, the theory of the Communists may be summed up in the single sentence: Abolition of private property.'[25]

But how can these communist goals be achieved? Marx and Engels's answer is a communist revolution: 'They [the Communists] openly declare that their ends can be attained only by the forcible overthrow of all existing social conditions. Let the ruling classes tremble at a Communistic revolution. The proletarians have nothing to lose but their chains. They have a world to win.'[26]

If Marx and Engels did not provide us with an explanation of the means of revolution, Lenin directly applied the theory of the 'dictatorship of the proletariat' to consolidate the class power of the proletariat and formulate the vanguard of the proletariat – the Communist Party – as a united fighting force with a high level of political consciousness and discipline. Overthrowing the bourgeois state under the leadership of the vanguard of the working class is the historical condition for causing a violent revolution. It is also the historical condition for the final dissolution of the vanguard of the working class and the 'withering away' of the proletarian state.

In 'State and Revolution', Lenin said: 'The supersession of the bourgeois state by the proletarian state is impossible without a violent revolution. The abolition of the proletarian state, i.e., of the state in general, is impossible except through the process of "withering away."'[27]

---

23   See Karl Marx and Friedrich Engels, *Manifesto of the Communist Party* (1848), at marxists.org.
24   Ibid., Chapter 2.
25   Ibid.
26   Ibid., Chapter 4.
27   Vladimir Lenin, *The State and Revolution* (1918), at marxists.org.

By interpreting Engels's thesis in *The Origin of the Family, Private Property and the State*, Lenin concludes:

> The state is, therefore, by no means a power forced on society from without; just as little is it 'the reality of the ethical idea', 'the image and reality of reason', as Hegel maintains . . . The state arises where, when and insofar as class antagonism objectively cannot be reconciled. And, conversely, the existence of the state proves that the class antagonisms are irreconcilable.[28]

Hence, Lenin's famous expression is: 'The state is a product and a manifestation of the irreconcilability of class antagonisms.'[29] I would extend this famous expression to the existence of party: the party is also a product and a manifestation of the irreconcilability of class antagonisms.[30]

In general, 'party' refers to a formally constituted political group that attempts to form or take part in a government, usually through the contestation of elections in peaceful periods. By means of either elections in peaceful periods or revolutions in wartime, the party is definitely a crystallization of class power. The party's final victory, which enables it to run the state, thus means the victory of one class or certain classes over others. The party and its form thus definitely manifest the result of class struggles in a contested historical process.

Now we face the thorny issue of 'the dictatorship of the proletariat': the conquest of power by the vanguard of the proletariat that pursues revolution, runs the state and rules over the people. As a form of political organization, unlike Lenin's assertion that the proletarian state will wither away, instead the party maintains its resilience and transforms itself into a party-state after the communist revolution.[31]

---

28   Ibid.
29   Ibid.
30   'Party' refers to a formally constituted political group that contests elections and attempts to form or take part in a government. 'State' means a nation or territory considered as an organized political community under one government or federal republic. In modern polities, the state is a bureaucratic and administrative organ that helps an organized political community function in a specific bounded area. But it definitely manifests as the result of class conflicts and struggles in a specific nation or territory.
31   Actually, in the modern Western state polity, all state forms have a party-state nature; it is not peculiar to socialist states in the third world. The single-party system controlled by the communists is often accused of being characteristic of the party-state, lacking the multiparty systems open to competition between all classes.

We face a few crucial questions once the party or the party-state of the proletariat fails to dissolve after the communist revolution: What is the justification of 'the dictatorship of the proletariat'? In 'Critique of the Gotha Program', Marx said, 'Between capitalist and communist society there lies the period of the revolutionary transformation of the one into the other. Corresponding to this is also a political transition period in which the state can be nothing but the revolutionary dictatorship of the proletariat.'[32]

All sorts of critiques, from both right and left, arise when this political transitional period becomes unlikely to end, and the prospect of dissolving the vanguard party and of the withering away of the state becomes distant. When the party-state finally turns out to be bureaucratic and oppressive, the dream of communism is dashed.

This seems like a historical irony but only because we lack a true class perspective. Very often, we look at the dictatorship of the proletariat and the form of party politics, but we avoid the enemies of the party, the real class forces, intentionally or unintentionally. We are not ready to prepare for a more protracted and bitter struggle for a communist revolution.

Acknowledging that class conflict still exists, the revolution is not over, and neither is the party nor the party-state.

The Study of the Chinese Communist Revolution

Wang Hui, a leading progressive Chinese scholar studies the Chinese Revolution, takes the party as a form in the revolutionary period, and does not perceive a problem so long as the party relied on the people's war, i.e. the 'mass line'.[33]

As Wang states, the idea of the mass line was first advanced by the Central Committee of the Communist Party of China in 1929, in a letter to the Fourth Route Army. A political project embraced a slogan: 'All for the masses; all rely on the masses; from the masses and to the masses', which Wang describes as more than just political propaganda, but indeed a description of an organic revolutionary politics.[34] The mass line is thus an inventive political form providing political energy in its formulation. It enables a process in which 'the masses become a political category and

---

32   Karl Marx, 'Critique of the Gotha Programme' (1970 [1875]), Chapter IV, at marxists.org.
33   Wang Hui, 'The Crisis of Representativeness and Post-Party Politics', Chapter 1 in this volume.
34   Ibid., p. 16.

the political party, part of mass politics; the two define each other and intermingle'.[35]

Echoing Russo's argument, Wang Hui laments the decline of 'inventive politics', whereby, in the mass line after the Revolution, and especially after the Cultural Revolution, this 'inventive' form of organizing vanished. The end of the mass line that engendered the political dynamism of the CCP occurred during the political process of the twentieth century. Wang notes, 'After the PRC was established, the Communist Party searched for a new path for its own renovation under the conditions following people's war. The failure of the Cultural Revolution signified the end of this search, as well as the beginning of the full integration of the party in to the framework of the state.'[36] He argues that the 'logic of state' controls parties, and that 'the boundary between party and state is vanishing'.[37]

As Wang explains, the end of the mass line is the consequence of the process of depoliticization, or the detachment of political form from social form. Like Alessandro Russo, he calls for new forms of post-party political experiment, or new forms of organizing, that might move beyond the old political-party model.[38]

The question that remains to us is this: Was the mass line purely a form of political organization, or a line of struggle that inherently engaged class forces and class struggle?

Mao was successful in mobilizing the mass line to fight foreign imperialism and civil war – a fight targeting a comprador bourgeoisie and landlords in the pre-Liberation period. But Mao was defeated when he mobilized the same mass line in the Cultural Revolution. The same invention of Mao's Marxism that laid the foundation for the success of the Chinese Revolution failed to accomplish socialist transformation in the post-Liberation period. Why?

In order to mine the Chinese revolutionary tradition, historian Elizabeth Perry adopts a perspective of cultural position to study the dynamics of the Chinese revolutionary leadership and their creative use of cultural capital and organizational innovation in mobilizing Anyuan's workers to support the revolution.[39] In certain ways, she agrees that Chinese communism was an alien import, and Marxism a *deus ex machina* of the Chinese

---

35   Ibid., p. 25.
36   Ibid., p. 71.
37   Ibid., p. 8.
38   Ibid., p. 29.
39   Elizabeth Perry, *Anyuan: Mining China's Revolutionary Tradition* (California: University of California Press, 2012), p. 4.

revolution.[40] She argues that the ability to translate revolutionary goals culturally, such as by using folk songs, music and stories over the course of the revolution, bestowed victory upon the Chinese struggle.

By highlighting the cultural factor in the nurturing of China's revolutionary past, Perry simultaneously downplays the importance of class struggle. By emphasizing the watchwords of the Anyuan strike – 'Once beasts of burden, now we will be human'[41] – Perry redefines the struggle for class equality as a workers' battle for 'human dignity and social justice' by the dispossessed, and thus characterizes the Chinese Revolution as a civil movement in a broad sense. Perry is sympathetic to the Chinese Revolution in a way that dismisses its class contents and goal of achieving a communist takeover.

Nevertheless, echoing Perry Anderson and others, she is correct in her assertion that,

> In contrast to Lenin's revolution, Mao's revolution was a protracted process. Building upon the Republican Revolution of 1911 and the Nationalist Revolution of 1925–27, the Chinese Communist revolution took nearly three decades to achieve political victory, from the establishment of the Chinese Communist Party in July 1921 until the founding of the People's Republic of China in October 1949.[42]

An Unfinished Revolution

The year 1949 did not see the final victory of the Communist Revolution. Instead, it signalled the beginning of a new era of continuous revolution.

By nature, China's Revolution of 1949 was an unfinished one. It was the product of 'socialism in one country' – a country surrounded by strong bourgeois states in the new world order. By 1949, what the CCP had achieved was national unification and the eviction of foreign imperial powers. The transition to socialism was yet to come, including the process of the 'withering away' of the party-state.

---

40   Ibid., p. 283.
41   Ibid., p.14.
42   Ibid., p. 3. See also Mao's own words: 'We have a Communist Party and a Liberation Army both tempered in decades of revolutionary struggle, and a working people likewise so tempered. Our Party and our armed forces are rooted in the masses, have been tempered in the flames of a protracted revolution and have the capacity to fight. Our People's Republic was not built overnight, but developed step by step out of the revolutionary base areas.' Mao, 'On the Correct Handling of Contradictions among the People' (27 February 1957), at marxists.org.

But this turned out to be an impossible mission, as predicted by Marx's theory of the dictatorship of the proletariat, as well as Lenin's thesis on the 'withering away of the state' in a concrete historical struggle. Let us first examine the international factors.

Proletarian internationalism was betrayed by both Western and Russian communism in the late nineteenth and twentieth centuries. The centre of revolution had no choice but to shift to the third world countries, especially for those nations that were incorporated into global capitalism and imperialism by armed force. As today, China in the first half of the twentieth century was at the centre of this incorporation and oppression, which was accompanied by a deepening process of class conflict and loss of life. When revolution came, it arrived in a single and insular nation. The betrayal, led by the West of the continuous process of communist revolution internationally, and of internationalism itself, threatened the existence of the socialist state. The Chinese Revolution was by nature a national and socialist revolution, as well as provisional and transitional. The state had a stake in safeguarding the fruits of revolution from its enemies in the Western capitalist world.

Given this betrayal by the Western communist movements, the historical conditions for the 'withering away of the state' or the dissolution of the party-state in China did not exist. When the Cold War started, the only option left to the CCP was to build a state as strong as possible, in order to protect itself from foreign powers. Not that its class enemies were extinguished; in fact, they surrounded it. In reality, enlarging and strengthening the state was a dream shared by many Chinese people in both the socialist and contemporary periods. It was these international circumstances that crippled the Chinese Revolution, to a certain extent. The conditions for the 'withering away' of the state faded.

Maurice Meisner was quite correct to comment that, 'Unlike Lenin or Trotsky, Mao Zedong was an eminently national revolutionary leader', and that 'The Chinese victors of 1949, by contrast, appear as somber realists; not seized by the same chiliastic revolutionary visions as their Russian predecessors, they were not to suffer similar disillusionments.'[43]

The dictatorship of the proletariat persisted. Yet, while Mao faced historical limits in the third world context, he was creative enough to turn 'the dictatorship of the proletariat' into a 'people's democratic dictatorship' in order to broaden the representativeness of the party-state.

---

43   Maurice Meisner, *Mao's China and After: A History of the People's Republic* (London: Simon & Schuster, 1999), p. 34.

On 30 June 1949, before the Liberation, Mao wrote the famous article, 'On People's Democratic Dictatorship'. In its opening, he states:

> The first of July 1949 marks the fact that the Communist Party of China has already lived through twenty-eight years. Like a man, a political party has its childhood, youth, manhood and old age. The Communist Party of China is no longer a child or a lad in his teens but has become an adult. When a man reaches old age, he will die; the same is true of a party. When classes disappear, all instruments of class struggle – parties and the state machinery – will lose their function, cease to be necessary, therefore gradually wither away and end their historical mission; and human society will move to a higher stage.[44]

He continued:

> To be overthrown is painful and is unbearable to contemplate for those overthrown, for example, for the Kuomintang reactionaries whom we are now overthrowing and for Japanese imperialism which we together with other peoples overthrew some time ago. But for the working class, the labouring people and the Communist Party the question is not one of being overthrown, but of working hard to create the conditions in which classes, state power and political parties will die out very naturally and mankind will enter the realm of Great Harmony.[45]

By creating the conditions for a 'people's democratic dictatorship', the CCP would definitely be criticized by the international community. Mao answered in this way: '"You are dictatorial." My dear sirs, you are right, that is just what we are. All the experience the Chinese people have accumulated through several decades teaches us to enforce the people's democratic dictatorship, that is, to deprive the reactionaries of the right to speak and let the people alone have that right.'[46]

'Why must things be done this way?' Mao asked, and answered:

> The reason is quite clear to everybody. If things were not done this way, the revolution would fail, the people would suffer, the country

---

44   Mao Zedong, 'On the People's Democratic Dictatorship' (30 June 1949), at marxists.org.
45   Ibid.
46   Ibid.

would be conquered . . . 'Don't you want to abolish state power?' Yes, we do, but not right now; we cannot do it yet. Why? Because imperialism still exists, because domestic reaction still exists, because classes still exist in our country.[47]

Mao was a lone fighter. This statement describes him even more accurately in reference to the post-revolutionary period.[48] After the 1949 Liberation, the epic duty shouldered by the 'dictatorship of the proletariat' was the construction of a socialist country.

Class Enemies: Real and Imagined

The period after the Chinese Revolution can generally be divided into two phases: that of socialist construction; second, the Cultural Revolution. The first phase sought to create conditions for socialist transformation, by which class contradictions based on private ownership of the means of production could be gradually resolved. Whereas the first period sought the socialist construction of an economic and material base, the second was a revolution to resolve political and ideological contradictions inside the party itself.[49]

While the majority of the leadership of the CCP shifted all of their political energy to focus on socialist construction, Mao never lost sight of politics and potential political enemies. The enemies with guns, and especially foreign imperial powers, were very easy to identify, as Mao reminded people. But who were the enemies after the Revolution? The landlord class and the old bureaucrat-bourgeoisie were gone. New enemies internally, however, continued to exist. There were at least five groups:

1. the old civil servants inherited from the Guomindang, the Nationalist Party, who worked in the new government;
2. the intellectuals of old learning who preferred a hierarchical society, and the liberal intellectuals and democratic people who believed in a Western parliamentary democracy;
3. the national bourgeoisie and its supporters, who were not willing to transform themselves;

---

47   Ibid.
48   Ross Terrill, *Mao: A Biography* (London: Harper & Row, 1980), p. 206.
49   Steve S. K. Chin, *The Thought of Mao Tse-Tung: Form and Content* (Hong Kong: Centre of Asian Studies, University of Hong Kong, 1979), p. 84.

4. the rich and middle peasants, both from the pre-Liberation period and newly emerged after land reform, who declined to join in the collectivization movement;

5. last but not least, the party revisionists and elites who might not agree to the direction of socialist construction and radical policies for social change adopted by the party.

Surely not all of these enemies could have been correctly identified, and may even have been wrongly accused and sentenced. Equally wrong would be the simple and essentialist identification of class enemies based on birth and social identity during the Cultural Revolution. But it would hardly be convincing to claim that there were no internal enemies or class conflicts at all.

Mao Zedong developed a theory of revolutionary dialectics, as Stuart R. Schram notes.[50] As the socialist revolution developed, Mao understood the forces of opposition as 'contradictions among people' as well as 'class contradictions'. As time went by, Mao's view on the opposition forces evolved. Who were the enemies during the course of socialist construction and Cultural Revolution?

Enemies after the 1949 Revolution were generally classified as 'counter-revolutionaries'. In contrast to Stalin's harsh suppression of internal enemies, Mao was much more lenient. In 'On the Ten Major Relationships' (25 April 1956) Mao stated:

> Counter-revolutionaries may be dealt with in these ways: execution, imprisonment, supervision and leaving at large. Execution – everybody knows what that means. By imprisonment we mean putting counter-revolutionaries in jail and reforming them through labour. By supervision we mean leaving them in society to be reformed under the supervision of the masses. By leaving at large we mean that generally no arrest is made in those cases where it is marginal whether to make an arrest, or that those arrested are set free for good behaviour. It is essential that different counter-revolutionaries should be dealt with differently on the merits of each case.[51]

Mao emphasized that counter-revolutionaries still existed inside the country, although their number had been greatly diminished:

---

50   Stuart R. Schram, 'Mao Tse-tung and the Theory of the Permanent Revolution, 1958–69', *China Quarterly* 46 (April–June 1971), pp. 221–44.
51   Mao Zedong, 'On the Ten Major Relationships' (25 April 1956), at marxists.org.

The effort to clear out those who remain hidden must go on. It should be affirmed that there are still a small number of counter-revolutionaries carrying out counter-revolutionary sabotage of one kind or another. For example, they kill cattle, set fire to granaries, wreck factories, steal information and put up reactionary posters. Consequently, it is wrong to say that counter-revolutionaries have been completely eliminated and that we can therefore lay our heads on our pillows and just drop off to sleep.[52]

Mao requested that the party adhere to the policy started in Yenan of killing none and arresting few in the process of clearing out counter-revolutionaries from places like government organs, schools and army units. He insisted that counter-revolutionaries were to be screened by the organizations concerned, but that they were not to be arrested by the public security bureaus, prosecuted by the procuratorial organs, or tried by the courts.[53] He concluded: 'As long as class struggle exists in China and in the world, we should never relax our vigilance. Nevertheless, it would be equally wrong to assert that there are still large numbers of counter-revolutionaries.'[54]

In 1957, Mao conceptualized the internal forces of opposition in a more sophisticated way. In the article, 'On the Correct Handling of Contradictions among the People', he further distinguished between two types of social contradiction – those between the people and the enemy, and those among the people. The two were totally different in nature. In this article, not only is the concept of enemies malleable, but so too is the concept of the people: 'The concept of "the people" varies in content in different countries and in different periods of history in a given country . . . There have always been contradictions among the people, but they are different in content in each period of the revolution and in the period of building socialism.'[55]

According to Mao, during the Sino-Japanese War, any social classes and social strata opposing Japanese aggression would be grouped within the category of 'the people', while the Japanese imperialists, their Chinese collaborators and the pro-Japanese elements were classified as enemies of the people. During the War of Liberation, the US imperialists and the

---

52   Ibid.
53   Ibid.
54   Ibid.
55   Mao, 'Correct Handling of Contradictions'.

bureaucrat-capitalists, the landlords and the Guomindang reactionaries, were the new enemies of the people, while the other classes, strata and social groups that opposed them all came within the category of the people:[56]

> At the present stage, the period of building socialism, the classes, strata and social groups which favour, support and work for the cause of socialist construction all come within the category of the people, while the social forces and groups which resist the socialist revolution and are hostile to or sabotage socialist construction are all enemies of the people.[57]

Unlike for Stalin, not all the class contradictions were antagonistic in the eyes of Mao: 'Within the ranks of the people, the contradictions among the working people are non-antagonistic, while those between the exploited and the exploiting classes have a non-antagonistic as well as an antagonistic aspect.'[58] Mao believed that the antagonistic contradiction between the two classes, if properly handled, could be transformed into a non-antagonistic one and resolved by peaceful methods.

Mao always preferred peaceful methods in dealing with people's contradictions, hoping to turn internal enemies into new humans:

> The people's democratic dictatorship uses two methods ... Towards the people ... it uses the method of democracy and not of compulsion, that is, it must necessarily let them take part in political activity and does not compel them to do this or that but uses the method of democracy to educate and persuade. Such education is self-education for the people, and its basic method is criticism and self-criticism.[59]

In search of a Chinese way to construct socialism, Stuart Schram comments that 'thought reform' was consistently used to transform people in general and class enemies specifically.[60]

In fact, Mao had a very clear vision of what kind of an ideal society the Chinese Revolution should lead to, which could be called the true

---

56   Ibid.
57   Ibid.
58   Ibid.
59   Mao Zedong, 'Closing speech at the Second Session of the First National Committee of the Chinese People's Political Consultative Conference' (23 June 1950), at Marxists.org.
60   Stuart Schram, *Mao Tse-Tung* (Harmondsworth: Penguin, 1975).

'Socialism with Chinese characteristics'. In contrast to Russian communism, Mao argues,

> We do not propose the slogans 'cadres decide everything' or 'technology decides everything,' or the slogan 'communism is the Soviet Union plus electrification'. But does it mean we do not want electrification? We want electrification just the same and even more urgently. The first two slogans were Stalin's way and rather one-sided. If 'technology decides everything', then what about politics? If 'cadres decide everything', then what about the masses?[61]

In order to distinguish his own approach from the Russian path of socialist transformation, Mao argues that,

> When discussing the socialist economy, Stalin said the post-revolutionary reform was a peaceful reform proceeding from the top to the bottom levels. He did not undertake the class struggle from the bottom to the top ... only proceeding from the top to the bottom and struggling against the capitalists. We proceed from the top to the bottom, but we also add the class struggle from the bottom to the top, settling the roots and linking together.[62]

The mass line and class struggle were always intertwined as the essential ingredients of the construction of socialism.

The Permanence of the Cultural Revolution

The climax of the Chinese Revolution was the Cultural Revolution.

Perry Anderson is right to say that revolution is a political act that serves as a complete overthrow from below of one state order in order to create a new one. He is also right to say that 'a revolution is an episode of convulsive political transformation, compressed in time and concentrated in target', and that it has 'a determine beginning – when the old state apparatus is still intact – and a finite end, when that apparatus is decisively broken and a new one erected in its stead'.[63]

---

61   Mao Zedong, 'Speeches at the Second Session of the Eighth Party Congress' (8–23 May 1958), at marxists.org.
62   Ibid.
63   Perry Anderson, 'Modernity and Revolution', *New Left Review* I: 144 (March–April 1984), p.

But Anderson is probably wrong when he argues that revolution is a punctual and not a permanent process. His refusal to acknowledge the permanent process of revolution is due to his negation of Mao's Cultural Revolution, which he takes as a kind of psychological or moral conversion, and an unnecessary extension of chaos into every corner of social space. In Anderson's view, the Cultural Revolution was initiated in order to prevent any reproduction in China of a bureaucratic class that, as Mao saw it, 'was leading the USSR after Stalin towards a class society indistinguishable from capitalism'.[64] In order to resolve this huge contradiction, Mao did not rely on the security organs, but turned to student youth and the younger generation to revolt. Anderson argues: 'Unleashing, against those he feared would take the Soviet path, mass turbulence from below, rather than decapitating them from above, Mao plunged the country into a decade of controlled chaos . . . The cruelties that followed were legion. Uncoordinated violence – persecutions and dissensions; humiliations, beatings, shootings; factional warfare – spread from city to city; in the counties, organized executions.'[65]

Finally, Anderson remarks on the Cultural Revolution that 'Its self-proclaimed goal was an egalitarian transformation of outlooks that would no longer accept the "three great differences": between town and country, between agriculture and industry, and – above all – between manual and intellectual labour. Such ideals were utopian in any society at the time, let alone one still as backward as China.'[66]

Anderson's negation of the Cultural Revolution is the reason that he negates Mao's concept of 'permanent revolution'. Through this approach, he repeats the right-wing argument of the evils of the party and the chaos of Mao's Cultural Revolution, romanticizes one-off revolution, and underrates the difficulty of class struggle. Mao's major contribution is nevertheless his theory of 'permanent revolution', the development of a dialectic of revolution for the communist movement in history and in the future. In contrast to Anderson's view that revolution should be a punctual process, Mao is more realistic in viewing the revolution as an 'interrupted' and 'continuous' process, in order to achieve the transformation from a capitalistic society into a socialist, and then communist, one.[67] Mao explains:

112.

64   Perry Anderson, 'Two Revolutions', *New Left Review* II:61 (January–February 2010), p. 65.
65   Ibid., p. 68.
66   Ibid.
67   See the discussion in Schram, 'Mao Tse-tung and the Theory of the Permanent Revolution', pp. 221–44.

Our nation is waking up, just like anybody waking from a night's sleep. We have overthrown the feudal system of many thousands of years and have awakened. We have changed the system of ownership; we have now gained victories in the Rectification Campaign as well as in the Anti-Rightist Campaign . . . I stand for the theory of permanent revolution . . . For example after the Liberation of 1949 came the Land Reform; as soon as this was completed there followed the mutual-aid teams, then the low-level cooperatives, then the high-level cooperatives. After seven years the cooperativization was completed and productive relationships were transformed; then came the Rectification. After Rectification was finished, before things had cooled down, then came the Technical Revolution . . .[68]

In 'Sixty Points on Working Methods' (2 February 1958), Mao further explained: 'Our revolutions are like battles. After a victory, we must at once put forward a new task. In this way, cadres and the masses will forever be filled with revolutionary fervour . . . From this year onward, simultaneously with the accomplishment of the continued socialist revolution on the ideological and political front, [we] must shift the foci of attention of the whole party.'[69]

He requested that his party comrades emphasize that, 'Red and expert, politics and business – the relationship between them is the unification of contradictions. We must criticize the apolitical attitude. [We] must oppose empty-headed "politicos" on the one hand and disoriented "practicos" on the other.'[70]

The concept of permanent revolution that arose by the time of the Great Leap Forward campaign of 1958 laid the theoretical foundation for the coming tides of mass movement, and eventually the Cultural Revolution itself. Mao's continuous revolution obviously is not simply intended to extinguish internal rivalries, but is also a call for a deepening of the revolution to resolve contradictions among people and between humans and nature. As Stuart Schram puts it, Mao's dialectic of revolution helped to 'translate a concept of man, society and the universe in ceaseless and unending flux which has no real parallel in Soviet thought, and which lies at the heart both of the Great Leap Forward of 1958, and of the Cultural Revolution'.[71]

---

68   Mao Zedong, 'Speech At The Supreme State Coference' (28 January 1958), at Marxists.org.
69   Ibid.
70   Ibid.
71   Schram, 'Mao Tse-tung and the Theory of the Permanent Revolution', p. 224.

In 'Reading Notes on the Soviet Text *Political Economy*' (1961–62), in which Mao notes: 'Socialism will "inevitably" supersede capitalism and moreover will do so by "revolutionary means" . . . The proletariat will "organize all working people around itself for the purpose of eliminating capitalism." Correct. But at this point one should go on to raise the question of the seizure of power.'[72] Mao insisted that the proletarian revolution could not hope to come upon ready-made socialist economic forms:

> 'Components of a socialist economy cannot mature inside of a capitalist economy based on private ownership.' Indeed, not only can they not 'mature'; they cannot be born. In capitalist societies a cooperative or state-run economy cannot even be brought into being, to say nothing of maturing. This is our main difference with the revisionists, who claim that in capitalist societies such things as municipal public enterprises are actually socialist elements, and argue that capitalism may peacefully grow over to socialism. This is a serious distortion of Marxism.[73]

This text touches upon the 'form of the proletarian state', which is the issue that has concerned Alan Badiou and Alessandro Russo the most. Mao frankly admitted that, though the proletarian state could take various forms, there was actually not much essential difference between the proletarian dictatorship in the people's democracies of China and the one established in Russia after the October Revolution. He pointed out that the soviets of the Soviet Union and the Chinese people's congresses were both representative assemblies, different in name only. If there were a difference, it would be located in the stronger base of support and higher degree of representativeness enjoyed by the people's congresses in China.

Mao asks, 'Is revolution harder in backward countries?' His answer is in the negative:

> In the various nations of the West there is a great obstacle to carrying through any revolution and construction movement, i.e. the poisons of the bourgeoisie are so powerful that they have penetrated each and every corner. While our bourgeoisie has had, after all, only three generations, those of England and France have had a 250–300-year history of development and their ideology and *modus operandi* have

---

72   Mao Zedong, 'Reading Notes on the Soviet Text *Political Economy*' (1961–62), at marxists.org.
73   Ibid.

influenced all aspects and strata of their societies. Thus the English working class follows the Labour Party, not the Communist Party.

Lenin says, 'The transition from capitalism to socialism will be more difficult for a country the more backward it is.' This would seem incorrect today. Actually, the transition is less difficult the more backward an economy is, for the poorer they are the more the people want revolution. In the capitalist countries of the West the number of people employed is comparatively high, and so is the wage level. Workers there have been deeply influenced by the bourgeoisie, and it would not appear to be all that easy to carry through a socialist transformation.[74]

Now we return to the basic question: *What is class struggle for?*

The dictatorship of the proletariat is intended to end the dictatorship of the bourgeoisie. This is the historical condition that creates the possibility for the class party to be dissolved. We have to understand clearly that, although resistance politics does not take the party form, oppositional forces will always come back to use it. The party is the locus of power, and the state is the site of class struggle. The devil is not the form per se, but the bourgeois power that controls it. The form can be malleable, and it might include party, network, platform, node, or digital. Without a continuous revolution – a permanent process without completion – the power of the bourgeoisie will come back in some form. In China, this class power returned and reformed according to historical circumstances, and these circumstances presented themselves most simply as conflicts between bureaucrats and the masses in the socialist period, as well as in the contemporary period. This is exactly the historical challenge that was faced by Mao Zedong and the people in the Cultural Revolution. When the Cultural Revolution failed, capitalism returned to China. In 1975 Mao stated: 'It is easy to establish capitalism in China.'

The issue of the 'dictatorship of the proletariat' was at stake during the course of Cultural Revolution. The return to order by Deng's political force was not a result of the persistence of the 'dictatorship of the proletariat' per se, but of its failure in concrete class struggles like those between the ruling cadres and the masses, between factory management and workers, and between school management and students.

The strengthening of bureaucratic organs, and hence the restoration of

---

74   Ibid.

party-state control over society, was a victory of the party revisionists and state elites who controlled the means of production in the name of collective ownership and a socialist market economy. These were the actual people, not to be construed as an abstract form of the 'dictatorship of proletariat' or an authoritarian state. The failure of the masses in the Cultural Revolution, presented as factionalism, group fighting and chaos, was not the result of a failure in exploring new forms of political experiment in organizing, but precisely of the weakness of mass power. The concept of the 'working class' is not itself problematic, and the core problem was the inability of working-class power to overthrow the bureaucracy or the institution of the state. Class relations still existed. Enemies survived.

The ideal of communism had largely vanished, but not its struggles.

3   Liberating Dictatorship: Communist Politics and the Cultural Revolution

Cécile Winter

Why should we assume that the word 'dictatorship' is necessarily reserved for the state? 'Dictatorship', it turns out, is among the vaguest of words, a word that designates – what? – the absence of an electoral procedure, the lack of alternation between parties in power, at least when a bourgeois uses the term. Or else it refers to the famous 'dictatorship of the proletariat', a phrase whose clichéd quality evokes the construct, as rigid as it was imaginary, called 'socialism'. I will return to this point.

Democracy, that belle whose beauty is rather banal, has many suitors eager to extricate her from all of her determining ties with the state, and to extol her as the non-state-like virtue impelling assemblies and mass movements. I seek to recognize and serve her younger sister, dictatorship, in my view even more beautiful, as well as more rare, and deserving all our efforts.

Without doubt, whoever speaks of dictatorship speaks of power. This is exactly what interests me: this power from below, as opposed to the ordinary power of the state. A fragile authority, it is not intended to last, having at its disposal – unlike the well-entrenched administrative and repressive institutions of the dominant machine – nothing more than the capacity for mobilization and formulation, the dedication, the energy on the part of its standard-bearers in rallying people to their cause, and finally their intelligent awareness of how far they can go with it.[1]

---

1   A remarkable brochure, Contre la démocratie"(Sébastien Lamarre and David Riffin, available at contreLademocratie.wordpress.com) written as an assessment of the great Québécois movement of 2011– 12 enacts precisely this movement in the direction of dictatorship: 'Now, there is such a thing as a positive affirmation of dictatorship. Writing the "Histories of Words" columns, I emphasized that the term "dictatorship" is intimately linked with speech . . . It is not about outdoing an adversary or exceeding an average, but, rather, about raising a group to a higher level . . . One must be able to demonstrate precisely that a political proposal combats capitalism and helps the greatest number, especially the weakest . . . The verbal act implied by the term "dictatorship" presupposes a return to the predominance of speech. The dictatorship *that would not be tied to the state* [my emphasis] would be based on the most vital part of assemblies, namely, discussions and debates, all the while rejecting the vote insofar as it would put an end to discussion before it had reached its logical conclusion. It remains for us to define the contours of such a political structure, in which the truth of an idea would rule over the widest range of opinion.'

I will argue that dictatorship is a measurement. It measures the true potential of a moment or situation. It measures what can really be changed, at that point at which one measures where one stands with regard to liberation and transformation.

For a paradigmatic example – by no means a random one – take the strike committee.[2] First of all, there needs to be the fact of a strike, or a declaration of a strike. Then there needs to be the strike committee – in other words, the capacity to formulate the cause to which those who are there have now committed themselves. Let us be precise. A particular workshop or factory has gone on strike – sometimes, indeed often, perhaps always, on the basis of a movement, a refusal, that has not yet had its say. But then: here we are – What do we want? What are we going to declare, comrades? There has to be a declaration, a platform, a watchword. There has to be this coalescence, this agreement, around a word, an utterance, a dictation. Let us put it this way: something has to be that was not before, that has not been part of the law of the place: it is on the basis of this new word that the assembled collectivity raises its hand, makes up its mind to be committed.

Let us recall Mao Zedong's formulation: in every situation, there is a right, a left and a centre. The left wants to move; the right wants to stay put. The general rule is that the centre, the great majority, remains under the heel of the right, through the law of inertia. You know what you are dealing with, anyway: let things stay the same; at least we're familiar with them. Committing yourself to something new is by definition risky. Should the left happen to make common cause with the centre, it does so on the basis of – what? An idea, a thought, an act of speaking; a rallying cry, which we will sustain together. This is why the authority in place – the boss, the government, the party committees, and the provincial and municipal agencies during the Cultural Revolution, and so on – is always demanding elections; they always appeal to the individual account and to the counting of individuals, which will end up confirming that indeed there exists what had already existed in the static, state-like impotence of its dissipation, and

---

2   'The factory is where we measure where we stand in relation to capitalism.' As an appendix to the present chapter, the text entitled, 'I Can't Do It, I'm Going to Do It: What Is a Political Intervention in a Factory? What Is the Political Statement of a Cell?' (unpublished), assesses the political experience of a Maoist workers' cell in the Parisian region, of which I was one of the members. It deals with the political role of workers and of the factory when they are liberated from the state–trade union problematic of 'class' and its 'representation', and thus locates itself wholeheartedly in the problematic opened up by the Chinese Cultural Revolution.

nothing else. The right calls for a vote,[3] the left for assemblies. This is the general law. The left is necessarily in the minority; if it happens, if it rallies people to its cause, it does so on the basis of a new act of speaking or dictation, inseparable from the collectivity brought together by and for this verbal act. The moving dialectic of what is said and of those whom it brings together institutes a dictatorship – and signifies, in addition, that the dictatorship will not last forever, for its duration and power depend upon this very movement. The stronger and more inventive this new collective capacity, the more effectively its new dictum will impose itself and become reality, giving way to a new watchword, to be sustained in turn by a new collectivity, and so forth.

For this reason, let us keep in mind that dictatorship is always, to begin with, a capacity 'from within the people' – a hitherto unseen gathering-together around one or several utterances.

It is on this basis that dictatorship works as dictatorship. It uses its power. Our strike committee goes after scabs, and summons the boss to appear before it. It will be noted that the younger and stronger a dictatorship is, the more the persuasion of the hesitant will take precedence over coercion, while, as the strike runs out of breath, the more coercion will prevail over persuasion. The wise committee will have a sense of where to stop in order to store up as much of the effort undertaken as possible.

'Now, the boss has to talk with us': this is the declaration of a strike committee in France from the beginning of the 1980s. Dictatorship makes authority appear before it. If the boss fails to show up, you occupy his offices, you go into his files, you display their contents, and so forth. I will maintain, therefore, that dictatorship replaces the imaginary of the enemy, and the imaginary enemy with a real face-to-face encounter. This is its second virtue, and the reason why measures in two ways. Measuring the collective capacity for uniting, this power will really measure itself against the old order's capacity for resistance. The movement will develop, and will rally other movements or people to itself. Or not. Here, dictatorship is the measure of what we will have been able to do, this time. I propose

---

3   Provided that the vote produces the result expected by the power in place. If, by some chance, the vote does not completely satisfy this power, it immediately forgets all its democratic speeches and resorts to coups and state terror. Just recall Algeria in the past, or Egypt today, or the pure and simple kidnapping by a Franco-American commando unit of the Haitian president Aristide, elected by more than 80 per cent of the population.

to take dictatorship as the measure of what is really possible, and as the real measure of the possible.

From this point, I will return to the question of revolutionary time, by designating as, precisely, revolution a time of dictatorship practised on the state, which dictatorship submits to an operation of forcing. History books, for that matter, refer to times of 'dual power'. There are clubs, and there is the assembly, committees, soviets. 'Power' here would designate the contradictory conjunction of state and dictatorship. When Mao asks 'Why Is It that Red Political Power Can Exist in China?', he gathers together and distinguishes between the two – between new agencies of dictatorship in the liberated zones and the embryonic skeleton of the new state, the liberation army.

Lenin anticipates, or hopes, that dictatorship will simply replace the state, resulting in something like a lasting Commune. This is why he can speak of a state that is already no longer really a state: a state that is constantly being forced, in some sense – otherwise, how could it 'wither away'? Once it becomes resistant to experimentation, with (or by) the test of experience, the contradiction reappears whereby meetings, and thus soviets, become increasingly rare, or get bogged down, and the new bureaucracy establishes itself; Lenin seeks practical solutions that take the duality into account, such as 'peasants and workers inspection teams'. Or else, to get around the aporia, he calls for the intervention of the workers as a body, for the political discipline of the workers, which therefore well deserves to be called the proletariat, as it itself takes the place of the state. The state, Lenin says, will be 'the body of armed workers': such an authority can only be that of one action. The intervention of the proletarian body in all its majesty must be even more short-lived. This unprecedented act indeed takes place – during the critical phase of the Cultural Revolution, when Mao, instead of further strengthening the authority of the army and giving it license to practice terror, will call on the workers as a body, as a body of unarmed workers, in order to put an end to the conflicts between factions of students in Beijing. So let us keep in mind: dictatorship, and the proletariat.

Discontinuity, then, to be sure. Not like the state, which of course has lasted for a long time. But, for all that, does it necessarily follow that what stops and starts again has to be declared, once and for all, finished, done, discredited?[4]

---

4   It is saddening – and at the same time disturbing – to see our formerly close comrade Sylvain Lazarus writing on the back cover of a collection of his political writings, with a preface by Natacha

We prefer the idea of going on. A thought resumes its itinerary.

Certainly, the desire for equality and justice, the idea that everyone must count: we can declare this desire to be as unchanging as it is eternal, surging back to the surface with every popular uprising. Always irrepressible, always frustrated, communist desire (that great semaphore planted from one century to another, as Alain Badiou phrases it) has asserted itself perhaps since the beginning of time as an insistent and powerful chant, rising above the masses of wretchedness and putting its trust in the heavens.

Nonetheless, I will maintain that the nineteenth century constitutes a break – thanks to capitalism, of course, which ushers in the a-theological era, as shown by Marx and Wagner. This should be taken seriously.

With Marx, the idea of communism comes down to earth. Humanity, he says, will finally be able to realize itself as humanity, for technical power now makes this possible, and capitalism, he adds, thus fashions the human beings necessary for this project. We enter into politics. We create an organization not subordinated to the borders of states.

All of this is really just from yesterday – hardly a century and a half ago. And yet, since then, what power, what richness of experience, has nourished this project, in such a short period of time.

Let us agree on one thing. The idea that 'it has to be', that 'it is determined by the course of history', was very ambiguous and unclear. For Marx, it followed from a coherent analysis of what capitalism is, but at the same time it immediately conveyed eschatological hope. Now, history is quite long, and quite contingent; to transform it into a purposiveness or a promise is to make it one's own nasty little god: for two or three generations, it was like a little pocket demon that, as it was applied, proved to be not only useless but extremely harmful as well. So we are in perfect agreement: neither transitivity, nor expressivity, nor automatic consequences, nor sleight of hand from one analytic framework to another.

It is, however, possible to treat the history of specific problems in a given order. And it must be done, if we don't want to let things drop.

Michel, 'The withering away of the State did not take place!!', in order to justify his renunciation of the communist idea. Are we to understand that the state should have withered away during the life-time of Sylvain Lazarus? We are mischievously tempted to write: of course, dear Sylvain, we have whatever little Kautskys we can get; dear Natacha, don't you think the ancient queen Semiramis must be convulsed with laughter in her tomb? And how can you then claim the word 'militant' for yourself? We now find ourselves compelled to deny it to you. What is a militant, if not first of all someone who agrees to work – for free – in the service of something that from every perspective transcends her? See Sylvain Lazarus, *L'intelligence de la politique* (Paris: Al dante, 2013).

Marx and Engels themselves could not avoid seeing this right before their eyes, and right away. Let us understand that such an insight also results from the force of the idea combined with the force of the investigation. Thus the young Engels, fresh from passionate discussions within the circles of the German young Hegelians, covers every square inch of England's workers' neighbourhoods (doing exactly what one must do), and, on the basis of what he sees and hears there, thinks: something must happen, something is going to happen.[5]

Let us accept as a childhood symptom the persistent trace of religious hope whose mark is a belief in immediacy – all the stronger for merging with the desire of someone who makes a strong, real commitment to a task, to believing in something like its accomplishment. Chartering one's raft for real and facing the first wave can hide the long, oceanic undulations that lie ahead.

Lenin is a consistent materialist. He writes:

> We are entitled to say with the fullest confidence that the expropriation of the capitalists will inevitably result in an enormous development of the productive forces of human society. But how rapidly this development will proceed, how soon it will reach the point of breaking away from the division of labor, of doing away with the antithesis between mental and physical labor, of transforming labor into 'life's prime want' – we do not and cannot know. That is why we are entitled to speak only of the inevitable withering away of the State, emphasizing the protracted nature of this process and its dependence upon the rapidity of development of the higher phase of communism and leaving the question of the time required for, or the concrete forms of, its withering away quite open, because there is no material for answering these questions.'

A few lines further, he states that thinking of socialism as 'something lifeless, rigid, fixed once and for all' is nothing more than an 'ordinary bourgeois conception', but he maintains the hypothesis of continuity: 'socialism will be the beginning, in all domains, of a rapid, genuine, truly mass movement forward', which he sees as 'ensuring further progress':[6]

The present-day Great Cultural Revolution is only the first of its kind. There will inevitably be many more in the future. In the last few years,

---

5   See Engels, *The Condition of the Working Class in England* (Oxford: Oxford University Press, 2009).
6   See Lenin, *The State and Revolution* (London: Penguin, 1993).

comrade Mao Zedong has often indicated that the issue of who will win in the revolution can only be settled over a long historical period. If things are not properly handled, it is possible for a capitalist restoration to take place at any time. All party members and the people of the entire country must beware of thinking that they can sleep soundly and that everything will be fine after one, two, three, or four Great Cultural Revolutions. It is imperative that we continue to pay the most careful attention and never relax our vigilance.[7]

I want to argue that, with the Chinese Cultural Revolution (the first of its kind!), the communist idea is liberated from every eschatological view: neither immediacy nor historical promise nor continuous progress. It is a question here of a history without limits or stages – a history about which one says only that it is 'very long': this time, which is indefinite in every sense of the term, is precisely what liberates communism as an idea and a project, whose treatment can never be anything other than current. From this point forward, communism is thus a political matter (a matter of politics).

I now want to try to show how this revolution actually carried out the liberation of communist politics as such, and how it put communist politics on the agenda. I will do this in four steps, roughly corresponding – as far as the first three are concerned – to the chronology of the revolution, and moving, in the process, from the most specific to the most universal and current lessons:

1. Unlocking socialism: paradox and avowal (1966)
2. The time of revolution strictly speaking (1967 and 1968)
3. Communism or capitalism (or the time of assessment)
4. A comment on the question of class

Unlocking socialism: paradox and avowal

Socialism presented itself as a particularly locked 'system': this locking was at once symbolic (with its compulsory and official ideology, its coded language – the notorious 'jargon' 'wood's language') and political, guaranteed by the single state authority constituted by the party-state that, from the highest government agencies to the smallest organizations and establishments, directs and controls all social activity. Now, it

---

7   See *Circular of the Central Committee of the Communist Party of China on the Great Proletarian Cultural Revolution*, at Marxists.org.

is in socialist China that free rein was given to a truly unheard-of political freedom, never before experienced in history, under the banner of
'mass democracy'. This was anything but an empty slogan, for it
included: total freedom of organization; freedom to travel throughout
the country for 'revolutionary exchanges'; the founding of an unlimited
number of organizations, with orders given to afford them every means
of publishing texts and newspapers, posters placed everywhere, and
tracts extending to millions of copies; the right – and the encouragement
– to pronounce oneself on any and every subject and to attack without
restriction all governing authorities and personalities on all levels; to
criticize them without restriction; to go through and display their files;
to undertake investigations into their pasts and to make them public –
and so on. As Hong Yung Lee sums it up simply in his book, *Politics of
the Chinese Cultural Revolution*,[8] 'Undoubtedly, the January Power
Seizure was a unique event not only in Chinese political history but also
in the history of mankind, for in this period a so-called totalitarian
regime governing a quarter of the world's population ordered its people
to seize power from itself for the sake of revolution.' Over the course of
1967, the initiative is left entirely to the masses. The army has to guard
strategic sites, the police have to keep watch over criminal activities,
and the masses are warned against 'economism'. That is all. Lee remarks
that the very fact that the Chinese political system survived such a test
shows its viability and its strength.[9]

All this thanks to the willpower and grace of a single man, Mao Zedong.
We know that he said, 'I did two things in my life: I invited the Japanese
to go home and I launched the Cultural Revolution.' Above the state and
the 'system', there is the power of speech of the great revolutionary leader,
the conviction and the faith attached to his person;[10] and this is due to the

---

8   This book, Hong Yung Lee, *The Politics of the Chinese Cultural Revolution*, has constituted the guiding thread of my study, along with brochures of the Foreign Languages Publishers of Beijing
preserved from the period, and Neal Hunter's book, *Shanghai Journal*.

9   A point whose truth we would maintain to this day. We could also say that the fact that the
Chinese state apparatus has kept the same name (Communist Party), considered as defying common
sense and as an admission of defeat, should also be considered as an effect of the Cultural Revolution
(things did not happen in this way in the USSR), which leaves open semantically the hypothesis of a
long-lasting struggle between the communist and capitalist ways and the possibility therefore . . . of
new cultural revolutions.

10   As well as gratitude, and love, absolutely. Only the bourgeois and the scoundrels who claim to
honour Homer, Mozart, Rembrandt and Archimedes, and the unknown Indian who invented the
zero, thus offering the world the decimal system, can mock the people's love for great revolutionary
leaders, who are, however, as rare, unfortunately, and as important for the destiny of humanity as the
great geniuses of science and art.

fact that, as a communist revolutionary, he himself stays above the state and above the level of the already-accomplished, in the service of what remains to be accomplished – eternally, 'the situation and our tasks'.

Mao officially launches the Cultural Revolution in May 1966. Revolution is declared in China. He immediately puts in place a directing agency; there is thus in fact, from the outset, a situation of double power, a stand-in for authority (pre-eminent from the viewpoint of the revolution) that will be called the Centre. The Centre comprises the 'Cultural Revolution Small Group', an ad hoc authority, and elements of the state apparatus, in some sense detached or split within themselves – more or less, the army, particularly in the person of Lin Biao, at the beginning of the process, and, very peculiarly, Zhou En Lai, the head of the government, who in a way realizes in himself, and performs the feat of putting into practice, this oxymoron: a communist head of state. Mao does not have the status of a reference point or of an icon during the Cultural Revolution; he is its effective political director, according to his methods: thinking while walking, observing, letting things develop, finding solutions gradually, proceeding more by general directives than by precise orders, inventing new methods, agreeing to move in a zigzagging manner. He does not just set off the Cultural Revolution, giving the masses unlimited political freedom under such slogans as 'four great freedoms' and 'it is right to revolt', launching in August 1966, before a crowd of millions of students,[11] this watchword: 'You must get involved in affairs of state; you must lead the Cultural Revolution all the way to its end'; he also directs it in all of its phases, making all the great decisions, effecting modifications this way or that way; it is also he who decrees its end – and to a great extent its failure – by endorsing the reconstruction of the party apparatus.[12]

Let us imagine for a moment this thing that is unthinkable in our society. Suddenly, the possibility is given on all levels, from the simple

---

11   I note that, on 26 November 1966, the date of the last great mass rally in Beijing, a total of 10 million young Chinese visited the capital.

12   We must therefore take seriously the statements in the Chinese articles, as always quite precise, of the type: 'this document was established under the personal direction of comrade Mao Zedong', or 'taking advantage of the absence of comrade Mao from Beijing, etc.', or again the meaning of the famous swim in the Yangtze before his return to Beijing in July of 1966: I am taking personal responsibility for this matter. As for the famous cult of personality centred on Mao and put in place by Lin Biao, that is another story, with its own purpose – just like the cult of personality centred on Lumumba established by Mobutu immediately after he had delivered him to his assassins. I will return to this (note, incidentally, these subtle distinctions whereby Mao is called 'comrade' in the editorials of the *People's Daily*, and 'president' in those of the *Hongqi*, the army newspaper, in the course of 1966).

workshop, hospital, or school, up to the highest state authorities, by way of all regional, municipal and local administrations, to criticize the leaders, to expose their flaws, to demand their files, to ask for their replacement, and so on. If this happened, it would cause a frenzy of activity, and people would have a field day. But is it not obvious that quickly, even very quickly, there would form two opposite camps spoiling for a fight – defenders versus attackers, each group as relentless as the other, the first in its determination to defend the authority in place and to serve as its shield, the second to bring it down? Why would it be surprising that two camps should arise, as antagonistic as difficult to tell apart in terms of their political content? Why would it be surprising that there should be factions?

Lee thinks that the Cultural Revolution has not degenerated into a civil war, through violent struggles between the two opposed camps that happened in various places but never became global, because, at least formally, everyone recognized the supremacy of Mao Zedong and Mao's thought, as well as the legitimacy of the Cultural Revolution, and recognized also the legitimacy of the socialist framework (structure?) of the society. Conversely, if Mao and his supporters could launch the Cultural Revolution without being too scared of war, it is because they trusted the strength of this structure (framework), which was supposed to provide strength enough to support its testing by a politicizing diagonalization.

Why was it necessary to put socialism in question? What is socialism?

In a word, China is a socialist country. Before the Liberation, it was more or less like capitalism. Even now, the system of eight salary-levels remains in place as well as distribution according to the work performed, exchanges through the intermediary of money, none of which differs much from the previous society. The difference is that the system of ownership has changed.[13]

The system of ownership has changed. This is hardly insignificant! It is what defines a socialist state: its role is to guarantee it.

But the reality of this change is not so simple. And herein lies the question. We know all too well what private ownership of the means of production is. Whereas the process of their socialization, to begin

---

13   'Recent' quotation of Mao Zedong in the brochure – of assessment – by Zhang Chunquiao dating from 1975, 'On Complete Dictatorship over the Bourgeoisie'.

with, is a process, and this process is always simultaneously uncertain and 'in progress', as the editorial in the *People's Daily* of 17 July, 1966 recalls.

But furthermore, and above all, assuming that a business is socialized 'in law', what guarantees that it is socialized in practice, that it really works for the good of the society as a whole. And who knows this? Who determines what this good is?[14] (Zhang Chunqiao, in the same brochure: 'The ideological and political lines . . . are the factors that determine in which class factories really belong. Our comrades can remember how a business rooted in bureaucratic or national capitalism would become a socialist business: didn't this happen when we sent to it one of our representatives from the commission on military control or from the public sector, in order to transform it by enforcing the Party line and its political measures?')

Therefore, nothing is guaranteed in fact. Everything is a question of orientation: of choice, decision, politics.

Here, then, is the paradox of a radical change opening onto fragility and uncertainty. Not only is restoration always possible: it is the natural tendency of non-intervention. The word 'vigilance' recurs in all the directives – which sheds considerable light on the political and symbolic operation of locking. The party is a rock: 'Our country is a great State of proletarian dictatorship. Our party is a great armed party of Marxism-Leninism and of the thought of Mao Zedong', and so on.[15] Socialism, that guarantee without a guarantee, that envelope of an intensified contradiction, declares itself a system. The contradiction is manifested as conflicts of line at the top.[16] And the corollary of locking – of the state-imposed pseudo-guarantee of the 'system' – is, necessarily, the logic of the purge.

---

14   The Congo, again. The most grotesque spectacle of the false transfer of property is offered by the badly named decolonization – as always, most outrageously, in the Congo. We can read, for example, in Gérard Althabe's *The Flowers of the Congo*, the description of the staging of the triumphal return of Tschombe (the actual assassin of Lumumba) waving around before the crowd 'the briefcase' – the briefcase supposed to contain the Belgian assets, which were ostensibly handed over to him graciously by the former colonial power in Brussels.

15   'Never Deviate from the General Orientation of the Struggle', in 'The Red Flag', *Hongqi*, newspaper of the army, 1966.

16   Lee rightly points out that the well-informed Chinese knew how to read between the lines of the different party publications, deciphering the clichéd official language, and thus recognizing the radical divergences of orientation that were dividing the Communist Party. This is because socialism covered up and locked down a radical conflict of orientation. It is the exact opposite in our society, where the various media say whatever they want to, except that they all say the same thing, since there is only one orientation shared by everyone – namely, the upholding of capitalism.

This paradox is very well exposed in the famous article of Yao Wen Yuan entitled, 'About the Village of the Three', which will mark the beginning of the Cultural Revolution.[17] In this article, Yao Wen Yuan recounts the history of an undertaking of critical propaganda put into practice by several well-known intellectuals since the beginning of the 1960s. It is about the assessment of the Great Leap Forward:

> Teng Touo used to characterize the party line for the edification of socialism as 'forced'. Taking advantage of the temporary difficulties of the period . . . the 'Village of the Three' perfidiously attacked the overall party line for socialist edification, the Great Leap Forward, and the people's communes . . . Let go and you will fall on solid ground, he wrote. Wasn't Teng Touo asking us to proceed towards bourgeois liberalization, to bow our heads in the face of the baleful tendencies that were manifesting themselves at the time and that were called 'making your way' (i.e. the restoration of an individualist economy) and 'extending individual plots of land and free markets, multiplying small businesses, assuming complete responsibility for their profits, establishing norms on the basis of the family'? . . . While asking that we took into consideration the huge contribution of the very cultivated persons to the work of management, they had in their own view to use this great knowledge for changing socialist companies into capitalist companies, didn't they?' So he concludes: 'A black line, against the party and against socialism, brought dark clouds into the Chinese sky', and, if we want to go on the socialist way, we must block the restoration of capitalism.

The paradox lies in the claim – and this will continue during the Cultural Revolution – that the real issue is a handful (a 'tiny handful') of pro-capitalist leaders who are nonetheless able to threaten a gigantic healthy body.[18] Hence the perpetuation of a logic of purge, associated with a general proposal formulated defensively (the point is to prevent the

---

17   'About the "Village of the Three": The Reactionary Character of the "Evening Words in Yenchan" and of the "Chronicle of the Village of the Three",' in *The Great Socialist Cultural Revolution in China*, vol. 1 (Beijing: Foreign Language Publishers, 1967).

18   Step by step, we will arrive at Liu Shao Shi, then president of the Chinese republic, who is effectively, absolutely, a supporter of capitalism (he rises up against the 'iron bowl' – that is, the guarantee of a daily meal for everyone; he clamours for the right to shut down entire factories, as is done everywhere in the world, including the USSR). See Lee, *Politics of the Chinese Cultural Revolution*, p. 133.

restoration of capitalism, which is 'on its way'),[19] while, in order to ensure this defence and to get rid of this 'handful', it is declared that nothing less than a general mobilization of the entire country is necessary.

There is a radical absence of measurement, which is the distinctive sign of 'socialism'. And it takes the courage and the audacity of a Mao to dare to tackle the question, to decide to shatter all the locks, to put this 'system' thoroughly to the test. A great confusion that makes clarity possible (as he likes to say, 'the more confusion there is, the more clearly we can see').

Thus the Cultural Revolution is begun as a gigantic critical undertaking ('700 million Chinese people, 700 million critics', according to 'We Criticize the Old World', an editorial in the *People's Daily* from 8 June 1966). In contrast with the different campaigns of the 1950s and 1960s, there can be no precise objective of transformation fixed in advance. Rather, the point is to open the floodgates, to liberate the voice of the people, to test the entire structure of the society. It is important not to lose sight of this critical commitment, marked by the logic of the purge (even if this time what is happening is a gigantic movement from below, light-years away from the Stalinist method). It of course renders problematic what might be the meaning of the proposition 'leading the cultural revolution to its conclusion', 'to its end'.

And so it happens that the famous poster of Nieh Yuan-Tzu is approved and put up – 'the first large-print poster of the twentieth century', attacking the party organization in the name of ideological principles. Party authorities are by no means slow to react: this is when the famous 'work teams' are sent into the universities under the direction of Liu Shao Shi and Deng Xiao Ping, and when the anti-interference movement, whose objective is clear, is triggered. That objective is to distinguish sharply between the inside and the outside of the party, and it entails the denunciation of radical student-critics, who bow their heads until the return of Mao (without whose intervention they would have been defeated even before the battle had begun). It is noteworthy that the first Red Guard organizations emerge from the work teams, drawing many children of cadres and brandishing the 'right class origin'. When they leave for the provinces, they wear their parents' military uniforms and prove authoritarian and arrogant in their attitude towards the local students. It is they who target the 'four old things' and old customs, cut women's hair, reject

---

19 'The struggle that has recently become more overt between the bourgeoisie working for the restoration of capitalism and the proletariat opposing it'. 'We Criticize the Old World', editorial in *People's Daily*, 8 June 1966.

works of art, and so on.[20] They oppose the extension of the movement, set up checkpoints in the train stations to control the class origins of the students arriving in Beijing and to send them back to their provinces en masse, and so on. Criticism of the work teams remains at this point the project of a small minority, and those carrying it out must fight for their 'rehabilitation'. But they are gradually becoming organized.[21]

The first great effect of the unlocking produced by the Cultural Revolution consists, then, in the critique and destruction of the shackles of the notion of class, as an ossified notion, based on exclusively economic criteria, and even on origin, this notion of class determining in advance the nature of the party – of the class party! – thus of the state, and from there the idea of imaginary representation, in principle establishing the legitimacy of the 'socialist' system.[22] Lee writes that the condemnation by the Centre of the theory of 'natural redness' had the effect that 'revolutionary organizations sprang up like bamboo sprouts after the rain'. While the party apparatus, in order to curb and contain the movement, is appealing to the 'workers' common sense' against 'student disorders', the Centre is encouraging these students to appear in factories and in the countryside.

From this point on, the major line of demarcation becomes: support for or opposition to the mass movement. It is here that the 'great and glorious' Communist Party undergoes its great test:

> Mobilizing the masses, deploying the mass movement on a large scale, putting up the large-print poster-newspaper, and giving free rein to the expression of opinions and to widespread debate – this is the only way in which the Cultural Revolution can develop both widely and deeply . . . Every member of the Communist Party must be put to the test in this great revolution, in the flames of the struggle of the masses. He must prove through his acts that he is the faithful servant of the masses of the people and that he genuinely takes the teachings of

---

20   Thus the kitsch imagery of the Cultural Revolution that is common in the West is in fact the imagery of its adversaries.

21   And they are now practising, as appropriate, discussion and the mass line, seeking to understand their adversaries' motivations and concern for loyalty. Take the example of a tract cited by Lee: 'Most of these comrades have the mistaken thought that believing in the work team is believing in the Party and that opposing the work team is opposing the Central Committee and Chairman Mao.' See *Translations on People's Republic of China* (Joint Publications Research Service, 1967), p. 42.

22   See, for example, the critique of the famous slogan, 'Heroic father, brave son', in the 1967 New Years' Day editorial of the *People's Daily*. 'This slogan has become a weapon for opposing the proletarian revolutionary line. It must be emphasized that the slogan, thus used, has the goal of propagating the reactionary theory of lineage preached by the exploitative classes.'

comrade Mao Zedong as the supreme directives in all his actions. This comrade has said: Every one of our cadres, whatever his rank, is a servant of the people.[23]

To say the least, this party does not pass the test:

> But it must be noted that resistance to the movement still remains rather strong and stubborn. The leaders of a great many organs of the party made mistakes with regard to their orientation and to the line they adopted. They organized counter-attacks against the masses. They even put forth slogans according to which opposing a leader of an organization or of a work team is opposing the central committee of the Party and socialism, engaging in counter-revolution. They have aimed the spearhead at authentically revolutionary militants, hunted down the revolutionary left, and repressed the mass revolutionary movement.[24] The bourgeois line is a line of repression of the masses and of opposition to the revolution.[25]

As a result, there now appears in the texts the designation of a new enemy – a second front, as it were – although its numbers too are said to be 'tiny': 'Currently, the characteristic feature of the activities of a handful of individuals within the Party who occupy positions of leadership but commit themselves to the capitalist path and of the activities of a small number of people who cling stubbornly to the bourgeois reactionary line is that they are acting behind the scenes . . .'[26]

Thus, beginning in late 1966, we can say that the Communist Party considered as a revolutionary political organization is a thing of the past: a party that went from 1.2 million members in 1949 to 17 million in 1961 and 23 million in 1973 is now 'a gigantic machine of interconnected interests, having become the establishment, recruiting those who want to make careers for themselves', according to Lee; favouring a slave mentality, according to the Red Guards; and encouraging 'blind obedience and servility', according to the 1 January 1967 *People's Daily* editorial.

That is the end of the legitimacy of the state-party, and with it of socialism considered as a system. A note in the Beijing editions that publish the

---

23   Editorial of the *People's Daily*, 21 July 1966.
24   Editorial of the *Hongqi*, 1966, 'A Program-Document of the Cultural Revolution'.
25   Ibid.
26   Ibid.

brochures of the Cultural Revolution, dating from the early autumn of 1966, announces: 'Beginning with issue number 8, this collection is changing its title from "The Great Socialist Cultural Revolution in China" to "The Great Proletarian Revolution in China."'

On this point, should the Centre – which now addresses itself directly to 'authentic communists' (in the same joint New Year's Day editorial in the *People's Daily* and the *Hongqi*), enjoining them to 'oppose servility resolutely' and, more or less already, 'to dare to go against the current' – have called for a new regrouping, political and strictly political, of the so-called communists? Would the repercussions and the effects of the Cultural Revolution not have been much clearer had this happened?

Perhaps the situation at this point is too tense and too much on the verge of breaking apart to risk intensifying it further. For the development of the mass movement and of free mass critique quickly led to clashes and confrontations: one side trying to occupy public buildings in search of 'black material' collected against them by the authorities, the other side mobilized in order to protect 'state secrets'.[27] The constitution of such a clash has been considered as in some sense a formal law of the situation of total liberation brought about by a confrontation between 'the masses' and the state power in place – a confrontation that almost automatically follows a path of inherent aggravation and acceleration, for want of a possible diagonal treatment by one or several declared policies. For such a confrontation – for or against the leaders of the state in place – cannot be considered as manifesting by itself the opposition of two political lines or orientations. This is precisely one of the fundamental lessons of the Cultural Revolution (and a fundamental declaration by Mao Zedong to his wife Jiang Qing, which, albeit sounding very simple,

---

27   See, for example, Lee, *Politics of the Chinese Cultural Revolution*, p. 96: 'When the work teams, after making their self-criticism (asked by Zhou En Lai) refused to comply with the demands of a "minority", the radicals chased them back to their original ministries. The Red Flag Group of the Peking Aviation Institute staged a twenty-eight-day sit-in in front of the Scientific and Technological Commission for National Defense, demanding a direct interview with Chao Ju-Chang, the head of the work team at their school. The East Is Red radical group at the Peking Geology Institute staged a demonstration in front of the Ministry of Geology, asking for an interview with the head of that work team, but the majority faction at that school, the Struggle Criticism Transformation Fighting Group, denounced the demonstration and physically attacked the radicals.' 'The Beijing University Xin Beida, which for the first time published articles criticizing Liu and Deng by name, was raided by the conservatives. Nonetheless, as the radical power grew, they frequently resorted to violent means themselves, such as forced entry into government buildings, sit-in demonstrations, and violent political meetings. Their already tense relationship with the PLA – Popular Liberation Army – deteriorated further, as the radicals tried to enter the PLA compounds searching for black materials.' (Ibid., p. 125)

is in my view one of the most important statements in this entire affair: 'The question lies in the content.' I shall return to this point.)

For the time being, there is indeed a clash between those who want to defend the apparatus in place (thus thinking that they are thereby defending the fundamental benefits of socialism in China) and those who are attacking it (thus considering that the new revolutionary situation is the measure of all things).

The repeated calls from the Centre to 'limit oneself strictly to struggle by means of reasoning, and to proscribe struggle by means of coercion, to protect the democratic rights of the masses of the people' – in other words, to treat the situation as being solely that of a discussion about the proper line to take, and so on[28] – remain largely ineffective. Likewise, the thesis claiming manipulation by the 'tiny number . . . of supporters of the capitalist way and of those who are clinging to the bourgeois reactionary line . . . they are scheming behind the scenes, manoeuvring the workers' and students' organizations that they have deceived, sowing discord, creating sects, inciting others to use coercion and violence . . . whereas they themselves "withdraw to the mountain-top in order to watch the tigers devouring one another", etc.'[29] This thesis, for all that it describes real attitudes on the part of a power with its back against the wall, nonetheless remains quite inadequate, like all theses of this kind. In both cases, at any rate, an attempt is being made to maintain the idea of a pseudo-unity that direct confrontation with the apparatus of power has smashed to bits.

As Mao himself admitted, 'when the students were fully mobilized, all kinds of contradictions in Chinese society were laid bare'.[30] Starting the Cultural Revolution was a decision involving a radical disruption, itself having, as we have seen, a formal character: a putting-into-movement, a putting-to-the-test. This time, the lid of socialism has been taken off. The apparatus of the party-state can no longer work. Getting out of the confrontation, such as it has been constituted, requires putting into

---

28   'It is normal that there should be different opinions among the masses of the people. The confrontation of different opinions is inevitable, necessary, and beneficial. The methods of argument based on facts and of persuasion by means of reasoning must be applied in the course of the debate. It is not permissible to engage in intimidation to put down the minority that supports different views. The minority must be protected, because sometimes truth is on its side. Even if it has erroneous views, it is still allowed to defend itself and to maintain its opinions. Every one of our revolutionary comrades must faithfully apply this decision developed under the personal direction of President Mao'. In 'Never Deviate from the General Orientation of the Struggle', editorial in *Hongqi*, 1966.
29   'Let Us Snatch New Victories', editorial in *Hongqi*, 1966.
30   Lee, *Politics of the Chinese Cultural Revolution*, p. 93.

place a new structure of authority, while at the same time clarifying, if possible, the question of content. At the end of 1966, there is talk of the new power, and people are thinking about the Paris Commune (as Lenin thought about it and as Marx had described it, with elected delegates who are subject to recall at any moment, and so on, in the idea of a 'new state').

Revolutionary time and questions of power (1967–68)

The point here is not to offer a narrative, much less an exhaustive history. Facts can be discussed and nuanced, but, through the schematic framework, the essential questions really do come to the surface.

I. Shanghai, political ability, dictatorship
a. The incident at Anting (November 9, 1966)[31]
Once the workers enter the lists of the revolution, the content manifests itself and the conflict becomes sharper. Independent workers' organizations have come into existence since the autumn, gathering together thousands and then tens of thousands of people. One of these organizations has asked the party authorities to recognize it as a revolutionary organization – in other words, to have the right to take part in the revolution. In the face of their refusal, a delegation of 2,000 workers seizes a train to go and appeal before the Centre in Beijing. The train is stopped in the little station at Anting. The authorities from Shanghai order the workers to return to their jobs, in view of their interpretation of the watchword, 'Grasp the revolution and stimulate production.' If they leave their jobs, they are traitors. The workers refuse to leave the train. A telegram arrives from Beijing, playing for time, issuing from a member of the 'Revolution Cultural Small Group'. The workers declare that it is a forgery. They are absolutely right. This is an example of political discernment. Although the telegram might have been authentic (really sent by the Centre), it is false politically. The Centre then sends another member of the RCSG, from the cadres of the party in Shanghai, Zhang Chunqiao. Having studied the situation, he agrees with the workers, recognizes them in his name as a revolutionary organization, and persuades them not to continue on their way to Beijing but rather to return to Shanghai. Here is another example of discernment: you have affirmed your autonomy and your political ability, so now what we need to do is not to appeal to the

31   The importance of this incident was recognized thanks to the discernment of Alessandro Russo.

central authority, but to deal with the situation by counting on our own forces.

b. The opposing camps and the taking of power

The worker-rebels and Zhang Chunqiao effectively demonstrate their political abilities during December by getting the better of the pro-party conservative workers' organization and – with greater difficulty – of the 'ultra-left rebels' who want to fight for the sake of fighting and distrust the leadership of Zhang. They are also capable of rallying under their direction the student-rebels and a significant fraction of the committed intellectuals of Shanghai.

In the meantime, in Shanghai and the rest of China, the party organs have launched a counterattack that consists of organizing chaos in the society by emptying the state treasury and encouraging workers by the thousands to abandon their jobs:

At the beginning of the campaign, in the name of grasping production, they repressed the revolutionary masses. Now, when the masses are breaking through the various barriers created by them and rising in rebellion, in the name of showing concern for peoples' livelihood and improving their livelihood, they are providing material incentives and corroding the revolutionary will of the workers by means of revisionist tactics such as additional wages and amnesties.[32]

What was happening all over Shanghai was that the cadres in charge of the purse strings were suddenly being very free with the state's money. As a result, vast sums were withdrawn from the banks. One previous complaint was that the workers had not been issued travel vouchers and funds to go off on 'longues marches', as the students had been. Now the cadres suddenly capitulated. Thousands of workers left Shanghai to make 'revolutionary liaisons', and those who stayed had a field day converting their windfalls into furniture and household goods.[33] There can be little doubt that the run of the banks was organized.[34]

---

32   From a Red Guard leaflet.

33   In the description given by Lee: 'in the communes the peasants share the communal reserves and the public funds; in the factories, wages are increased, promotions are given, and people are paid arrears and bonuses. 70,000 workers quit their jobs in the oil-fields of Taking. Many high-level cadres also quit their positions.' (Lee, p. 139)

34   From Neale Hunter, *Shanghai Journal.*

They are hoping in vain to undermine the revolutionary will of the masses by means of material stimulants. They are causing the stoppage of factories, the interruption of transport by buses and trains. They went so far as to compel the dock-workers to stop working, seriously interfering with the activity of the port and damaging the international prestige of our country. They are squandering state property to their hearts' content, increasing wages and material advantages at their whim, and granting all sorts of benefits belonging to the state . . . thus conspiring to divert a serious and major struggle into the baleful path of economic conflict . . . This is why we are seriously warning the party in Shanghai that no conspiracy seeking to derail the struggle by means of the sabotaging of production, the stopping of communications, and the increase of wages and material advantages can ever succeed.[35]

In reaction to the acts of sabotage and walking off the job organized by the Party Committee, the taking of power by the revolutionary camp is at that moment well under way.

On 4 January 1967, the rebels in effect take control of the great organ of the press, the *Wen Hui Bao* (after having obtained the support of Zhou En Lai, and with the personal approval of Mao after the fact). On 5 January, they publish a 'letter from the people to the municipality', on behalf of eleven rebel organizations:

At the beginning of the movement, under the pretext of 'producing', they repressed the revolution, objecting to the fact that we were doing it. They called us saboteurs. [Having failed in this manoeuvre,] they had recourse to a new ruse . . . Our workers of the revolutionary revolt have thwarted the vast conspiracy intended to combat the revolution by sabotaging production. Revolutionary worker comrades, it is time to take action.

On 9 January, the *People's Daily* publishes this letter with its own note of support: 'This endorsement finally removed the distinction between the authority of the government and that of the mass organizations and convinced the latter that they could exercise the authority hitherto reserved solely for the Party committees.'[36] The same day sees the

---

35   These sentences are taken from the 'Urgent Notice' sent out by thirty-two revolutionary organizations in Shanghai on 9 January.

36   Lee, p. 143.

publication of the 'Urgent Notice', which decrees ten measures including the return to Shanghai, the directive to resume one's job, the return of funds allocated in exchange for experience, and the punishment of offenders. This time, the response from the Centre comes even faster than before. On 11 January, the *People's Daily* widely publicized greetings from the Central Committee of the CCP, the State Council, the Military Affairs Commission, and the RCSG:

> You have developed a sound policy. Your proletarian organizations are the core towards which you are rallying all revolutionary forces. You sided with the proletarian revolutionary line embodied by president Mao and thwarted in time the plot for a new counter-attack by the bourgeois reactionary line. We appeal to everyone to follow the example of the experiences of the revolutionary rebels of Shanghai and to take action unanimously in order to repel the new counter-attack by the bourgeois reactionary line.[37]

On 9 January the rebels take control of the train station and get all the trains running again, mobilizing the students for odd jobs, setting about persuading the conductors to go back to work, and putting those with some experience in positions of technical control.

In the Shanghai docks, thousands of student volunteers helped the rebels to unload a cargo, sometimes working sixteen-to-twenty-four-hour shifts. To coordinate the city-wide economic activities, the rebels set up the 'Fire Line Committee', which consisted of fifty members nominated by the workers in various factories, the municipal economic bureau and the universities. The Committee functioned as the highest decision-making organ for the Shanghai economy, concentrating its efforts on restoring economic order and production. On 14 January, *Wen Hui Bao* for the first time used the term 'power seizure' in the context of encouraging the workers to take over control of factories for production. By that time, the rebels were already parading the party leaders through the streets, and what was left of the city administration was completely crippled. Thus, the workers' take-over of the factories led to de facto power seizure of the Shanhgai Municipality. Zhang Chunqiao confirmed that the combined effects of the workers'

---

37   Hunter, *Shanghai Journal.*

spontaneous initiative and the Centre's post facto support of their action led the Shanghai Revolutionary Committee to the power seizure.[38]

'Probably deeply impressed by the Shanghai worker's movement, the Centre finally adopted power seizure as an official policy on 22 January.'[39]

c. Naming and content
The proclamation of the Shanghai Commune takes place on 5 February. What this in fact involves is a great rally celebrating the unification of the different revolutionary organizations of Shanghai – under the direction of Zhang Chunqiao. The Commune is thus a name for the revolutionary camp's ability to unify itself and for its already tested ability to exercise real power, in revolutionary circumstances. Let us note, moreover, that, like the Paris Commune, this one was established to make up for the defection and flight of the authority in place, following a gesture of political affirmation by the popular workers' camp.

This authority of the Commune designates therefore, in my opinion, the authority of dictatorship, as I proposed the concept at the beginning of this text – that is, a non-state agency of power, not intended to last as a state form, but, while it is being practised, a form of effective and real power, demonstrating the capacity of a revolutionary camp to come together on a particular content, on watchwords, and consequently on a line of action. All these elements characterize the Shanghai experience.

Three weeks later, at the request of Mao, the Shanghai Commune changes its name and its composition: henceforth, it is called the Revolutionary Committee, and includes, besides representatives of the mass organizations fewer in number, representatives of the army and the cadres in greater numbers. The Revolutionary Committee thus designates a new form of state authority, resulting from an act of forcing by an authority of dictatorship, and carrying its trace.

The experience of the Cultural Revolution, it seems to me, shows precisely how far the test of establishing a dictatorship gives the measure of what can be accomplished, particularly in relation to the state. The choice, with regard to the forcing of an existing state, is either dictatorship – a real 'seizure of power', which draws its energy from a seizure of

---

38   Vol. 10 of the series *The Great Proletarian Cultural Revolution in China* (Beijing Foreign Language Publishers, 1966).
39   Lee, pp. 144–5.

power over oneself, entailing an effectively revolutionary forcing – or the logic of the *coup ∂'état*. This means that, from a political point of view, the determinant issue is not the question of power seized as such, but rather the political capacity within the people itself.

In fact, Shanghai, unlike the rest of China, did not experience the subsequent formation of factions and the violent confrontations between them.

II. Elsewhere

This revolutionary success had to do with the significant politicization of the city, with the fact that the rebel forces there were led by workers rather than by students, and, last but not least, with leadership by a dynamic political cadre in the person of Zhang Chunqiao. The leading trio in Shanghai – Zhang Chunqiao, Wang Hongwen (spokesperson for the worker-rebels in Anting), and Yao Wenyuan (the revolutionary intellectual who authored the famous article on the 'village of the three') – is in itself exemplary. But it is precisely these three, and only these three, who emerged as political cadres in the course of the Cultural Revolution – and who were, with Jiang Qing, Mao's wife, who directed the RCSG, designated as the 'gang of four' and arrested after Mao's death, then judged and imprisoned until their deaths, after the *coup ∂'état* by Deng Xiao Ping.

For, elsewhere, things took an entirely different turn. Lee describes in detail the events in Canton. At the urging of the RCSG, a group of rebel organizations coordinates a 'seizure of power' there, beginning on 22 January. It is notable that, in the heart of this group, a veritable left opposes it, judging that the rebel camp has not yet established political supremacy. Actually, the provincial party committee 'cooperates' with this seizure of power while at the same time fiercely opposing it in reality. There ensues a terrible aggravation of the contradiction between the two camps, which constitute themselves as two antagonistic factions. This situation is the strict opposite of that in Shanghai: in Shanghai, the establishment of an agency of dictatorship demonstrating the left's political ability to unite the centre under its leadership, permitting a real measurement of power relations; in Canton, a logic of the 'coup', which, in stark contrast, sharpens the contradictions at the heart of the people, to the point of provoking civil war. It is then the army that takes the reins of power that the leftists are struggling to exercise in a real way, and that puts an end to the economic chaos and reorganizes production, but under the aegis of the former cadres, putting the conservative camp back in charge. The army then turns against the rebel camp, distributes 6 million copies of an article denouncing as false the seizure of power of 22 January, and engages in reprisals (including arrests). Zhou En Lai arrives in Canton and organizes a compromise, declaring that the January seizure of power was a mistake on the part of the rebels but that their general orientation remains sound, while the opposing faction may be said to 'have conservative leanings' without really being reactionary. The army, charged with putting this compromise into practice, in fact adopts an equivocal attitude, paying lip service, under pressure from the Centre, to the rebel organizations, but in fact supporting the other faction. The army then loses its credibility, and thus its ability to restore unity. From this point on, the two factions are in a face-off, and the confrontation begins with an armed attack by the conservatives on the rebels. It happened on 19 July 1967, which is exactly the date of 'the incident of Wuhan'.

Now, on the basis of my own experience of those years in France, I can fill in some of the features of the two opposing camps – defenders and attackers of the power in place. On the side of the defenders, there are of course many apparatchiks, protecting their position and their turf – and with them, a very large mass of 'good workers', skilled people, often working in big factories and benefiting from the advantages linked with their jobs, advantages that are not only material. They have good reasons for being proud of their work, of their contribution to the development of the country, and they enjoy the esteem that their role confers on them. They are justly proud of socialism, and ready to defend it. But the revolution under way is in fact in the process of demonstrating that socialism in itself is neither a solid shelter nor a system. They do not constitute an independent political force endowed with its own vision, and therefore finally depend on masters of whom they take no notice for the time being, but who will let them know later that their time has passed. In France, this camp was represented by the Communist Party and the municipal and labour apparatuses linked with it, defending above all the positions it had conquered in the agencies of the state apparatus and the factories, where the workers who supported it often held positions as foremen. They form *cordons sanitaires* around the factories whenever student troublemakers try to get near them. They hit hard, they love order, they detest everything that does not stay in its place, everything that causes mixture: young people, students, women in meetings, foreigners. But this precisely testifies to their dependence. They neither represent nor propose a political orientation; they defend an established position that they believe is solid but that is in fact fragile, because it depends on their capitalist masters. Because they have chosen not to associate or to identify themselves with the vital forces of the people, the capitalist camp will have little trouble getting rid of them.[40]

In contrast, we can easily picture the leftists, the hard-liners motivated solely by their own revolt and led by their student 'little generals'. It suffices to recall the French Maoist group La Gauche Prolétarienne. They scream for a total seizure of power, combat all authority, demand the dismissal of all the cadres, the bringing down of the entire old order. Unfortunately, parallel to this, sounding the trumpet incessantly, flexing their biceps, and very fond of publicity stunts and other spectacular activities, they are incapable of maintaining an autonomous line by relying on their own strength, with the result that these ferocious enemies of authority spend their time whining that people are being mean to them and begging for support from the Centre, for help from the army, for the intervention of the police to pull them out of all the tight spots in which they get themselves stuck, and so on. Their ambition and egocentrism are immeasurable, as is their total lack of responsibility towards their own camp – and when things turn out badly, they will know how to offer their services to the other side.[41]

Each in its own way, both camps are the 'playthings of larger forces', all the more fierce in their struggle for 'power' insofar as their vision of it is imaginary, since it is not subordinated to a political proposal and measured by a real conflict of a political nature.

Consider, for example, what Wang Li, one of the members of the RCSG, has to say about this:

---

40   In France, the Communist Party and its unions, far from trying to organize recently arrived workers of foreign origin, opposed their struggles head-on once they could no longer use them. As a result, their base of support, skilled workers, 'the aristocracy of workers', was without energy or strength at the moment of the dismantling of the factories, and let itself be dispersed without a fight – the death-knell sounded for them with the dismantling of the Lorraine steel basin. The PCF, far from learning any lesson here, intensified its campaign against foreigners in the heart of the workers' suburbs, putting in place all the themes taken up later by the far-right Le Pen party. In other words, this was a political suicide; the unions and the PCF itself were liquidated as part of the deal, whose sole beneficiaries were the employers and the fascists.

41   In France, when the big names of the Gauche Prolétarienne, hailing mainly from the *grandes écoles* and the upper crust of the Parisian intelligentsia, saw that the 'seizure of power' wasn't going to happen overnight, they immediately forgot their grandiloquent calls for 'civil war' in order to become either the editor of a big mainstream newspaper, or a religious dogmatist, or an advisor to ministers or banks.

Therefore, we must be concerned with the essential thing, power. When we have power, we can dispose of the black materials and the white materials by ourselves. If we don't have power, and if we don't take [firm] hold of it, in the future they will reverse verdicts and collect black material on us. Therefore, the most important and essential thing is power itself.[42]

Let us compare this statement with that of the rebel workers of Shanghai in their 'message to president Mao', written to celebrate their own 'seizure of power': 'In keeping with the proletarian revolutionary line that you embody, we are undertaking a fierce battle, aiming to strike deadly blows against the new attack by the bourgeois reactionary line.'

The political weakness of the left and the complete lack of authentic political cadres anywhere other than in Shanghai constituted the tragedy of the Cultural Revolution. On this point, Mao's hope of seeing a new generation of revolutionary leaders forged in the struggle was bitterly disappointed. (It is, by the way, possible that political cadres never arise as such from a struggle, which is why it is necessary that there be political organizations that have already formed cadres so that a struggle entering into a dialectic with their proposals and their thought might be able to make new cadres arise from this process. It is here that Alessandro Russo's comment on the 'depoliticizing nature' of the communist party acquires its full weight.)

Later, Wang Li was in effect manoeuvred out of power because of his 'ultra-leftist' positions. However, the whole of the RCSG was marked by this tendency, including Jiang Ching, as witnessed by this remark of Mao to his wife, to whom I have already referred: 'You have been calling them such and such chiefs, and they are called "persons on duty" or "service personnel." This is mere formalism. Actually, chiefs are necessary. The question lies in the content.'[43]

In search of a way out of the formalist confrontation, Mao, the revolutionary leader, intervening through directives, and Zhou En Lai, the communist head of government, clarifying the directives and running from one camp to the other, thus find themselves practically isolated – seasoned old chiefs doing piecework in order to embody the clear-sightedness of the Centre.

Mao's directive concerning seizures of power is formulated as follows:

---

42   Lee, *Politics of the Chinese Cultural Revolution*, p. 153.
43   Ibid., p. 169.

In those places and establishments where the seizure of power is necessary, we must apply the policy of the revolutionary triple union (that is,
'leaders of mass revolutionary organizations truly representing the
great masses, representatives of the People's Liberation Army, and key
revolutionary cadres') in order to create a provisional organ of power
that is revolutionary and representative, and whose authority should
be proletarian. It would be good for this organ of power to be called the
revolutionary committee.

Note that the mention of the party as such has disappeared, and that the
organ of power described here falls into the category of an organ of dictatorship, or at least derives from it. There are recurrent appeals not to
condemn all cadres categorically, as well as not to condemn rebel groups
whose orientation is good, even though they may have made mistakes,
since you learn to swim by swimming. It is a mistake to have 'seized
power' without having established a great alliance. It is also a mistake to
establish a new power without the participation of the rebel masses and
the leadership of the revolutionary left. After the Canton experience, it is
recommended that any seizure of power should be approved in advance
by the Centre, and not after the fact.[44]

However, except for the few provinces where the direction on this line
is taken over by leading party cadres (such as Heilongjiang), in many
cases, as in Canton, the new directives are used by the conservatives as an
opportunity to take their revenge on the rebels. The Centre, faced with
the absence of cadres and the political weakness of the left, now finds
itself compelled to appeal to the army to 'support the left' and to create the
conditions for a new unity. This does not seem so bizarre if we remember
that the Chinese army, a 'liberation army', was created, trained and
conceived as 'charged with the political tasks of the revolution'. But it
remains an army, a state structure, legitimist by definition; and its
commanders are everywhere connected with the cadres in place. Mao
enjoins the army to 'support the left' in a letter to Lin Biao, dated 22
January. A discussion takes place between them on this subject, Lin
objecting that the army is not 'entirely trustworthy', Mao replying that
this will raise its ideological level. Precise directives are given on how to
recognize and support the left. Lin Biao prefers to fall back on 'ideology'

---

44   I cannot help mentioning here this mischievous remark of Zhou En Lai's in Canton:
'Theoretically, the leftist faction has been right, but not permanently. Correctly speaking not all the
leftists of today will be leftist tomorrow, *[since] it is not easy to be leftist in practice*' (emphasis added).

and on a purely ideological interpretation of the whole affair. It is to him that we owe the publication of the famous Little Red Book. He will promote the cult of Mao's thought, the Cultural Revolution conceived as a movement for the study of the thought of Mao and for individual ideological revolutionizing, the slogan 'fight against egoism and criticize revisionism' being intended to replace 'the fight against leaders embarked on the road to capitalism' (we are in fact very close to Liu Shao Shi's famous 'perfecting of the individual'). However, it is not true that 'immobilism being on the move, nothing can stop it'.[45] The struggle intensifies. As in the example of Canton, the army takes the side of the conservatives and attacks the rebels (Lee: 'Finally, there was no reason for the PLA to support the radicals except for the order from the Center'), firing on them in Sichuan. Despite investigations, sanctions, reshufflings, calls to return to the line ('The Center readily conceded that the masses tended to make many mistakes as they changed from a position of oppression to one of exercising power, but the Center still demanded that the cadres respect the authority of the masses' organizations'), the army's inability to play the role assigned to it, combined with the weakness of the left, leads to an exacerbation of the conflicts. At Wu Han, on 20 July, the members of the conservative faction kidnap Wang Li, present on the scene as an emissary from the Centre, as well as the person accompanying him, under the benevolent eye of the army. The RCSG responds to this act of open rebellion with a proposal of insurrection, 'calling on the masses to seize the military power from the "handful of power holdings in the army." The net result of this maneuver and counter-maneuver was large-scale armed struggle and complete chaos.'[46]

Moving back and bringing an end by any means to the armed confrontations then becomes the top priority for the Centre. Immediately after the self-criticism of Jiang Ching – with regard to her call to attack the army – the campaigns to 'rebuild the party' and 'rectify class ranks' are decreed. The properly revolutionary time of the Cultural Revolution will

45   *Hongqi* editorial no. 5, 1967. The temptation of a high army officer to 'freeze socialism', as in the USSR, is quite understandable. It is also understandable that a marshal with presidential ambitions should consider organizing the cult of the political leader whose real acts he wants to annul. I have already cited Mobutu organizing, for his advantage, the cult of Lumumba just after having delivered him to his assassins.

46   Lee, p. 250. Immediately after the Wu Han Incident, the more radical Peking Red Guards, led by the Peking University Chingkangshan, advocated the 'third round of the great exchange of experience', in order to renew the revolutionary momentum in the provinces', 'the seizure of the political power by armed forces', and the 'settlement of the issue by war, in order to assault the rival mass organizations'. Lee, *Politics of the Chinese Cultural Revolution*, p. 259.

thus end with a return to the party's state legitimation, and to a 'simple' logic of the purge. Mao personally gives the signal for retreat and, as much as possible, directs it by touring the provinces, from which he will return with directives urging moderation towards the cadres, and the doing away with such distinctions as 'conservative' and 'radical' between mass organizations. He maintains, however, their right to continue as organizations, inviting them to Beijing to resolve their conflicts and arrive at an agreement. He takes care to avoid as much as possible the settling of scores and Stalinist tactics. 'We must pay attention to policy in dealing with counterrevolutionaries and those who have made mistakes. The target of attack must be narrowed and more people must be helped through education. The stress must be put on the weight of evidence . . . it is strictly forbidden to extort confessions and accept such confessions'.[47] Above all, to replace the missing political leadership, he comes up with the idea of relying on the workers as a body. A strategic retreat:

> It was therefore obvious that what was needed most for the formation of the revolutionary committees was effective political leadership from the top . . . Confronted with these dilemmas, Mao improvised a new format, the Worker's Mao's Thought Propaganda Teams, as the interim political authorities which would first bring an end to the factional struggle and then supervise the 'campaign to rectify the class ranks' and the 'rebuilding of the Party'.[48] Compared with the students, the workers were less divisive, achieved the three-in-one combinations more easily, and set up revolutionaries committees more quickly . . . Furthermore, the workers were genuinely annoyed with the factional struggles on the campuses and were willing to 'help the students'. On July 29, a large crowd of workers gathered in the front of the Tsinghua campus, which was now divided and fortified by the two factions for the final showdown. As the workers forced their entry onto the campus, the students fired at them, killing five workers and severely wounding seven [hundred]. Next day, Mao summoned the leaders of the five major Peking universities and urged them to unify themselves, admitting that he was the 'black hand' that had sent out the workers. All over China, the revolutionary committees, very tired of the endless factional struggles, responded enthusiastically to the Peking model by sending workers not only to the schools but also to factories with serious

---

47   Lee, p. 291.
48   Lee, p. 276.

factional problems and in some cases even to Party organs. The Worker's Teams usually consisted of a large number of people drawn from different factories. They dealt with both factions quite fairly. They first brought an end to the armed struggle and then worked to formalize the great alliance. Then they proceeded to conduct the campaign to purify class ranks and to rebuild the Party structures.[49]

As I noted at the beginning of this chapter, the question is to go on, move further, test the propositions of the previous stage. We can see how precisely the Cultural Revolution backed itself to the experience made by Lenin and tested Lenin's propositions. Mao calls to study Lenin's works and quotes him frequently as the time of drawing the lessons of the experience approaches.

Communism against capitalism (the time of assessment)

At least apparently, the screen of socialism, of the party, and of its *langue de bois* was reconstituted, and with it came declarations of victory. In fact, as Lee describes it, if the task of rebuilding the party was confided by Mao to the Shanghai revolutionaries – the revolutionary nucleus stays on top for the time being thanks to Mao – the further down one goes in the ranks, the clearer it is that victory belongs massively to the enemies of the Cultural Revolution.

Mao: 'In the past we could easily fight the war of conquering South and North, because our enemy was clear. Compared with that kind of war, the GPCR was much more complicated. The main reason was that the demarcation line between enemy and friend was unclear, because of the confused mix of ideological mistakes with antagonistic contradictions.'

In fact, we have seen how, tested by the Cultural Revolution, socialism proved to be nothing more than the straitjacket of an intensified contradiction – but also what a great capacity it had to function as a screen-discourse. Hence the extreme confusion, the difficulty in discerning the enemy, the tendency to magnify him out of all proportion with a lens lacking definition, even while underestimating him, according to formal or crudely ideological criteria. This is why it is true that Lin Biao, who devotes himself to freezing the situation with large doses of hyperbolic slogans, and along with him all the apologists for the 'socialist

---

49   Lee, p. 285.

system', are indeed the servants and puppets of Liu and Deng, who prefer to manoeuvre the party apparatus without too much flowery talk according to a logic of interests, while their overtly capitalist proposals (such as no longer ensuring the right to work) do not really occupy the foreground. For this reason, I have underscored the relevance of the change of the Revolution's name, from 'socialist' to 'proletarian', proletariat and bourgeoisie designating the subjects of a real conflict between two political orientations and two lines. But we have seen that it is perhaps only in Shanghai that this opposition between two lines was articulated clearly – I quote again the 'message to the entire population of Shanghai': 'We revolutionary rebels profoundly understand that if we do not see the Cultural Revolution through, our production will stray from its proper course and assume a capitalist orientation.'

In other words, the logic of the defence of socialism, threatened on all sides by the restoration, and more generally the logic of 'the defence of social benefits', proved that it was without value. It is a logic of obfuscation. Perhaps we can retain the word socialist only as an adjective characterizing 'a state form linked to a new regime of property and law, and about which we know nothing, except that it cannot take the form of a party. The orientation, the line, the politics that opposes itself to capitalism is communism. Only from this perspective is it possible to see clearly' ('The question lies in the content'). In other words, if the notion of the defensive strategy can be decisive from a military and tactical point of view (defending a place and time of dictatorship, which, if it was able to constitute itself peacefully, will be necessarily and obligatorily attacked, against the logic of 'coups', and so on), prior to that, the notion (although often promoted under the name of 'resistance') has no political value. Clarification, the possibility of constituting a camp, only comes from a gesture projected forward (which is indeed the case in our Shanghai example), from an invention, or as the waning Cultural Revolution is going to put it, from a 'communist newness'.

In April 1969, Mao declares:

It seems to me that, without the Cultural Revolution, it wouldn't work, for our basis was not solid. Judging on the basis of what I have seen, let us not say in all of them or in a crushing majority of them but, I am afraid, in the fairly large majority of factories, leadership was in the hands neither of real Marxists nor of the working masses. Not that there weren't good elements among those who directed the factories.

There were . . . But they followed the line previously put forward by Liu Shao Shi, which simply amounted, in their case, to practices such as material stimulants, benefits for command posts, no place of honour given to proletarian politics, distribution of bonuses, and so forth . . . However, there are actually also bad elements in the factories. This shows that the revolution is not over.[50]

The next years, until Mao's death, when China is still thanks to him 'in revolution', will be those of assessment, which is to say of the clarification of the stakes, of invention, and of study. Of study, to begin with. In those days, this quotation from Mao was held in great esteem: 'Why did Lenin say that it is necessary to practice dictatorship over the bourgeoisie? This question must be well understood. If it were not, we would fall into revisionism. This must be brought to the awareness of the entire country.'[51] And again: 'Let philosophy be liberated from the lecture hall and from philosophy books, and become a sharp weapon in the hands of the masses.'[52] Experience has shown that the decisive question is that of the clarification of the stakes within the people and from their point of view. And this has value in general; the decisive question is that of the clarification of the stakes within the people and from their point of view. And for that it is necessary to politicize, to pinpoint what is essential, to give oneself the means to think the situation as a factual ensemble and as a local reflection, and to do this on a large scale, on the scale 'of the entire country'. During these years, study groups flourish just about everywhere in China. And they actually produce something new, precisely communist novelties: for the first time, they disturb the lines separating the manual and the intellectual, the very conception of work, the relations between human beings and their relation to what they do.

They do so, first of all, through their very existence: meeting and studying during work time is an immense victory in itself.[53] It also means

---

50   Quoted in Zhang Cunqiao, 'On Complete Dictatorship over the Bourgeoisie'.

51   Cunqiao, 'On Complete Dictatorship over the Bourgeoisie'.

52   *Selected Philosophical Essays by Workers, Peasants and Soldiers*, (Beijing: Foreign Languages Editions, 1972).

53   Again taken from our cell's text of assessment: 'You just concluded: the workers (in our factory) are a bit at home now. Yes, the best example is the story of the mosque. Imagine, at 2:30 because that's the time for prayer, you see a guy who goes to the bathroom, who washes himself, puts on a djellaba, and he walks into the workshop, there's the director, the chief, he goes in, and at least fifteen people do the same, he leaves the workshop and goes to pray in the mosque, which is about 200 meters from the workshop, he prays and he returns quietly to his place, where during this time the chief has replaced him. Because this happens during work hours. For the afternoon shift, it's at 6 o'clock. The

that work itself is no longer and can no longer be what it has been. It can now be subjectivized as a task to undertake, a task in which every single person has a part: what one does, why one does it, how one does it.

I marvel at the *Selected Philosophical Essays by Workers, Peasants, and Soldiers*.[54] They discuss and outline solutions to essential problems, such as: having been nominated by my team to a position of leadership – president of the revolutionary committee – how must I balance the time devoted to meetings, to the study of files, and my continuing participation in the work in the fields with the other members of my team? In organizing a study group made up of technicians and workers, can we create the conditions permitting us to perfect a high-precision apparatus while our factory does not have available all the equipment judged necessary? And here is the story of the mailman, who, 'armed with the thought of Mao Zedong', braved the storm, for, aware that his mission was to serve the people, he considered that delivering her son's letter or her pension check to the an old peasant woman was a task that could not wait.

Do the scruples of the first author make you laugh? This is because you think that, for eternity, there are those who command and those who execute: no doubt you belong to the first group.[55] The essay, however,

---

mosque is a big office formerly occupied by a chief. Now they've put down some carpet and the workers have the key. This makes them happy – very, very happy. You know, for us, the mosque isn't important, it's not really what we want, but it's very important nonetheless. There is something here that's like the factory in Shanghai (the one that was filmed by Joris Ivens and Marceline Loridan in the series "How Yukong moved the mountains"). Picture this, at the time for prayers, a guy calls out, Allah is great, and people walk by, they walk by or they don't, and the director or the head of personnel sees that, closes his eyes, and turns away. It's like in a film . . . But what counts is that this happens during work hours. There are people who don't go to pray but they're happy to see this, like you and me, we're happy to see it not because we go to pray but because we see that the worker is at home in the factory, in some way. Incidentally, in the Chausson factory, we didn't support those who wanted to draw up a petition so that there could be a mosque in the factory, because it would have been a mosque where people went to pray after work. In those circumstances, the cell decided that it had nothing to do with this question, that this had to do only with Islamist policy and that as a result the Islamists had only to work things out without us. They didn't succeed, by the way. Here, during work hours, a guy walks across the workshop to go into a room whose key the workers have, and he does something that has nothing to do with work. This means that the worker is at home in the factory after all. He isn't a slave. This is a practice that concerns the worker himself, taken individually. This means that he has been recognized on a point that doesn't concern work, or his social condition, but himself: which goes to show that he is someone who's here and this guy needs to pray in the factory. And he did it. He succeeded in doing it.' ('I Can't Do It, I'm Going to Do It: What Is a Political Intervention in a Factory? What Is the Political Statement of a Cell?')

54   Foreign Language Publishers, Beijing.

55   You are perhaps a feminist, modern and full of energy, demanding equality of responsibilities between men and women. Busy with important tasks, you don't have time for housework, and have 'better things to do'. Besides, you have a cleaning woman to clean your house and watch your children. And should it happen that she needs a half-day off for matters of concern to her, you flatly refuse, and you scream at her: 'Fatoumata, how can you ever think of letting me down like this?'

takes on the question that carries within itself the possibility of the extinction of the state. Do the authors of the second essay, who find among other things that working at night will permit them to alleviate the effect of the vibrations that daytime movement causes in their badly insulated factory, strike you, who are so proud of your own technical capacities, as pitiful, as ridiculous? No doubt you are among those who plan on perpetually looting, for their own profit, the soil and the sub-soil of Africa: whereas their way of seeing has tremendous importance for whoever hopes one day to rid himself of the colonial scourge. Do you find the mailman's story childish? No doubt you cherish the notion that work must not and cannot be anything more than profit and compulsion, belonging among those who consider themselves or who believe themselves to be strong by their own free will, and who have firmly made up their minds anyway never to serve anyone. Whereas we salute this magnificent watchword: to serve the people, as the first invention of a new concept and a new measurement of work[56] which for the first time gives it, and makes available to everyone, the possibility of a horizon and of an overcoming.[57] 'Have the world as your horizon', the brochures of the period would often say.

Communism or capitalism, in terms of content, of line, and of point of view explicitly orienting choices and practical proposals. Such, it seems to me, in the hour of assessment, is the inestimable contribution of this amazing Cultural Revolution. A failure, if we think that this extraordinary undertaking of examination has in fact shown that the pro-capitalist forces triumphed and will doubtless have allowed them to assert themselves more rapidly and more arrogantly. But a victory in the sense that communism asserts itself here for the first time, not as the ineffective vision of a future state but as the point of view that alone gives us a grasp of the situation, and as the practical orientation of the people's projects. The conclusion of the brochure of Zhang Chunqiao, moreover, testifies to the fact that both sides are fully aware at once of the terms and of the power relation of the opposing forces:

---

56   Lenin: 'Before work is transformed into a primary vital need . . .' (Lenin, *The State and the Revolution*): 'One day, working will be a pleasure, an offering to the brotherhood' (From a leaflet written by Chinese students in 1912, as quoted in Henri Bauchau's biography of Mao).

57   Analyzing Marx's 'reflections on the Jewish question', Ivan Segré brilliantly shows how freedom can be conceived only as fulfilling itself for and in others, counter to the bourgeois fantasy of the isolated individual (but are the bourgeois really running around naked in the woods relying entirely upon themselves for survival?) whose freedom is an intrinsic property limiting and limited by that of others.

Do you want to make a wind of communization blow? Asking this kind of question in order to spread rumours is a tactic to which certain individuals have quite recently had recourse ... We would rather direct the attention of our comrades to the fact that another kind of wind is blowing, which is called *embourgeoisement*. In the grip of this sinister current, certain individuals are throwing themselves into a frenzied race for honours and riches, and far from blushing, they brag about it. Among those who are spreading rumours about the 'wind of communization' figure new bourgeois elements that, having appropriated what belongs to the public, fear that the people will 'communize' it. They take a very particular interest in preaching to the young and to adolescents that material stimulants are like a fermented cheese that, if it has a strong smell, is no less tasty. All these people have much more acute senses than do many of our comrades. While some of our comrades think that study is a task that can be reduced, they sense instinctively that the present movement of study is an urgent task as much for the proletariat as for the bourgeoisie.[58]

The machine-tool factory in Shanghai created a university within itself. Here, the thinking went at the time, is an example to follow and the point of view from which to reflect on the reform of the entire educational system, oriented around the idea of resolving the contradiction between manual and intellectual labour. But, as Lee had observed, 'factory management can be motivated to run a school attached to their factory well only when the whole rationale of managing the factory is defined in terms of its broad contribution to the society. But when the performance of the factory is evaluated by "profitability" and "efficient management", such a system puts an unnecessary financial burden on the factories.'[59] This university created in the movement of the Cultural Revolution will be eliminated, along with all of the study groups, with the coming to power of Deng Xiao Ping.

Similarly, all projects and achievements having to do with the idea of resolving the contradiction between city and country, by developing in the countryside small units of autonomous production, will also be scrapped.[60] Not to mention all the small services spread around the

---

58   Zhang Cunqiao, 'On Complete Dictatorship over the Bourgeoisie'.
59   Lee, p. 132
60   At the beginning of the 1970s, wanting to get a footing in our workers' suburb, we rent a movie theatre and put up posters inviting people to attend the screening of the film *Red Flag Canal*. The film

countryside – the postal service, for example – which from a capitalist point of view are simply irrational.

A comment on the question of class

During the Cultural Revolution, the notion of class clearly took on a political meaning. 'Bourgeoisie' and 'proletariat' designate the subjects of the political conflict between capitalism and communism. We have seen that this notion was one of the major issues at stake in the first stage of this revolution, with the party apparatus, through the 'work teams', emphasizing the objective determinations of class membership, even making it a question of heritage and of 'lineage', whereas the revolutionaries and the Centre emphasized subjective determinations, particularly the relation to the revolution.

Did this mean that objective determinations had to be considered henceforth as erased – that, in the movement under way, they should not be taken into account? This too was an issue at stake in the discussions and conflicts: we easily recognize in the position that consists in considering them as totally meaningless the radical idealism of the ultra-left. It is clear that one's relation to property and ownership, and one's place in the process of production and in the division of labour, are things that matter, that are even of the highest importance. And if indeed one wants to be able to transform them, it is not judicious to begin by ignoring them or by claiming to obliterate them with the stroke of a pen.

During the Cultural Revolution, the facts amply proved this. We have seen the essential role played by the workers when it comes to grappling with real questions of power, or to succeeding in ending false factional and formal power struggles; and perhaps even more, we have been able to experience the decisive character of their capacity for discerning the

---

relates the construction, during the Cultural Revolution and thanks to it, of a canal winding along the side of a mountain, designed to permit the irrigation of an arid zone and the installation along its course of small hydraulic power stations. It shows the difficult work on the mountain, the public meetings, the discussions about the distribution of forces between work on the canal and agricultural work (the contribution of this or that team, village, etc.), the studying of the Little Red Book . . . To our great surprise, the room is full, and, despite our technical amateurism (a comrade improvises a translation of the Chinese text, etc.), the attention in the room is intense. And at the end, when you finally see the water starting to flow, the entire room stands up to applaud. Those comrades who had been compelled to leave their mountains in the Rif and Kabylia for the factories and workers' hostels of the Paris suburbs certainly had no trouble grasping the significance of this canal. And at the moment when the clear water started to flow, we were all together, they on the screen, we in the room, the Chinese officials who had come for the inauguration, the crowd of peasants shouting hurrah, we French militants and our worker comrades lit up with joy, applauding fervently. A moment of pure happiness.

real stakes of the struggle, and for forming thereby the framework of a popular camp. And how could we deny that all this has to do with their singular place in the process of production, with the school of the real constituted by the factory, and with the measure that can be taken there of 'where we stand in relation to capitalism':[61] with the discipline of acting as a body of which, for this reason, workers are capable, a discipline forged by workshop labour itself, as Marx emphasized, but also by their long apprenticeship in measure-taking, with regard as much to what is possible as to specific consequences?[62]

But all this is contingent on political and ideological orientation. Where does the struggle between the two classes, the bourgeoisie and the prole-tariat, take place? Well, above all, essentially, and in an absolutely determining way, within the working class – as the Cultural Revolution, but also the other movements of the 1960s, have demonstrated on a large scale. But already in their own lifetime, Marx and Engels had been able to observe that in fact the workers could not be confused with the mass of the wretched 'having nothing to lose but their chains', since they had been able to see Western workers turning into essential stakeholders in the colonial consensus. From the point of view of the workers, the question of orientation is answered precisely in the political relation that they main-tain with the poorest and the most wretched, who are in fact more numerous than they are: insofar as it is possible for them, perhaps not always and forever, but often enough for it constitute an orientation, indeed to negotiate their role in the process of production against certain material advantages, and a social recognition that will place them above the mass of the wretched.

Alberto Moravia, in his eloquent testimony as a clear-eyed stroller, grasps precisely this in the Cultural Revolution. Unlike those commenta-tors who assign to the mass of peasants nothing more than a very marginal role in the whole affair, he sees in this revolution the assumption of the peasant and of the peasant's point of view as having to dominate Chinese society and give it at once its style and the norm of its ambitions. He wants to speak of simplicity, 'of a style of simple life and arduous strug-gle', of a certain taste for austerity that we are not obliged to confuse with a religious morality of asceticism, but only to take quite simply as a taste

---

61   'The factory, where one measures where one stands in relation to capitalism, as we used to say in our cell.' ('I Can't Do It, I'm Going to Do It: What Is A Political Intervention in a Factory, What Is a Political Statement of a Cell')
62   'Like an army that would be special within it'. (Ibid.)

for few objects, but beautiful ones, fewer but better, as against the capitalist flood of junk and the constant compulsion to keep lusting, again and always, for ever more junk. It is therefore in the encounter with peasant tastes and ways of seeing that it is possible to give oneself the proper orientation, which would detach itself from the watchword 'Let's catch up with England in twenty years', which means: let's submit to its norms. 'What direction should we give to our production?', in the words of the Shanghai text: What do we want? What are our priorities? Why?[63] How? – and so on.

In the world as it is today, the decisive question is certainly that of the relation of the workers to the mass of casualties, the tens and hundreds of millions about whom capitalism does not give a damn, whose labourpower has reached the value of zero, and who find themselves doomed to abandonment, to the ghettos, or to something worse.[64]

Thus, the communist political point of view divides and splits the classes as defined by their position and role in the social edifice and, consequently, by the system of their interests in the existing social order. At the end of the day, if the point is to end the great contradictions and thus the very existence of classes, in terms of a political movement we have to understand that unification on the basis of the new will succeed here and there in winning out over the calculation of interests derived from the old order. Thus, coming together on the basis of a 'content' is the important thing. With the Cultural Revolution, the idea of 'class interests' represented by a party, and so on, was in effect done away with, and so,

---

63   As Mao says, in a quotation that was also held in esteem during the Cultural Revolution, 'In all things, a communist must ask himself the question "why?"'; and, in the famous editorial of 1 January 1967: 'A certain number of muddleheaded people oppose revolution to production. These comrades do not ask themselves with what goal people are cultivating the field, weaving the cloth, and tempering the steel.'

64   In order to show the importance, even of a thoroughly tactical kind, in a limited conflict, of reflecting on the choice of orientation, a group that had emerged from a French Maoist political organization intervenes in the struggle of undocumented immigrants which, in the first decade of the present century, became rather vigorous. It emphasizes the identity of undocumented immigrants as workers, and organizes demonstrations in the course of which they spread out through the streets of working-class neighbourhoods in Paris under the watchwords 'a worker matters', 'work matters'. Magnificent watchwords. As they pass, these demonstrations elicit surprise, applause, encouragement. They are good news. Unfortunately, the group in question then 'translates' this matter into a demand: for regularization on the basis of work, which amounts to dropping the majority of undocumented immigrants for the sake of negotiating for those who can produce evidence of work contracts drawn up by the book. This is precisely what the CGT union – formerly the big union associated with the French Communist Party – is doing at the same time, much more effectively and with much more capacity for negotiation than this small group can have. This is why it disappears, as follows logically, during this episode.

therefore, was everything that had been offered as a vision in terms of the composition of interests, alliances (of classes, and so on).

But then, what about the intellectual petite bourgeoisie and the famous 'middle classes'? As concerns them, the line of demarcation that was proposed is articulated in a sharp and clear manner: 'In order to determine whether an intellectual is revolutionary or not, there is a decisive criterion: it is knowing if he wants to become assimilated and if in effect he does assimilate himself to the masses of workers and peasants. If the intellectuals do not assimilate themselves to the mass of workers and peasants, they amount to nothing.'[65]

It should be noted how prominent a place, how essential a role, is accorded here to the intellectuals: in this famous editorial, the tasks concerning the workers and peasants, together forming '99 per cent of the population', do not take up any more space, in fact even a little less, than what concerns the intellectuals. And who, then, if not they, can take responsibility for 'bringing this to the awareness of the whole country?' Who else is going to sit down on the ground in order to write down ideas, propose a formulation, and carry it elsewhere? Who else will be saluted and attended to as an indispensable and excellent expert when the corrupt cadres will have run off with all the useful equipment? There is nothing comparable in the bourgeois order to what revolution offers to students and intellectuals: and this is truer of the Cultural Revolution than of any other to this day.

The point is that this can only be a matter of personal destiny and luck. But here is the paradox: the apologists for personal destiny known as petit-bourgeois intellectuals also prove to be the most anxious to maintain, when it comes right down to it, the division of society into classes as such – which means, above all, the famous 'middle classes'.[66] They can smell from a mile away that the revolution will mean their disappearance. Just look at Amílcar Cabral, who proposed that 'the petite bourgeoisie should commit suicide as a class by putting itself at the forefront of the struggle for liberation'. But the petite bourgeoisie as such means to defend, even more than its right to property, its right to irresponsibility. It quickly labels as totalitarian whatever threatens its privilege to say and do anything by its proper fancy without owing anybody an explanation. And the fact is that the revolution – the dictatorship, precisely – does threaten

65   This quotation from Mao is taken from the editorial of the *People's Daily*, 1 January 1967.

66   During periods of reaction. The 1960s witnessed, on the contrary, the spontaneous and fairly rapid development of a movement to install students and intellectuals in the factories.

it. Let us look to Lenin again, expressing his hope to see the disappearance one day of 'today's average man, capable, like Pomialovski's seminarians, of recklessly squandering the riches of the state, and of demanding the impossible'.[67] What better description could there be of the ultra-left, as sectarian and radical as it is fickle, criticizing 'grand alliances' and 'triple unions' (like Kuai Ta Fu, the red guard leader at Tsinghua University in Beijing), all the while maintaining its right to the immediate about-face? On the other side, the revolutionary students were seen working tirelessly at the port of Shanghai.

When all is said and done, it is quite true that two lines, two conceptions, two great orientations, two gigantic subjects are opposed here, which the Cultural Revolution quite aptly names 'proletariat' and 'bourgeoisie': 'Which of the two, the proletariat or the bourgeoisie, will win in a socialist country?' – again from the famous New Year's editorial. Taking on, depending upon the place and the group, different colourings, their opposition traverses and splits the socially defined classes: 'proletariat' tending towards the viewpoint of a generic humanity – thus leading towards the disappearance of classes – bourgeoisie towards the preeminence of private interests – thus leading towards their separation and preservation. We could therefore say that on one side there is the necessity and the injunction for a movement, on the other the rights and needs of the man who owns a seat: as Victor Hugo put it, 'The bourgeois is he who finally has the right to sit down'; or, as Zhang Chunqiao said, 'Let others go on; as for me, it's the last stop: I'm getting off.'

My conclusion will be in the form of Russian dolls: envelopings and interlockings, neither linearity nor mere negation nor smooth transitions.

The State

There is no question of ignoring the question of the state. All the more so since the imperialist-capitalist tendency is precisely to divide up and shatter states. If questions of political lines could unfold as they did in China, this is because China was (this is perhaps no longer true today) in itself something like a metonymy for the world: as big as the world. Whereas now, and in any case everywhere else, what is being reformulated is the question of the local and the whole in a space that cannot necessarily be

---

67   Lenin, 'The State and the Revolution'.

superimposed on that of states – but perhaps indeed this was a possibility, a risk, that the Cultural Revolution could not take. While it is clear that it is better to have great states.

Is it better to have a socialist state? Certainly, if we take that to mean, and to mean only, a state that attests in its laws, and in its law, that the regimes of property and of work have been transformed, without there being any guarantee implicit in this. Do we know anything more about it? Is it possible or on the agenda? We do not have the information that would allow us to say.

Dictatorship

This will be for us the determining element, our compass, our instrument for measuring, the object of all our attention. It is only from dictatorship that we could, among other things, learn a bit more about the question of the state, which it determines, but which does not determine it. What constitutes it is the capacity within the people to deal with contradictions, to unify a camp on the basis of an affirmative content, thereby giving the measure of the possible in a situation.

Politics

In other words, the ability to clarify terms of discussion, to formulate the stakes, to conduct towards this end the necessary investigations, to propose strategies of displacement – in short, to define a line and the lines of opposition, to dare to pronounce oneself on the content, the time and the place. I have argued that only a communist politics – that is to say, a politics effectively related to the communist orientation in the here and now of the tasks that we have just mentioned – makes it possible for an invention rather than a submission to emerge, and, with this invention, the contours of a new unity and strength.

The Communists

In other words, the question of militant activists and cadres, which, we have seen, can in no way be circumvented. The question of organization remains entirely open. In view of the totality of accumulated experience, I will dismiss the idea as well as the name 'party', since it has proved inappropriate to politics and appropriate only to the state. But the fact is that, even without calling themselves parties and even operating on a very small scale, organizations prove capable of exuding and promoting servility and careerism, rather than novelty and audacity in thought. So would it suffice to have a communist Centre that would call to itself the potential militants and cadres who would emerge from the struggle? Given the experience of the Cultural Revolution, this is by no means clear; we have seen how much the Centre was lacking in reserves of cadres who could be mobilized and who were capable of conducting investigations, of proposing watchwords, of arriving at assessments of experience. Thus the question of grouping, of how to form an organization that would be 'politicizing rather than depoliticizing', really does present itself. One definitely wants, in any case, to reject the distinction between militants and cadres, to prohibit absolutely all full-time employees or organization 'officials', to bring together only people for whom politics is extra work, unpaid work, and who have demonstrated their autonomy – that is to say, their own connection with the great masses, to speak Maoist, and their capacity to produce on the basis of their own work proposals, concepts, watchwords, assessments.

4 Althusser and Mao: A Political Test for Dialectics

Claudia Pozzana

In the enigmatic relationship between philosophy and politics, as Badiou calls it, the issue of dialectics occupies a constitutive place. Modern communism crosses originally philosophy on the ground of dialectics, and in particular on one of the most dense and arduous concepts of the Hegelian system, the *Aufhebung*, as in the famous definition of communism in *The German Ideology*: 'the real movement which abolishes the present state of things' (*die wirkliche Bewegung, welche den jetzingen Zustand aufhebt*). The embarrassing polysemy of the *Aufhebung* is well known. It can be rendered as suppression, sublation, supersession, destruction, abolition, or, as recently proposed by Slavoj Žižek, 'the survival of the sublated thing in an abridged edition'.[1]

The class party, especially in its Stalinist version, has stabilized the instability of the *Aufhebung*, and in general the enigma of the relationships between politics and philosophy in the 'worldview of the Marxist-Leninist party'. Dialectical materialism was for Stalin literally this worldview. On the contrary, during the political configuration of the 1960s, when the value of the class party was subject to a worldwide mass political testing, the issues of the balance between politics and philosophy and the value of dialectics were inevitably reopened. In other words, the political 1960s were the condition for an indispensable rethinking of the philosophical categories of Hegelian dialectics with respect to revolutionary classism.

Althusser, under the condition of that political configuration, deeply explored the constitutive instability of the intersection of modern communism and materialist dialectics. His declared interest in Mao's philosophy has been one of the strongest points, as well as one of the thorniest issues, of his intellectual itinerary.

I propose a reading of a probable philosophical encounter between Mao Zedong and Louis Althusser. Of this encounter there are more

---

1   Slavoj Žižek, *Less Than Nothing: Hegel and the Shadow of Dialectical Materialism*, (London: Verso, 2012), pp. 319–20.

philosophical clues than there is philological evidence, with the added complication that Althusser himself, in his memoir, tells the story of his refusal of an invitation by Mao, which apparently is a mere imaginary construction.[2] But the point of reality of a 'missed encounter' should be explored on philosophical grounds, and in particular with reference to the instability of the relationship between politics and philosophy in the 1960s. These temporal circumstances are decisive, and deeply mark the value of the theoretical issues at stake.

Althusser, Reader of Mao

The key point is the relationship between the philosophical concept of 'over-determination' and Mao's *On Contradiction*,[3] which Althusser cites as the main reference for his theoretical elaboration on this point.

It should be noted that 'overdetermination' was the first original philosophical concept formulated by Althusser in 1962, in his essay 'Contradiction and Overdetermination',[4] the third of the essays in *For Marx*. It was also developed the following year in the essay 'On the Materialist Dialectics'.[5] This was the 'second movement' in Althusser's philosophical itinerary. The first two essays in *For Marx* ('Feuerbach's Philosophical Manifestos' and 'On the Young Marx')[6] represent the 'first movement' (the one on Feuerbach is somehow an 'overture'), which aims at discussing the fundamental discontinuity between the *Economic-Philosophical Manuscripts of 1844* and *The German Ideology* of 1845. The issue concerns 'humanism': the well-known anti-humanistic position of Althusser[7] focused on the political nature of the crisis which post-Stalinist

---

2   ". . . j'étais au Parti, mais . . . j'avais un très fort penchant pour le maoïsme (Mao m'avait même accordé une entrevue, mais pour des raisons "politiques françaises", je fis la sottise, la plus grande de ma vie, de ne pas m'y rendre, peur de la réaction politique du Parti contre moi, mais en fait qu'aurait pu faire le Parti à supposer même que la nouvelle d'une rencontre avec Mao eût fait l'objet d'un communiqué public et officiel? Je n'étais pourtant pas un tel "personnage"!).' 'I was in the Party, but they also knew I had strong leanings towards Maoism (Mao had even granted me an interview, but for reasons to do with "French polities", I made the stupidest mistake of my life by not going to see him, fearing the political reaction of the Party against me. But what could the Party have done, even supposing that news of my meeting with Mao had become known through an official, published communique? I was not really that much of a "public figure"!).'
Louis Althusser, *Future Lasts Forever: A Memoir* (New York: The New Press, 1993) p. 234.
3   Mao, *On Contradiction* (1937), at Marxists.org.
4   Louis Althusser, 'Du *Capital* à la philosophie de Marx', in Louis Althusser Étienne Balibar, Roger Establet and Paul Macherey, *Lire le Capital* (Paris: Maspero, 1965).
5   Althusser, 'On the Materialist Dialectics',1963, at Marxists.org.
6   Louis Althusser, *Pour Marx* (Paris: Maspero, 1965), pp. 20–84.
7   Louis Althusser, 'Marxisme et Humanisme', *Cahiers de l'I.S.E.A.* 20 (June 1964).

humanism denied, reducing it to a moral crisis of Marxism. While affirming Marxism as a scientific invention – the discovery of the continent of history – Althusser emphasized its experimental character in political invention. The thesis that philosophical elaboration was immediately transitive to revolutionary politics (even with the finesse of postulating a role for philosophy of representing politics in science and science in politics, as well as distinguishing between theoretical and political practice) was one of the strong points of Althusser and his school up to the political caesura of 1968. But it was later transformed into the opposite, i.e. a factor of weakness, to the point of producing the resounding split of his philosophical school.

What was at stake was neither the history of philosophy nor that of Marxism, but rather the political impasse of the socialist states, which the pro-Soviet communist parties tended to reduce into the terms of a moral crisis. 'Stalin's crimes' were presented as the result of insufficient 'humanism', and therefore it would have been advisable to search for the authentic roots of communist political thought in the young Marx. For this reason, the *Manuscripts of 1844*[8] were very successful at that time among the philosophical circles of the communist parties.

This opening movement of Althusser's thought, although manifesting an extraordinary philosophical acuity, did not actually contain original concepts directly elaborated by him; but he made his point by explicitly borrowing the concept of *coupure épistémologique* from Gaston Bachelard and that of *problématique* from Jacques Martin. The goal was to refute the view of the continuity of Marx's intellectual itinerary, which was a key argument for the 'humanism' of the communist philosophers of the moment, and to stress the importance of Marx's theoretical breakthrough. *The German Ideology*[9] *and The Communist Manifesto*,[10] Althusser argued, marked a *coupure épistémologique* through which Marx developed his own original theoretical *problématique*, very different to that of the early texts, still influenced by the conceptual systems of Hegel and Feuerbach.

The first movement of Althusser's itinerary aimed at clearing the obstacle that blurred the novelty of Marx's theoretical invention, and more essentially hindered the understanding of the political nature of the crucial issue at stake in that very moment. But only the 'second movement' of Althusser's itinerary tackled the crux of the situation – that is to

---

8   Karl Marx, *Economic and Philosophic Manuscripts of 1844* (Mineola, NY: Dover, 1961 [2012]).

9   Karl Marx and Friedrich Engels, *The German Ideology* (1845–46), at marxists.org.

10   Karl Marx and Friedrich Engels, *Manifesto of the Communist Party* (1848), at marxists.org.

say, the value of the class category for thinking politics. With the concept of 'overdetermination', Althusser scrutinizes the concept of contradiction in materialist dialectics through a philosophical lens – namely, the conceptual device that in Marxism-Leninism advocated political antagonism on philosophical grounds.

In short, the fundamental issue irreversibly opened by the political configuration of the 1960s, which Althusser allowed to emerge philosophically in a radical way, was: How could the philosophical concept of contradiction be used to advance the crucial political tasks of the communist revolutionary organization?

The main objective of the concept of overdetermination was to establish the discontinuity of materialist dialectics with respect to Hegelian dialectics – a novelty that for Althusser remained insufficiently theorized in the Marxist tradition.

We should here remark that the insistence with which Althusser emphasizes the discontinuity with Hegel, the need for a *coupure épistémologique*, and so on, are issues definitely under condition of the fundamental questions of the political configuration of the 1960s. It is clear that today the questioning of dialectics by Badiou and Žižek is very different in nature, because they are under condition of an entirely different set of political questions. The problem of our time is no longer that of the examination of the political value of the class party, but of how to invent new forms of post-party egalitarian political organization. It is therefore inevitable that the questions posed fifty years ago by Althusser to Hegelian dialectics are completely different from those raised by contemporary philosophers today, but I believe that Althusser's questioning was not without consequences.

Althusser considered Mao Zedong the theorist who argued most strongly for a discontinuity with the Hegelian dialectics, through the development of three original philosophical concepts in *On Contradiction*:[11] the concept of the main contradiction, that of the main aspect of contradiction, and above all that of the unevenness of development of contradictions in every real process. However, the 'deep theoretical reason' of those concepts was, for Althusser, still to be grasped.

The philosophical stakes were to prove that Marxist philosophy was an invention in no way indebted to the Hegelian problematic. Althusser

---

11   Mao Zedong, *On Contradiction*, (1937), at marxists.org.

affirmed that, on the one hand, Mao's philosophical concepts cannot have originated from the Hegelian matrix, but on the other hand, Mao had not yet theoretically formulated the point of discontinuity with Hegel. Althusser seriously doubted that the discontinuity of Marxist dialectics with Hegel could be assured by simply isolating the 'rational kernel' already present in Hegel, and freeing it from the 'mystical shell' of 'speculative philosophy' and all its conceptual apparatus.

Althusser remarked that the Hegelian model had a highly rigorous and systematic structure, based on the principle of 'a simple process with two opposites', entailing an original unity that splits into two. Althusser maintained that Mao, Lenin and Marx, in their political and theoretical practice, rejected this model of simple original unity, since they dealt exclusively with complex processes in which there was always 'not secondarily, but primitively, a structure of multiple and uneven contradictions'.[12] The problem was that Mao, Lenin and Marx did not clearly exclude the existence of a 'simple process with two opposites' conceived as 'the essential original process of which the other processes, the complex ones, would be only the complications'.[13]

In other words, for Althusser, the great Marxist leaders had ended up giving credit, or at least not explicitly excluding, the Hegelian dialectical principle of the 'splitting of the original One'[14] upstream of each process, while rejecting it in both theoretical and political practices. They did so, Althusser says, in order to simplify, 'to cut short', or 'inadvertently', but at the expense of a rigorous theoretical demarcation, which resulted in reactivating the value and the logical operation of the Hegelian model.

It was true that, for all of them in their practice, the 'simple contradiction', far from being an original universal, was the result of a long process produced under exceptional conditions. But the great Marxists have formulated ('to cut short') the essence of dialectics essentially in Hegelian terms, as in Lenin's formula 'the splitting of the One' (which Althusser cited), or in Mao's formula (which he did not cite), 'one divides into two'. Althusser remarked that, although effective in polemical terms, those formulations were extraneous to actual revolutionary practice, and they finally led to unreserved credit of the Hegelian model.

---

12   Althusser, *Pour Marx*, Chapter 4.
13   Ibid., p. 174.
14   Ibid., p. 173.

Althusser noticed that Hegelian dialectics was supported by the radical assumption of a simple unity that splits and 'evolves within itself by virtue of negativity', but whose essential purpose, in all its development, was to restore its original unity and simplicity, albeit in a higher form. The philosophical concepts that describe this process of splitting and restoration of original unity, such as the concepts of 'alienation' and 'negation of the negation', as well as the famous *Aufhebung* (the synthesis that exceeds and at the same time preserves the original terms), are not, according to Althusser, merely part of a 'mystical shell' that could be detached from the rational kernel via a 'reversal', as in the famous metaphor of an upside-down dialectic. They are operational concepts intimately related to the basic principle of a 'simple process with two opposites'. Althusser stated that, each time the structural discontinuity between Hegelian and Marxist dialectics is not clearly formulated, those concepts once again become operative.

The elaboration of the concept of 'overdetermination' aims to bring about theoretical clarification on that discontinuity. For Althusser, 'overdetermination' was a deeper connotation of Marxist dialectics. It fully discloses the theoretical value of the concept of an 'uneven development of each process', which Mao Zedong established systematically and which all the great Marxists have always 'practised'. The concept of 'uneven development', according to Althusser, can be reformulated as the concept of 'structure in dominance' of the 'complex whole'. Marxist dialectics considers the complexity of a process as never derived from an original contradiction, but structured around a dominant, which is determined, or rather 'overdetermined', by the subjective and objective circumstances, in national and international forms, in the cultural, economic and environmental elements of a historic–social world.

The concept of 'overdetermination' expressly refers to Mao's idea that any revolutionary politics should tackle processes that always develop unevenly. Unevenness means that at different times multiple circumstances determine the primacy of one contradiction over the others (the main contradiction) and of an aspect of the contradiction over the other – namely, the transformation of the main aspect into the secondary, and vice versa. In this sense, the concept of 'overdetermination' was strongly indebted to Mao's dialectical conception, and fully intended to stress the distance from the Hegelian model. On the other hand, the fact that the rejection of the simple process with two opposites was not set out formally was for Althusser a weak point that lead back to the Hegelian matrix of the re-composition of the One.

Mao's Philosophical Predicament

After outlining the intensity of the issues that Althusser attributed to Marxist philosophy, and in particular to Mao's conceptual device, let us discuss the original question about the 'encounter' between Mao and Althusser. Although we have no evidence of Mao's alleged invitation to Althusser, it is clear that Althusser himself invited Mao to a philosophical dialogue, addressing him with the utmost respect of a communist towards a great revolutionary leader. We do not know if Mao actually received this invitation, meaning that he did not necessarily read Althusser's text. However, there are philosophical traces that show how, at that time, Mao was restlessly grappling with the same philosophical problem posed by Althusser: how to deal with the tendency to restore the Hegelian matrix. Althusser maintained that, without an explicit rejection of the 'simple contradiction', it was inevitable that all the basic concepts of Hegelian dialectics would be reactivated. All of those concepts, Althusser remarked, focus on ensuring the glorious return of the original One, which in the Hegelian perspective becomes even more 'concrete' after going through all the phenomenal vicissitudes of the dialectical processes.

In the 1960s, Mao did not process systematic philosophical texts comparable to those of the 1930s, *On Practice*[15] and *On Contradiction*. The most relevant intervention on the topic was actually the 'Speech on the Philosophical Problems' made in 1964, one year after Althusser's texts. It is likely that, at the Translation Bureau of the Central Committee of the CCP, there was a specific group assigned to translate *La Pensée*, the philosophical journal of the PCF in which the essays by Althusser were published. The tense controversy with the pro-Soviet European parties made these translations essential for the central apparatus of the CCP. This is even more probable given that Althusser's essays discussed Mao's philosophy, and evaluated it highly. We can therefore assume that at least a summary had passed through Mao's secretariat, if not the full translation, and it is possible that he was more or less directly aware of the existence of these texts.

The traces that we find in the 'Speech on Philosophical Problems' are

---

15   Mao Zedong (毛泽东), *Shijian lun* (实践论), in *Mao Zedong xuanji* (毛泽东选集) ('Collected Works by Mao Zedong') (Beijing: Renmin chubanshe, 1968 [1937]), vol. 1.

indirect but significant. The speech focused on the same issues raised by Althusser. Firstly, Mao outlined a predicament concerning the philosophical issue of whether Marxist and Hegelian dialectics were mutually compatible. It was symptomatic how stubbornly Mao affirmed the discontinuity of Marxist dialectics, aiming at rejecting Hegelian conceptual devices, in particular the concepts of 'negation of negation' and of *Aufhebung*.

Even more significant was the *vis polemica* against Yang Xianzhen (杨献珍), the head of the philosophical school of the CCP, who formulated the thesis合二而一 'the Two combines into One', whereas Mao in those years had summed up the core of Marxist dialectics in the thesis 一分为二 'One divides into Two'.[16] He did so in order 'to cut short', Althusser would have said. He was also in good company, as he repeated the synthetic formula of Lenin in *Philosophical Notebooks*.[17] In fact, Yang Xianzhen did not oppose Mao's thesis, but argued that 'the Two combines into One' was compatible and even complementary to 'One divides into Two', and ultimately its logical conclusion.

Mao associated Yang Xianzhen with Hegel, and concluded that in both cases his was 'the position of the bourgeoisie on the issue of the synthesis of opposites'.[18] However, if Yang Xianzhen 'represented' the interests of the German philosopher, he was able to do so because, in the formula 'One divides into Two', the problem that remained unsolved was the issue of the 'simple contradiction' – in other words, the splitting of the original One. It was this unsolved problem that ultimately allowed Yang to bring Mao back to Hegel.

Mao resisted vigorously, emphasizing the crucial thesis of the unevenness in the development of contradictions. He stressed the idea that the simple contradiction is always the result of infinitely prolonged multiple processes. Even the 'unity of opposites' of hydrogen and oxygen, said Mao in the wake of Engels's *Dialectics of Nature*,[19] creates water only after millions of years of reiterated contradictory processes in the physical world.

---

16   VYang Xianzhen 杨献珍, 'Guanyu «he er er yi» de wenti shensu' (关«合二而已»问题的申诉) ('A Recourse on the question "Two combines into One"'), in Yang Xianzhen wenji (杨献珍文集) (Collected Works by Yang Xianzhen), (Shijiazhuang: Hebei Renmin Chubanshe, 1967), vol. 3, pp. 62–9.

17   V. I. Lenin, *Philosophical Notebooks* (1895–1916), at marxists.org.

18   Mao Zedong, 'Guanyu zhexue wentide jianghua' (关于哲学问题的讲话) ('Speech on Philosophical Problems'), in *Mao Zedong sixiang wansui* (毛泽东思想万岁) ('Long Life to Mao Zedong's Thought') (Tokyo: Nihon Kokura henshu, 1969 [1964]), pp. 548–561.

19   Friedrich Engels, *Dialectics of Nature* (1883), at marxists.org.

In other words, Mao pointed out the unlimited multiplicity of contradictions and the ceaseless transformation of opposites. On the other hand, from the Althusserian perspective, since Mao did not systematically confute the original One, it became difficult for him to reject the key points of the Hegelian conceptual device. It is true that he categorically excluded them, but he did so in hasty and indecisive statements. Mao's declaration, 'the negation of the negation does not exist', was not enough to confute it conceptually.

Similarly, Mao's rejection of the *Aufhebung* as the 'synthesis into the One' remained an aspiration that was not supported by strong philosophical arguments. For example, to show that this 'synthesis' involves the destruction of one of the opposites by the other, Mao used a metaphor that creates more problems than it solves. He says that one of the opposites not only destroys the other, but 'eats' it: 'As occurred in the *Aufhebung* with the Guomindang army? We ate it morsel by morsel.'[20] However, in metaphorical terms, in this example we know that, in the totemic meal, 'sons', after 'devouring the father', 'internalize his authority' (perhaps in an 'abridged form'?).

Metaphors aside, building a philosophical perspective capable of excluding the original One (in order to prevent the return to the Hegelian matrix) was in those circumstances a huge philosophical problem that Mao was unable to resolve. As I have mentioned, from the 1960s onwards Mao did not write any systematic philosophical texts, and the formula 'One divides into Two' was mostly a shortcut, which Mao finally used as a proverbial motto and never really formalized theoretically.

On the other hand, even Althusser failed to solve the problem of how to exclude 'the original One'. The concept of 'overdetermination' was in a sense a powerful 'signal' of the radical nature of the problem, but did not build an ontological perspective able to answer to it. It is important to note that Alain Badiou, not surprisingly a Maoist, created an 'ontology of the multiple without One', which takes into account the warning of his philosophical master Althusser while following a completely different path deriving from the ontological consequences of the inventions of twentieth-century mathematics, and not primarily from Marxist politics.

---

20   Mao Zedong, 'Guanyu zhexue wentide jianghua', p. 557.

A Dual Heritage

In order to begin my inevitably provisional conclusions, I would argue that Althusser's intellectual legacy involves at least one crucial issue of contemporary philosophical research. When Badiou calls the general horizon of his philosophical research 'materialist dialectics',[21] he reproduces verbatim the formula of his master Althusser, albeit in a completely different key. On a political level, it is more complicated to divide Althusser's legacy. I agree with Althusser's idea that egalitarian politics should be strongly theoretically consistent, and that political errors are also theoretical errors. The question is whether these theoretical errors are also philosophical errors (regardless of whether or not one can say that philosophers commit 'errors'). Everything that comes from that intellectual and political conjuncture of the 1960s converges into the exhaustion of the previous bridges that claimed to channel philosophical questions into political questions, and vice versa.

The basic structure of this transitivity was the 'class party', and it was precisely this point that showed the greatest difference between Althusser and Mao. In the presence of the events that began in 1966–68, Althusser met a radical political obstacle when he attempted to read the Chinese events theoretically in a famous essay of 1967 entitled 'Sur la Révolution Culturelle',[22] published anonymously in *Cahiers Marxistes-Léninistes* by his students. This anonymity was not only due to his membership of the PCF, at that time fiercely anti-Maoist, but also likely due to a deep political impasse. On one hand, he enthusiastically praised that political event which he declared 'unprecedented', and that 'all French Communists' were to examine carefully. On the other hand, the specific novelty of the events was described by means of a device so symmetrical that it was unable to grasp its stormy and unpredictable character. The novelty of the GPCR was seen correctly in the new mass organizations, but in order to theorize this innovation Althusser made use of a vaguely sociological typology as elegant as it was formalistic. The analysis took place around a 'triptych' in which the 'party' guaranteed the 'political revolution', the 'trade unions' guaranteed the 'economic revolution' and the 'new organizations' would have guaranteed the ideological mass revolution. The latter was the point that he considered unprecedented. When only one

21   See Alain Badiou, *Logiques des mondes. L'Etre et l'Evénement, 2* (Paris: Seuil, 2006).
22   Louis Althusser (attr.), 2013, 'Sur la Révolution Culturelle', in *Décalages* 1: 1, Article 8, Berkeley Electronic Press, at scholar.oxy.edu.

year later, in mid 1968, the new mass organizations in China revealed a radical political exhaustion that led to self-destruction, there was nothing left standing of this tripartite typology. At this point Althusser returned firmly to the PCF.

Mao's path was much more complex and enigmatic. Although he refrained from systematic philosophical interventions during the Cultural Revolution at the political level, Mao manifested a restless experimental activism. The core of political experimentation was the question of the value of the class party. This was the point that he and Althusser had in common. But Mao did not retreat in the face of this immense difficulty, and when in 1968 he realized the political exhaustion of the Red Guards, he continued to do everything he could to maintain the prospects of experimental egalitarian inventions.

5 Communism, the Void

Alex Taek-Gwang Lee

The Return of Nothing

Through his theoretical discussion in 'The Underground Current of the Materialism of the Encounter', an essay impressive for its attempted transformation of Marxist materialism, Althusser writes about 'raining'.[1] His essay begins with the very discovery that 'this book is about another kind of rain, about a profound theme which runs through the whole history of philosophy, and was contested and repressed there as soon as it was stated'.[2] What is 'another kind of rain'? The hidden history of materialism: 'the "rain" (Lucretius) of Epicurus' atoms that fall parallel to each other in the void; the "rain" of parallelism of the infinite attributes in Spinoza and many others: Machiavelli, Hobbes, Rousseau, Marx, Heidegger too, and Derrida'.[3] The main thesis Althusser proposes here is that of 'the existence of an almost completely unknown materialist tradition in the history of philosophy: the "materialism . . . of the rain, the swerve, the encounter, the take [*prise*]"'.[4]

What is this 'unknown materialism'? Althusser's aim is clearly stated: he would like to establish an alternative materialism to 'a materialism of necessity and teleology'.[5] For him, necessary and teleological materialism is a disguised form of idealism. Against materialism in the rationalist tradition, he coins the concept a 'materialism of encounter' – it is equivalent to what he also calls 'aleatory materialism' or materialism of contingency. Interestingly, Althusser says that he intends to develop the four concepts of this unknown materialism – the rain, the swerve, the

---

1   I would like to thank Jason Barker, who read my first draft and gave me useful comments.
2   Louis Althusser, 'The Underground Current of the Materialism of the Encounter', in *Philosophy of the Encounter: Later Writings, 1978–1987*, ed. Francois Matheron and Oliver Corpet, transl. G. M. Goshgarian (London: Verso, 2006), p. 167.
3   Ibid.
4   Ibid.
5   Ibid., p. 168.

encounter and the take. This poetic configuration of terms, which Althusser does not manage to elaborate in a *systematic* manner (system-building of course goes against his philosophical approach), remain in frustratingly summary form in Althusser's text. Nonetheless, what light does he throw on these concepts?

These are the key concepts of ancient atomism found in Epicurus. Althusser focuses on Lucretius's image of the rain falling in parallel in the void, an image based on Epicurus's hypothesis: 'the nature of the universe is bodies and void'.[6] For Epicurus, the void is not transcendent to the universe; it is something in between bodies: 'the atomic is a solid body which has no share of void included in it; [and] void is an intangible nature'.[7] The bodies (atoms) and the void are the origins of things and the beginning of the world. He argues that 'in totality [of things] nothing unprecedented happens beyond [what has happened in] the unlimited time which has already passed'.[8] Lucretius elaborates Epicurus's theory of atoms in his poem, *The Nature of Things*:

> Another basic principle you need to have a sound
> Understanding of: when bodies fall through empty space
> Straight down, under their own weight, at a random time and place,
> They swerve a little. Just enough of a swerve for you to call
> It a change of course. Unless inclined to swerve, all things would fall
> Right through the deep abyss like drops of rain. There would be no
> Collisions, and no atom would meet atom with a blow,
> And Nature thus could not have fashioned anything, full stop.[9]

Lucretius states further that 'if . . . atoms do not swerve a little and initiate the kind of motion which in turn shatters the laws of fate, but leave effect to follow cause inexorably forever, where does that freewill come from that exists in every creature the world over?'[10] This is the very reason why Lucretius puts an emphasis on the swerve of atoms – to prove the possibility of free will emerging out of necessity. Although concurring with Lucretius's hypothesis, Althusser does not agree with the absolute dimension of free will. Althusser warns of the idealism in Epicurus's

---

6   Brad Inwood and L. P. Gerson, eds, *The Epicurus Reader: Selected Writings and Testimonia* (Indianapolis, IN: Hackett, 1994), p. 75.
7   Ibid.
8   Ibid., p. 88.
9   Lucretius, *The Nature of Things*, transl. A. E. Stallings (London: Penguin, 2007), p. 42.
10   Ibid. p. 43.

conceptualization of the *clinamen* preserving the possible existence of freedom even in the world of necessity:

> In order for swerve to give rise to an encounter from which a world is born, that encounter must last; it must be, not a 'brief encounter', but a lasting encounter, which then becomes the basis for all reality, all necessity, all Meaning and all reason. But the encounter can also not last; then there is no world. What is more, it is clear that the encounter creates nothing of the reality of the world, which is nothing but agglomerated atoms, but *that it confers their reality upon the atoms themselves*, which, without swerve and encounter, would be nothing but abstract elements, lacking all consistency and existence. So much so that we can say that the *atom's very existence is due to nothing but the swerve and the encounter* prior to which they led only a phantom existence.[11]

This passage seems to follow from what Althusser claims in terms of determination in the last instance by the economic. For him, 'the existence of overdetermination is no longer *a fact* pure and simple, for in its essentials we have related it to *its bases*, even if our exposition has so far been merely gestural'.[12] From this perspective, he declares that 'a revolution in the *structure* does not *ipso facto* modify the existing superstructures and particularly the *ideologies* at one blow'.[13]

However, Althusser draws on Lucretius here to justify his shift in emphasis. As André Tosel points out, this means that Althusser reverses 'the "structuralist" primacy of reproduction over genesis'.[14] He comes to think reproduction as the consequence 'under the recurrence of the accomplished fact that which is the result of a genesis of elements that have "taken" and formed a structure which is a conjuncture',[15] and revises his earlier arguments about the relationship between contradiction and structure.

It seems that the crucial factor in Althusser's late work is his perspective on the transition of social structures with reference to Epicurus's

---

11   Althusser, 'Underground Current', p. 169.
12   Louis Althusser, *For Marx*, transl. Ben Brewster (London: Verso, 1969), p. 113.
13   Ibid., p. 115.
14   André Tosel, 'The Hazards of Aleotory Materialism in the Late Philosophy of Louis Althusser', in Katja Diefenbach, Sara R. Farris, Gal Kirn and Peter D. Thomas, eds, *Encountering Althusser* (London: Bloomsbury, 2013), p. 17.
15   Ibid.

atomism.[16] What preoccupies him is the contingency rather than the encounter itself in his discussion of ancient atomism – even though he clarifies that the latter is the condition of the former. As Lucretius states, 'nothing can be brought to nothingness once it is made, then there must be first bodies made of stuff that lasts forever'.[17] Thus, it might be argued that Althusser identifies Lucretius's concept of nothingness with his early concept of structures determined in the last instance. However, where previously Althusser had placed the emphasis on structure, in his later work he rather posits the void as the locus of the cause.[18]

The Materialism of the Encounter

Althusser's change of emphasis is also revealed clearly when he discusses Machiavelli, whom he considers a political philosopher in the tradition of the unknown materialism. His purpose in introducing Epicurus's and Lucretius's atomism into the latter edifice is to reformulate politics against the materialism of necessity and teleology of vulgar Marxism. His aim is to move the focus of Marxism from the structure to the void, the place in which 'nothingness' becomes the condition of the contingent encounter. Let us consider Althusser's argument:

> The reader [overlooks] the fact that a philosophy is simultaneously at work here too. A curious *philosophy which is a 'materialism of the encounter' thought by way of politics*, and which, as such, does not take anything for granted. It is in the political *void* that the encounter must come about, and that national unity must 'take hold'. But *this political void is first a philosophical void*. No Cause that precedes its effects is to be found in it, no Principle of morality or theology (as in the whole Aristotelian political tradition: the good and bad forms of government, the degeneration of the good into the bad). One reasons here not in terms of the Necessity of the accomplished fact, but in terms of the contingency of the fact to be accomplished. As in the Epicurean world, all the elements are both

---

16   For this discussion, see Chang-Yol Yang, 'Read Atomism for Althusser', in T. Jin, ed., *The Althusser Effect* (Seoul: Greenbee, 2011).

17   Lucretius, *Nature of Things*, p. 19.

18   Ted Stolze interestingly argues that Althusser's relationship to Epicurus's atomism involved Deleuze. According to him, 'Althusser and his circle seem to have been quite favorably disposed toward certain of Deleuze's early works (such as a 1961 essay on Lucretius and the already classic book on Nietzsche published in 1962)'. See Ted Stolze, 'Deleuze and Althusser: Flirting with Structuralism', *Rethinking Marxism* 10: 3 (Autumn 1998), p. 51.

here and beyond, to come raining down later . . . but they do not exist, are only abstract, as long as the unity of a world has not united them in the Encounter that will endow them with existence.[19]

What Althusser recognizes here is the link between the political idea and the philosophical thought in Machiavelli's theory of princes – 'unification will be achieved if there emerges some nameless man who has enough luck and *virtù* to establish himself somewhere, in some *nameless* corner of Italy'.[20] However, Machiavelli's philosophical aspiration must be realized by some 'body'. How is this possible? In his writing, Machiavelli says nothing about who will be the prince and where will be the place of this coming to be. His philosophical consideration of the Italian situation is based on the political consciousness of 'the powerlessness of the existing states and princes'.[21] The prince and the place are totally abstract emptiness, so to speak: the void. They could not be realized unless the 'unity of a world' unites them in the 'Encounter'.[22]

Machiavelli preserves the locus of the political for the *nameless*: the *demos* – in other words, those who for Rancière have no name and no part in the society. Althusser's adaption of Lucretius finally finds itself justified in the discussion of Machiavelli's politics of the void. On this point, it seems that Althusser's attempt to reformulate Marxism involves making the *nameless* emerge from the realm of possibility, those masses who could transform social structures while starting out from the void, the lacuna that preserves the political event. For Althusser, capitalism is the complex totality of conjunctures containing repetitive diversion, the *clinamen* in Lucretius's sense. The structure remains an event, and its reproduction is always interrupted by the repetition of the encounter. However, what is at stake here in the concept of *nameless* is a potentially new concept of politics.

Unfortunately, Althusser does not enter into the detail of how such politics might be possible. Althusser separates his aleatory materialism from Marx's idealist materialism, which conversely affirms freedom as a human ideal. He criticizes Marx's dialectical understanding of the bourgeoisie. What is problematic in orthodox Marxism lies in its pretensions

---

19   Althusser, 'Underground Current', pp. 173–4. Emphases in original.
20   Ibid., p. 172. Emphasis in original.
21   Ibid.
22   The hidden reference for Althusser's understanding of Machiavelli as 'the first theorist of conjuncture' is Gramsci. For this discussion, see Mikko Lahtinen. 'Althusser, Machiaveilli and Us: Between Philosophy and Politics', in Diefenbach et al., *Encountering Althusser*, pp. 115–23.

to be able to overturn capitalist exploitation *in toto*: the bourgeoisie as a totalizing subjectivity able to unify the specific mode of production originally freed from within the previous one. In Althusser's terms, the idealism of freedom in Marxism assumes that 'the bourgeoisie is produced as an antagonistic class by the decay of the dominant feudal class'.[23] Such an assumption is problematic, because it presupposes the free bourgeoisie predestined to accomplish capitalism. Althusser argues that 'the bourgeoisie is indeed nothing other than the element predestined to unify all the other elements of the mode of production, the one that will transform it into another combination, that of the capitalist mode of production'.[24] In short, the bourgeoisie is one of the floating elements in one of the multiple encounters realizing an original capitalist mode of production.

From this perspective, the classical principle of Marxism is renounced, which guides the burier of the bourgeoisie: the proletariat – another class dialectically produced by the ruling class, predetermined to comprise the communist mode of production. Accordingly, the necessity is not the result of what has been accomplished in the encounter, but the representation of what has been accomplished is able to impose its structure and its rules of reproduction.[25] This is the reason why Althusser puts an emphasis on contingency rather than encounter as such, and analyzes Machiavelli's politics of the void. The void is the place in which the encounter between elements would happen, the nothingness at which the dominant representation cannot be reached – the unknown and incomprehensible contingency.

Althusser's turn from contradiction to contingency somewhat tends towards the conclusion that social change depends on 'a wait for the unexpected'.[26] What he attempts to do is to define the state of *demos* as something else by a shift from structural causality to the void. This implies that there is no possibility of theorizing the structural determination, but merely 'the conjunctural interplay and rearrangement of the elements of social reality'.[27] The problem of the late Althusser is clear when he claims that the consolidation of a specific structure is a matter of repetitive encounters. The structure cannot be so much fixed as rather always already intervened upon by material practices in relation to social

23   Ibid., p. 201.
24   Althusser, 'Underground Current', p. 202.
25   See Tosel, 'Hazards of Aleotory Materialism', p. 18.
26   Panagiotis Sotiris, 'Rethinking Aleatory Materialism', in Diefenbach et al., *Encountering Althusser*, p. 37.
27   Ibid., p. 35.

relations – which is to say, to adopt a different discourse, the Real resisting the symbolic representation of structure. The 'aim' – or perhaps the unintended and unforeseeable outcome – of aleatory materialism is to reject the teleological dialectics of Marxism, with the result that only 'nothingness' be allowed in politics. However, the novelty does not emerge from nothingness as such. Nothingness is not political in itself.

The problem is that Machiavelli's concept of the *nameless* is merely the condition for politics; the nameless is not subjectivization through the political situation. The political subject is the dialectically interrelated materiality within the structural conjuncture, producing the form of ruptures. The decisive question raised at such moments is how such subjectivization can be actualized. Paradoxically, the possibility of subjectivization emerges from the negation of possibility. This is why it is necessary to consider carefully the concept of the void, which presumes the configuration of social forms. The void is not the genetic moment of the conjuncture from without, but rather always already from within.

Aside from his interest in Lacan and Spinoza, Althusser's conceptualization of the event for the materialism of the encounter cannot easily be reconciled with Gilles Deleuze's materialist metaphysics. For Deleuze, there is 'a double series of events which develop on two planes, echoing without resembling each other'.[28] He distinguishes 'real events on the level of the engendered solutions' from 'ideal events embedded in the conditions of the problem'; but 'the ideal series enjoys the double property of transcendence and immanence in relation to the real'.[29] That is to say, one event cannot be stabilized and ossified by representation: there are 'real events on the level of the engendered solutions' and ' ideal events embedded in the conditions of the problem'.[30] An event is the exception to the axiom of representation and emerges in its groundlessness. This is clearly distinct from what Althusser aims at in his formulation of aleatory materialism.

In Deleuzian terms, the later Althusser's agenda could be regarded as an attempt to liberate 'materialist thought from the "principle of sufficient reason"', while Deleuze writes a materialist metaphysics that wrests from this principle an anomalous turn'.[31] What is this materialist metaphysics?

---

28   Gilles Deleuze, *Difference and Repetition*, transl. Paul Patton (New York: Columbia University Press, 1994), p. 189.
29   Ibid.
30   Ibid.
31   Katja Diefenbach, 'Althusser with Deleuze: How to Think Spinoza's Immanent Cause', in Diefenbach et al., *Encountering Althusser*, p. 167.

It is materialism without the ground or determination. Deleuze intends to articulate 'a determination which is not opposed to the indeterminate and does not limit it'.[32] Meanwhile, Althusser conceptualizes the void as nothingness before the accomplishment of the factual: 'the non-accomplishment of the fact, the non-world that is merely the unreal existence of the atoms'.[33]

What then is the discrepancy between Althusser and Deleuze in their respective discussions of immanent causality? For Deleuze, there is no void. In Deleuzian terms, being is a single materiality in differential expression, the differentiation of the One. For Althusser, meanwhile, the absent whole or nothingness is the causality precedent to any structure. In this sense, we could find another thought parallel to Althusser in the politics of immanence, or multitude escaping from the state apparatuses. Deleuze seems to me a key figure here and, it might be argued, Rancière too shares his view, while at the same time criticizing the limitations of a Deleuzian politics.

The Politics of Immanence

In a short interview with *Le Magazine Littéraire*, dedicated to Deleuze, Rancière suggests an interesting explanation of Deleuze's aesthetics; Rancière argues that Deleuze is a philosopher who identifies the end of the representative aesthetic regime, 'a regime that desires to break with the representative tradition'.[34] In this way, Rancière continues, Deleuze completes the destiny of aesthetics in the name of philosophy. He seems to provide an idea for understanding Deleuze's aesthetics in particular, and for analyzing the relationship between an event and representation in general.

Rancière identifies the key aspect of Deleuze's aesthetics in terms of 'figuration'. Deleuze, an accomplished Spinozist, always presupposes a pre-figurative dimension, even if he clearly adapts 'figures' for the way of thinking. Like Heidegger's notion of *sous rature* ('under erasure'), Deleuze's concept of figures implies a preliminary mode of life before and after thinking – what Deleuze argues postulates not any separation between life and thinking, but rather 'a life' as pure immanence. For

---

32   Deleuze, *Difference and Repetition*. p. 275.
33   Althusser, 'Underground Current', p. 170.
34   Jacques Rancière, 'Deleuze accomplit le destin de l'esthétique', *Le Magazine Littéraire* 406 (2002)

Deleuze, immanence is 'not immanence to life, but immanence that is in nothing is itself a life'.[35]

For Deleuze, allegory and metaphor are not the imitation of reality or materiality. Above all, the category of immanence is the very condition for Deleuze's philosophical project; hence the question as to how immanence works as the image of thinking. Regarding Deleuze's philosophy as an inquiry into immanence, it is not accidental that Rancière connects Deleuze's philosophy to aesthetics. This does not so much mean that Deleuze assimilates philosophy into aesthetics as philosophy, but rather pits an aesthetic dimension against the ethical differentiation of social hierarchy. This is where Rancière, in my view, suddenly finds his resemblance to Deleuze. That is to say, the immanent dimension presumed in Deleuze's philosophy is nothing other than the aesthetic confusion by which Rancière formulates the political escaping from the hierarchical governance of the police – in other words, the representational system of the social and the given distribution of the sensible.

For Ranicére, an aesthetic dimension cancels the social discrimination and status differentiation, and serves as another distribution of aesthetical senses, which deconstruct and reconstruct habitual knowledge. There is a likeness between Deleuze and Rancière in their reformulations of the concept of an aesthetic dimension. Rancière regards the aesthetic dimension as the condition of the political. For both Deleuze and Rancière, aesthetics is not the enemy of 'the aesthetic', as for Adorno, nor the institutionalization of the aesthetic, but rather the assemblage of the sensible, or desire. In *The Flesh of Words*, Rancière discusses Deleuze's theory of literature, arguing that Deleuze sees literature as 'the development of formula'. The Deleuzian notion of formula is similar to Aristotle's concept of plot – the plot in opposition to symbol (σύμβολον).[36] This means that formula has no hidden metaphysical sense in it, just performance for the mechanism of formality as such.

As Rancière says, Deleuze regards Melville's 'Bartleby' not as 'the story of the quirks and misfortunes of a poor clerk, nor [as] a symbol for

---

35   Gilles Deleuze, *Pure Immanence: Essays on a Life*, transl. Anne Boyman (New York: Zone, 2005), p. 27.
36   According to Aristotle, symbol is meaningful as far as it is related to convention. He says that 'a *name* is a spoken sound significant by convention, without time, none of whose parts is significant in separation', and continues: 'I say "by convention" because no name is a name naturally but only when it has become a symbol'. See Aristotle, *'De Interpretatione': The Complete Works of Aristotle*, ed. Jonathan Barnes (Princeton: Princeton University Press, 1995), p. 25.

the human condition'.[37] For Deleuze's theory of formula, Bartleby is privileged, in the sense that the formula of the story is 'summed up in the materiality of a linguistic formula' – the formula of pure mechanism forming 'the essence of the comic'. What Rancière touches on here is that of the play of words, the pure mechanism of Bartleby's performance with language – 'I would prefer not to . . .'

The performance Deleuze praises in his analysis of 'Bartleby' reminds us of the Brechtian concept of *Grundgestus* – that is to say, the a priori which determines knowledge or senses. *Grundgestus* is in opposition to *gestus*, revealing the contradictions of the real and the antinomies of the social system. This is the very principle by which a play works in itself. In this way, *Grundgestus* is a primitive dimension precedent to any representation of gestures. Comparable to this, however, Deleuze rejects the way in which a critic reads the meaning of story and symbol in literary texts, not least literary texts providing story and symbol only. What might be stressed here is that, for Deleuze, literature trapped by a representative meaning system is not 'aesthetic' – of course, this implies that Deleuze uses the term aesthetics as a sort of 'dimension', in which the hierarchy of representation becomes confused and the conflicts of forces as the effect of a formula is betrayed.

Deleuze (like Brecht) presupposes the a priori of representation, and hence a question arises here: What is the a priori in Deleuze's aesthetics? Is it an aesthetic dimension and the moment of breakdown of the political? For Rancière, Deleuze is a philosopher who can discover the power of an aesthetic dimension, a formula of aesthetics. However, he presents the problem of 'Deleuzian politics' by pointing out the theoretical impasse that Deleuze postulates in the discussion of the emancipation internalized in the concept of a formula. Rancière argues that 'under the mask of "Bartleby", Deleuze opens to us the open road of comrades, the great drunkenness of joyous multitudes freed from the law of the Father, the path of a certain "Deleuzism" that is perhaps only the "festival of donkeys" of Deleuze's thinking'.[38] The road Deleuze opens leads not to political justice, but rather to contradiction – 'the wall of loose stones, the wall of non-passage'. In short, literature opens 'no passage to a Deleuzian politics'.

Why does Rancière argue in this way? I think what Rancière really wants to express here is the impossibility of Deleuzian politics, but the

---

37   Jacques Rancière, *The Flesh of Words: The Politics of Writing*, transl. Charlotte Mandell (Stanford: Stanford University Press, 2004), p. 146.
38   Ibid., p. 164.

possible point where 'Deleuzism' produces its own political aspect in terms of a formula – the pure play of a single gesture by which Deleuze clears 'the way of Deleuzism'. Rancière observes his outstanding disagreement with representation in Deleuze. Yet the break itself with representation cannot be achieved in a simple way. It is not easy to achieve it even if the artwork were to be consigned to a liberty in relation to radical immanence. Reality does not resemble the way in which one thinks that the plane of immanence can be separated from representation or the symbolic. Modernism teaches us that the artwork obtains its own autonomy while escaping from representation. As Rancière says, the aesthetic regime of art is not a simple autonomy of an artwork – it seems autonomous, but is always already blended with heteronomy.[39]

In this sense, it is proper to say, as Rancière claims, that Deleuze completes the destiny of the aesthetic regime of art. Deleuze solves the problem of autonomy in modernism or avant-garde aesthetics. In the regime, the will to produce the artwork is not the problem of a simple autonomy, but rather the weight of the unconscious, the void – hence, the artwork is passive, not voluntary. It is not an *object* of free will. This means that the rule of an artwork depends on the event. It is crucial that Deleuze's immanence is not an autonomous dimension; it is 'an' immanence, not a simple one – it is absolute in the sense that it must be always allegorized in its turn, achieved as figuration. What Deleuze aims at accomplishing is to repeat (or re-present) this tension between an absolute immanence and the representative. Deleuze must re-introduce the very traits of representation in order to figure the immanence pushed up to the extreme.

The Problem of Equal Things

It seems to me that Rancière points out the weak point of Deleuze, in which the latter supposedly regards aesthetic performance as the festival of Dionysus – as resistance to the dominant aesthetic of representation. Arguably this is another mistake comparable to that perpetrated by the Freudian Marxists under the slogan of liberating sexuality from social repression. Focusing on desire as such, Deleuze establishes an alternative way to affirm life and thinking at the same time in terms of absolute immanence. In summary terms, Rancière's argument seems to put an emphasis on the aspect of Deleuze's aesthetics which divulges the limit of

---

39   See Rancière, 'Deleuze accomplit le destin de l'esthétique'.

aestheticism, but his assertion also points out that Deleuze seems uninter-
ested in explaining the connection between aesthetics and politics. What
Rancière raises here is an unavoidable issue if one's aim is to search for
the way to link aesthetics to politics – the classical problem of philosophy
about how an aesthetic sense can be transformed into, or combined
towards, a political cause. This is at any rate what Rancière shares with
Deleuze, in the sense that the latter also develops the idea of an aesthetic
dimension as a political moment.

For Rancière, however, the 'Deleuzian difficulty' lies in the way in
which Deleuze opposes 'a horizontal world of multiplicities' to the dualis-
tic and vertical world of model and copy.[40] By this gesture, argues
Rancière, Deleuze overlooks what he really achieves, that is, a question
as to the political attribute of representation as such, and reserves the
contradiction in his aesthetics. The main focus of Rancière's criticism
here is that Deleuze reduces the aesthetic dimension of multiplicities to
the role of the eccentric – in short, Deleuze's aesthetic tacitly accepts
aesthetic elitism. In this way, Rancière continues, he falls into the simple
dichotomy between the exemplary and the multiple, the eccentric and the
imitative.

Arguably, the Deleuzian molecular revolution does not insist upon
such elitism, but rather on an absolute equality abolishing any social hierarchical order involved in institutional power. Rancière knows this well,
and goes further beyond the common misunderstanding of Deleuzism.
He picks up the theoretical shortcoming of Deleuze's discussion of the
relationship between aesthetics and politics and warns of the possible
misuse of Deleuzism in terms of revolutionary politics. Deleuze 'manifests the power of the work as an encounter of the heterogeneous, that is
to say not simply as the unpredictable composition of impersonal multiplicities but purely as an encounter between two worlds'[41] – the vertical
world of representation and the horizontal world of multiplicities. Thus,
for Rancière, this model of two worlds is not political enough.

The metaphysics of literature presupposes the atom of equality, and is
not limited to the human individual. Even all animals and plants can be
equal in the world of literary metaphysics – the equality is like
Schopenhauer's terms of compassion, which is 'the affect unique to the
writer since it exceeds the order of relations between human

---

40   Rancière, *Flesh of Words*, p. 157.
41   Ibid.

individuals'.[42] This idea deconstructs the community of brotherhood and nullifies any privilege over what exists within the past community. The politics depending on the metaphysics of literature 'leads from the equality of human individuals in society to a greater equality that only reigns below, at the molecular level'.[43] This allows for the possibility that the atom of equality can be connected to the principle of the universe as in the case of Schopenhauer, the one that emphasizes the ontological equality rather than the equality demanded by actual workers and poor people in society.

Rancière's reading of Deleuze seems to reveal a problem here; he presupposes Deleuze's notion of the eccentric as a permanent status, but Deleuzian ontology does not presume such an identical state with being. In a Deleuzian sense, 'fabulation' is the expression of immanence as such, the state of becoming, and the eccentric is the moment of flowing of pure immanence. The expression of immanence is life as a differential synthesis of sensation. It makes possible not so much the conscious self or person, but rather a 'being of sensation'. This is the core of Deleuzian ontology – the ontology of life. Life as immanence cannot be inserted into 'a categorical or discursive synthesis providing the unity of their manifold for an "I think"'.[44] The 'being of sensation' is not *sensus communis* – its preexisting materiality for itself. The sensation is precedent to any subject (not being as such), and becoming is the return of the sensation into the static and inert being captured by the representative discourse of community.

In this sense, all actuality is always connected to virtualities; more importantly, the virtual is not negative to the actual – it is not the limit of actuality, but the non-actualized something in it. For this reason, the synthesis of sensation is the very attribute of a subject that is similar to the situation of *demos* that Rancière presupposes for the political. Deleuze posits the plane of immanence in which an object and a subject actualize into concrete realities. Ontologically speaking, the *demos* are what can only be sensed, even though they make themselves visible by demanding the equality of their own parts in the community. Their discursive recognition already assumes the declaration of their different sensation from *sensus communis*, the habitual 'I think'. In this way, the Deleuzian concept of sensation brings forward the necessary condition for an event: *demos* is

42   Ibid.
43   Ibid., p. 158.
44   John Rajchman, 'Introduction', in Gilles Deleuze, *Pure Immanence*, p. 9.

the actualization of the virtual and a different synthesis of sensation from the agreed one of communal sense.

Consequently, what really gives rise to the differential sensibility of *demos*? If aesthetics is just passive and involuntary, we should consider a pre-existing something before the discursive or representational dimension of *sensus communis*. When the *demoi* declare themselves as not common, not subjects belonging to the agreed sensation in community, the political of an event begins to get on track. Hence, the actual problem is the declaration of the subject to insist upon its own sensation against the normative representation and struggle with the given political regimes. This is where aesthetics can be transformed into the political.

What is needed is an aesthetic realization of the politics of minorities praised by Rancière. As Deleuze said, 'all kinds of minority questions – linguistic, ethnic, regional, about sex, or youth – resurge not only as archaisms, but in up-to-date revolutionary forms which call once more into question in an entirely immanent manner both the global economy of the machine and the assemblages of national States'.[45] However, the real problem is how such questions become manifested in an idea.

The Reassertion of Politics

In *Less Than Nothing*, Slavoj Žižek recounts two types of materialism: first, scientific naturalism such as neurological sciences and Darwinism; secondly, discursive historicism such as those of Foucault and Derrida. He also points out 'the two sides of the spiritual reaction' to them: 'Western Buddhism' and 'the thought of transcendental finitude (culminating in Heidegger)'.[46] According to Žižek, these positions, whatever their theoretical aims, cannot properly explain the dimension of 'pre-transcendental gap/rupture, the Freudian name for which is the drive'.[47] What Žižek brings to light here is the problem of materialism. Alain Badiou had of course already established in *Logics of Worlds* a key methodological distinction between dialectical and 'democratic materialism', the materialism which verifies the axiom of conviction on only bodies and languages without truths.[48]

---

45   Gilles Deleuze, *Dialogues* (London: Continuum, 1987), p. 147.
46   Slavoj Žižek, *Less Than Nothing: Hegel and the Shadow of Dialectical Materialism* (London: Verso, 2012), p. 6.
47   Ibid.
48   Alain Badiou, *Logics of Worlds*, transl. Alberto Toscano (London: Continuum, 2009), p. 3.

Badiou's assessment of materialism is of prime importance. For him, materialism as such is not at all political, even if it is democratic. 'Democratic materialism' is merely the representation of multiple things, and only privileges ontological individuation. Multiplicity is nothing to do with the political dimension of beings, if it is limited to bodies and languages. There are truths beyond such limits. Thus, questions as to what materialism is should be expanded to what truths are which are not included within materialism as such. The truths are the hidden source of the material dimensions, the determinants to be the one rather than the multiple. According to Badiou, the one is the result of operation within the regime of multiple things.[49]

The one, which integrates the two worlds, the political and the non-political, is what is excluded from politics. The problem of materialism is related to the one. Badiou draws a distinction between the count-as-one and 'the one is not'. The one is ontologically the result of a retroactive procedure which re-presents the inconsistent multiplicity as an – i.e. one – inconsistent multiplicity. This nothing consisting of the multiple is the void, which is not presented in the situation's presentation of its count.[50] The void is universally included in every situation; its attribute of not belonging is why it is universally included. Without such nothing, the multiple cannot be presented in the set. In this way, Badiou opposes the ontology of presence to the ontology of presentation – that is, a thinking of the multiple. Ironically, each situation needs the void to be presented, yet the void remains uncounted, not to be presented. There is the void, but not included in the presentation; the void does not belong to any situation, but is included in every situation. What this amounts to is the failure of totality: 'the one is not'; but one is unity, not totality. Badiou names this in-consisting totality as 'Chimera':[51]

If the Chimera is reflexive, this means that it presents itself. It is within its own multiple-composition. But what is the Chimera? The multiple of all non-reflexive multiples. If the Chimera is among these multiples, it is because it is not reflexive. But we have just supposed that it is. Inconsistency. Therefore, the Chimera is not reflexive. However, it is by definition the multiple of all non-reflexive multiples. If it is not reflexive,

49   Alain Badiou, *Ethics: An Essay on the Understanding of Evil*, transl. Peter Hallward (London: Verso, 2001), p. 24.
50   Alain Badiou, *Being and Event*, transl. Oliver Feltham (London: Continuum, 2005), p. 55.
51   Badiou, *Logics of Worlds*, p. 110.

it is in this 'all', this whole, and therefore presents itself. It is reflexive. Inconsistency, once again. Since the Chimera can be neither reflexive nor non-reflexive, and since this partition admits of no remainder, we must conclude that the Chimera is not. But its being followed necessarily from the being that was ascribed to the Whole. Therefore, the Whole has no being.[52]

If the Chimera, the multiple of all multiples, includes itself, it is complete unto itself and is not to be included; conversely, if it does not include itself, it is suited to part of itself and is to be included. This is the way in which the whole has no being. Therefore, every situation conceals the danger of the void in its structure of the count of the count. To eliminate the void, the situation counts it repeatedly, but not to completion. It is left over from the impossibility of the count. The disruption of the void is the revelation of the uncounted impossibility – so to speak, the event. In this sense, the one of politics, the one world formed by an operation, does not exist ontologically, but rather eventally as 'ultra-one'. However, capitalism splits the one world into two worlds – of the wealthy and the poor. This split goes deeper than just the two worlds. People are themselves divided into two parts as well.

The Idea of Communism and After

Since World War II, 'Asia' has been the grandiloquent name for the way in which capitalism separates peoples into two camps, communism and anti-communism, and now more recently the political and the non-political. The Cold War is not just a metaphor in 'Asia', but rather the theatricality through which the utopian idea of modernization is intermingled with extreme violence, both of the 'ideological' and 'political' variety. In Asia, the nation-state as such paradoxically functions in such a way as to introduce – and to *stage* – the capitalist mode of production into the so-called 'Asiatic mode of production'. The ideology of the Cold War still succeeds in mobilizing farmers and workers to consolidate the US-stage-managed world system by employing their passion in the service of 'the ideal of the nation-state'. The geography of Asia must be seen in the context of an enlarged and imagined community of US-led anti-communist geopolitics. Anti-communism is not just another political

---

52   Ibid.

edifice, but enforces the cleansing of politics as such through violence. In short, anti-communism might be considered as an ongoing geopolitical project for depoliticization. Then again, the situation I am describing here is by no means the product of historical necessity. This strange paradox instead involves the type of aleatory encounters that throw the dominant narratives into question, and call for more sustained investigations, not just of 'our history', but, as Althusser was fond of saying, of our 'historical present'.

6 The Affirmative Dialectics

Alain Badiou

The fundamental problem in the philosophical field, today, is to find something like a new logic. We cannot begin with some considerations about politics, life, creation or action. We must first describe a new logic. Or more precisely a new dialectics. It has been the way of Plato. But after all, it is also the way Marx proposed. The work of Marx is not first a new historical vision, a new theory of class struggle, and so on, but from its very beginning a new general logic in the wake of Hegelian dialectics. Marx was perhaps the first, maybe after Plato, to create an explicit relation between revolutionary politics and a new dialectical framework. We have the same problem today. To be sure, we have to rectify something after two centuries of successes and failures in revolutionary politics, and, in particular, after the failure of the state-form of socialism. But we also have to find a new logic, a new philosophical proposition adequate for all forms of creative novelty. And so the question of dialectical and of non-dialectical relations is a pressing difficulty. If you want: our problem is the problem of negativity. Or more precisely: the relationship between logical negativity and the concrete process of politics under the Idea of communism.

When the logical framework of political action is of the classical dialectical type, what is fundamental is negation. The development of the political struggle is fundamentally something like 'revolt against', 'opposition to', 'negation of'. And the newness – the creation of the new state, or the creation of the new law – is always a result of the process of negation. This is the Hegelian framework: you have a relation between affirmation and negation, construction and negation, in which the real principle of movement, and the real principle of creation, is negation. And so the very definition of the revolutionary class is to be *against* the present state or *against* the present law in the precise sense that revolutionary consciousness, as Lenin would say, is basically the consciousness that one stands in a relation of negation to the existing order.

But this vision as such cannot be sustained today. We are living a sort of crisis of trust in the power of negativity. And we know two forms of this crisis.

Adorno thinks that the classical Hegelian dialectics was too much affirmative, too much submitted to the potency of the Totality and of the One. He proposes a sort of hyper-negativity, the name of which is 'Negative Dialectics'. We know today that, in this way, we have finally nothing else than an ethics of compassion, a vision where the hero of our consciousness is the suffering human body, the pure victim. And we know also that this moralism is perfectly adequate to the capitalist domination under the mask of democracy.

On the other side, Negri, but also Althusser, think that Hegelian dialectics was too much negative, too much subjective and too much indifferent to the absolute potency of Nature, of Life, of the movement of History. They find in Spinoza a model of philosophy which is finally without negation. We know today that, in this way, we have an acceptance of the dominant order, across the conviction that this order is full of newness and creativity, and that finally modern capitalism is the immediate strength which works, beyond the Empire, in the direction of a sort of communism.

The first hypothesis abandons the idea of Communism for an ethic of suffering, and some variations concerning the human rights. The second abandons the communist hypothesis for a sort of new hope concerning the potency of nature and the immanent creativity of capitalism itself.

What I seek to do in all my work is to propose a new dialectical framework which is not a return to the young Marx or to Hegel, but which is neither the negative dialectics of Adorno, which is like the aesthetics of human rights, nor the affirmative construction of Negri, which destroys all forms of dialecticity and is like a Nietzschean *Gai Savoir* of History.

I think the problem today is to find a way of reversing the classical dialectical logic inside itself, so that the affirmation, or the positive proposition, comes before the negation instead of after it. Or in some sense, my attempt is to find a dialectical framework where something of the future comes before the negative present. I am not suggesting the suppression of the relation between affirmation and negation – certainly revolt and class struggle remain essential – and I am not suggesting a pacifistic direction, or anything like that. The question is not whether we need to struggle or oppose, but concerns more precisely the relation between negation and affirmation. So when I say that there is something non-dialectical, whether with regard to the Apostle Paul or to the field of concrete political analysis, formally it is the same idea. We have to try to understand exactly the conditions under which we may still have anything like the possibility of concrete negation. And I believe this can only effectively be realized in the field of primitive affirmation, through something that is primitively affirmative and not negative. It is a question of event and subject, in my terminology. Ultimately, I am saying something very simple. I am saying first that to open a new situation, a new possibility, we have to have something like a new creativity of time and a new creativity of the situation. You have to have something that is really an opening. I name this opening 'event'. What is an event? An event is simply that which interrupts the law, the rules, the structure of the situation, and creates a new possibility. So an event is not initially the creation of a new situation. It is the creation of a new possibility, which is not the same thing. In fact, the event takes place in a situation that remains the same, but this same situation is inside the new possibility. For example, for Paul, the event is the resurrection of Christ, and this event does not directly change anything in the Roman Empire. So the general situation, which is the Roman Empire, remains the same. But inside the situation there is the opening of a new possibility by the event. In the political field it is the same thing. In Paris, May 1968, for instance, there was no real change in the general situation of the state: de Gaulle remained in power and the government was still functional with its police, and so on. But there was an opening of a new possibility, and this is what I call an event. After that, there is the possibility of the materialization of the consequences of this new possibility, and the elaboration of these consequences is the creation of a new subjective body.

A new subjective body is the realization of the possibility that is opened by the event in a concrete form, and which develops some consequences of the new possibility. Naturally, among these consequences there are different forms of negation – struggle, revolt, a new possibility of being against something, destruction of some part of the law, and so on. But these forms of negation are consequences of the birth of the new subjectivity, and not the other way around. It is not the new subjectivity that is a consequence of the negation. So there is something really non-dialectical – in the sense of Hegel and Marx – about this logic, because we do not start with the creativity of negation as such, even if the site of negativity is certainly included in the consequences of something which is affirmative.

I can here return to my book, many years ago, about Paul. This book was written ultimately to propose a clear example of this new logic – that is, a new logic for *all* truth procedures, and thus for those in the political field as well. Paul offers a very clear example of how to think the relation between an event and a new subjectivity – this was my main point. Paul provides a new, very acute perspective on how this logic operates in the field of law, and specifically in the relation of the new subject to the old law. And in a very explicit manner, Paul explains that, when you have an event that is really the creation of a new possibility in the situation, you must first create a new body and affirm a new subjectivity before all negation and all negative consequences. The first thing is to create, to affirm the new subjectivity. What, then, is at the very beginning of the new subjectivity and of the new subjective body? It is the group of people who affirm that there is really a new possibility – they affirm the affirmation. In the case of Christianity, they affirm the resurrection. After that, there are a lot of practical and symbolic consequences in all of the situations. But it is interesting to see in the example of Paul that the very beginning of something new is always something like a pure affirmation of the new possibility as such. There is a resurrection – you have to affirm that! And when you affirm the resurrection, and you organize that sort of affirmation – because affirmation is with others and in the direction of others – you create something absolutely new, not in the form of a negation of what exists, but in the form of the newness inside of what exists. And so there is no longer negation on the one hand and affirmation on the other. There is, rather, affirmation and division, or the creation that grounds the independence of the new subject from within the situation of the old. This is the general orientation of the new logic.

In this orientation, we can propose a new examination of all the old words in some field of knowledge or action. As an exercise, I propose to discuss the word 'democracy'. Today, democracy is really the common term of all the ideological dispositions of the imperialist states – of pretty much all the reactionary states, in fact. Therefore, we must declare a first rupture by saying that we do not accept their ideological line, which ultimately amounts to the idea that one cannot resist their 'democracy' without being a terrorist, an ally in despotism, and so forth.

But this means we are in a situation wherein we have to clarify for ourselves not only the content of the concept but also whether we want to use the word. Is there today a possible good use of the word 'democracy'? That is my subjective question. It is not exactly a theoretical one. Why?

Because I can always name as 'democracy' something else. There can be both good and bad uses of the word democracy today. And there is probably something really confusing in the use of the word itself. Because it is immediately, generally understood in terms of its present meaning, which is basically the meaning given to it by all the reactionary forces in the world today.

I have decided ultimately to keep the word. It is generally a good thing to keep the word, because there is something problematic about leftists saying, ' I am not interested in "democracy" at all, because it has become practically meaningless.' But it is true that when you talk about democracy you are always participating on the terrain of the common ideology. The situation is difficult because we have to criticize the actual 'democracies' in one sense, and in a different sense we have to criticize the political propaganda made of the term 'democracy' today. If we do not do this we are paralyzed. In this case we would be saying 'Yes, we are in a democracy, but democracy can do something else', and we would be ultimately in a defensive position. And this is the opposite of my conception, because my position is to begin by affirmation, not at all by a defensive position. So, if we keep the word, we must divide the signification of the word classically, and differentiate between good democracy and bad democracy, between the reactionary conception of democracy and the progressive conception of democracy. But what is the basis of that division? In classical Marxism there is a clear basis upon which to divide everything, and we divide according to the class distinction. We can distinguish popular democracy from bourgeois democracy, or perhaps, to be more contemporary, from yuppie democracy. And the possibility of that sort of division is also the possibility of thinking democracy as something other than a form of state. It is a distinction not only between popular democracy and yuppie democracy, but between true democracy and democracy as a form of state, as a form of oppressive state, as a class state.

But this strict duality is not convincing in the framework of a new dialectical thinking. It is too easy to determine negatively popular democracy as being all that state democracy is not. To escape the game of negation and negation of negation, I now present three understandings of democracy – not a division into two, but into three. That is always my trick. When I am in a difficulty with a division into two, I create a division into three. And it is why, generally, as Agamben was the first to remark, I have finally, for every problem, four terms. Hegel has three terms, because after the negation and the negation of negation, he has the totality of the process, the becoming of the absolute knowledge as a third term. But me, after two different affirmations – the conservative one and the affirmation of the new possibility – I have two different negations. This is because the conservative negation of novelty by reaction is not the same as the negative part, against the conservative position, of the new affirmation.

I give the three primitive terms in the question of democracy. First, there is democracy as a form of state, which is really democracy in its commonplace meaning – that is, representative democracy or the parliamentary ideology. Second, there is democracy understood as movement or a 'democracy of places', which is not democracy directly in the political sense, but perhaps more in the historical sense. So when democracy takes place, it is democracy in the form of an event. This is the sense of democracy in the work of Jacques Rancière, for example. For Rancière, as for me, democracy is the activation of the principle of equality. When the principle of equality is really active, you have some version of our understanding of democracy: that is, democracy as the irruption of collective equality in a concrete form, which can be protest or insurrection or popular assembly, or any other form in which equality is effectively active. So, this understanding itself has many forms, but we can perfectly understand precisely what this form of democracy is, and it is in fact a recurrent form of revolutionary democracy. But you know it is much more a form of a sudden emergence in history, and ultimately of the event, than of the consequences of the event or of the creation of the new political body. Thus, even if the moment of revolutionary rupture is a true meaning of democracy, it is not exactly the political concept of that meaning. I think it is much more a historical concept of democracy – that is to say, a concept that is in relation to the event. And so we have to find a third sense of democracy, which is properly the democracy of the determination of the new political subject as such. This is my ultimate conception. Democracy for me is another name for the elaboration of the consequences of collective action and for determining the new political subject.

But finally, we have four terms: classical representative democracy, which is a form of state-power; mass-democracy, which is of historical nature; democracy as a political subject; and, finally, the process of progressive vanishing of the state, which is the historical and negative inscription of politics in History, under the name of communism.

So we substitute for the clear classical opposition between the dominant false democracy and the true popular democracy a sort of complex, with three places: State, Revolutionary Event, and Politics; three process:

affirmation of the people's access to politics outside the state, negation of this access by the state, victory of the political organization of people. And as a totalization of the complete complex, a point of communism by the concrete results or all that, results which are proofs of the weakness of the state, and finally of the possibility of its vanishing.

Another example is precisely the relationship between politics and power. Classically, the goal of political action is to seize power, to destroy the state machinery of the enemies. The name of all that is a master name of all political classicism: revolution. Today, at the beginning of constitution, at the beginning of a new subjective body, it is not possible to be inside the state, or more generally to aim for power. The word 'revolution' cannot be our master name. So we have to be entirely on the outside of state power. But the state is always in the field of political questions and in the space of action. If our political subjectivity is not inside the state, if to the contrary it is on the outside, the state is nonetheless in the field of our action. To take a concrete example from my direct experience, if we have to do something about workers who are without papers, say African immigrants, and we want to organize and to change things in this field, we will quickly find that the state is in our space. We will have to confront new laws and decisions of the state. And we will have to create something that will be face to face with the state – not inside the state, but face to face with it. So, we will have a 'discussion' with the state, or we will organize various forms of disruption. In any case, we will have to prescribe something about the state from outside. We will have to prescribe something that establishes a relation with the state. And the big difficulty is to maintain the possibility of being outside while prescribing something that concerns the inside. There is, then, a sort of topological difficulty in the development of politics – namely, the relation between the outside and the inside. Because the state is always inviting you inside and asking that you not be outside.

I have had many very concrete experiences of this. For instance, I will go with some workers to discuss matters with some minister or other because the state refuses their 'regularization'. And always this state representative will ask, 'Who are you?' And we always answer, 'We are a political organization with people.' And the reply is always, 'OK, but who are you?!' The problem is simple: to be somebody is to be inside the state, otherwise you cannot be heard at all. So there are two possible outcomes. Either finally there is a discussion and some political results, or else there is no room for discussion because we are nobody. It is once more the precise question of affirmation: How can we be somebody without being on the inside? We must affirm our existence, our principles, our action, always *from outside*.

I know that some critics of my thinking who also want to represent possibilities of a complete transformation of our situation object that I am too 'outside' this process – that I am ultimately a 'prophet', and not really an active player in the immanent and concrete world. I completely disagree with this sort of objection, because it forgets in its theoretical analysis of global society the real logic of prescription, and finally the necessity of a new conception of affirmative dialectics. Without the French Revolution, without the great revolt of workers in France, without the real and concrete movement of the Parisian proletariat, Marx certainly would never have fathomed this concept of proletariat. The movement is not from the concept of proletariat to the proletarian movement. The real becoming is from the revolt of workers to the new proposition. So, finally, the true discussion is not at all about the concrete analysis of global society, but really about our relation to the state. The real question is whether to be outside or inside the state. The fundamental idea is: to be in the new affirmative dialectical framework, you must be outside the state, because inside the state you are precisely in the negative figure of opposition. And so, once more, the negativity, the appearance of negativity, comes first.

I want to insist on the fact that the new logical framework is not only a vision of politics, or even a vision of some particular practices. It prescribes, much more generally, a sort of anthropology.

First, I think we are animals, I speak of human animals and living bodies, and in contrast to all classical humanism I include in our definition of animals a lot of things. Ultimately, it encompasses all our concrete existence as such, without anything else and without any supplement. And I really think that capitalist anthropology is the conviction that, fundamentally, humanity is nothing else but self-interested animals. It is a very important point. I think we have to do some propaganda on this point. Modern capitalism is always speaking of human rights, democracy, freedom, and so on, but in fact we can see concretely that, under all these names, we find nothing else but human animals with interests, who have to be happy with products, and its subject is something like animals-in-front-of-the-market. And this is really its definition of the human. We have a hierarchy at the bottom of which are the poor, who are before the market but without means, and at the top of which are the rich, who are also before the market but who have far greater means, and the protection of all this is really nothing else but capitalist anthropology. And the possibility of being something else than animals in this sense is really the becoming subject of a human animal. And it is by the incorporation of a new body, which is something else than being in front of the market, that you become something like a subject. 'Infinite' is another name for this process, because what we have in this kind of incorporation is an affirmation of a new possibility with infinite consequences. The new possibility has infinite consequences – this is always the case.

So, we can say that human rights, rights that are the subject's rights, are in fact the rights of the infinite. Jean-François Lyotard wrote this formula for the first time in his most important book, *Le Différend*. And I assume this point.

But what is finally the anthropological question? I propose that this question is: What exactly is the singularity of mankind, of human beings? We know that, today, there exists a species of human animals, defined by their inclusion in the global market. And, in contrast, we can name 'Humanity' the capacity of becoming the subject to an event, to something that happens. The capacity of accepting the possibility of an incorporation in a new subjective body; the capacity of drawing its practical consequences in the situation of incorporation which itself is the becoming of the new subject. And in the becoming of the subject, beyond the support of all that which is one or some human animals, there is something infinite, a new creation of something infinite, and the name of this infinite something is for me: truth.

So we can say that the incorporation of the subject is the incorporation of some human animals to something like the process of truth. And that is the global field of what we can name humanity or human beings, in the context of affirmative dialectics.

I agree ultimately with the young Marx on one point: only in the successive creation of new forms of subjects is there something like a generic humanity, because generic humanity is infinite humanity – it's the same thing, and the human animal in front of the market is not at all generic, but absolutely particular.

All that is like a new hypothesis about the subject, and it is also a new hypothesis about human life, about what it means for humans to live. In my book *Logics of Worlds*, I oppose human rights in their ordinary meaning to the rights of the infinite by opposing today's 'democratic materialism' to the project of 'dialectical materialism', which is a possible name for affirmative dialectics. What makes these forms of materialism antithetical is their respective understandings of human life: either there is nothing but languages and bodies, or else there is a third term, something like the production of 'truths' that cut through the hegemony of our animal existence. The title of the conclusion of *Logics of Worlds* is: 'What is to live?' This is clearly the final question of a political anthropology.

In fact, there are two completely different conceptions of human life. The first reduces human life to common animal life: satisfaction of all natural desires, happiness, security, and so on. The second one is what we are speaking of: human life has to be identified with incorporation to a truth-body. So, a human being is properly 'living' only when he or she is the agent of a passage from particularity to universality, from local process to genericity, from a singular world to an eternal truth. Maybe this second conception is a slightly heroic one. More generally, the communist hypothesis, today, is an affirmation and a practice which is so independent and so opposed to the contemporary strength of planetary capitalism that to sustain it, as we do here, is neither 'realistic' in the common sense of the word nor concrete, as the world as it is proclaiming that we must be. In fact, we know that many philosophers affirm that the time of heroism is passed.

But maybe Althusser was right to affirm that philosophy has no history. The fact that an idea is old-fashioned is not, for the philosopher, an objection against this idea. In any case, even if my conception is a slightly heroic one, I affirm before you: it is mine. And certainly I am too old to change on this point.

7 The Sixties and Us

Alessandro Russo

Without new theoretical perspectives on modern egalitarian politics, no new political invention can exist. Lenin's famous statement, 'Without revolutionary theory there can be no revolutionary movement', modulated in the contemporary register, means the urgency of re-theorizing the set of modern political innovations into a new conceptual framework from the French Revolution onwards. For this purpose, it will be decisive to ponder each great inventive political moment as a singular exception endowed with its unique issues at stake. The necessary starting point will be a rethinking of the sixties, which is not only the last great political egalitarian moment, but is also so impervious to previous historical-political conceptualizations that any attempt to study and carry out research on it operates within an almost deserted intellectual field.

In this chapter, I will discuss several points about the urgent reorganization of the study of the sixties. Beginning with the most political one, exploring the essence of the sixties is an inescapable task, because no new possible political experiment can skip the issue concerning which attitude to assume in regard to the singular intellectual horizon of the previous political moments, and the last one in particular. Without rethinking the political problems they left unresolved, the compulsion to run into the same deadlocks is almost inevitable.

The other important reason for reconsidering the sixties in depth concerns the ambiguous and paradoxical relationship that governmental circumstances have with the last great moment of egalitarian politics. We should see it as the denial of a fundamental debt. The government of a certain social-historical world cannot fully disregard the existence of such a moment, albeit that it denies its political value. There has even been the 'thorough negation' in China for four decades. But this 'negation' works with all the logical paradoxes of which we learned from Freud onwards concerning how you can 'affirm' something just by 'negating' it. Through 'negation', one can admit the existence of something that would have been subject to 'censorship'.

What is peculiar about 'governmental negation' is that, on the one hand, it proclaims egalitarian moments as absolute chaos, which the new government has completely put in order. On the other hand, negation is a means that enables the new dominant subjectivity to take note that political mass activism enabled an escapable real issue to surface. The egalitarian activism had in fact revealed that something essential of the old governmental order had lost any credit in the eyes of the common people, and that it was therefore necessary to suppress it to enforce the effectiveness of a new order.

Therefore, no governmental 'negation' may be 'thorough'. It actually establishes a peculiar debt in the same political moment it proclaims to be mere disorder. As a rule, the new governmental order does not recognize the nature of this debt as such, but deliberately confuses the right and the wrong, the true and the false. You can never reflect on a moment of egalitarian politics by relying on governmental judgment.[1] Conversely, knowledge of the governmental forms of a particular historical social world must start by examining the political inventions that preceded it, since the former are their 'hollow imprint'.

A Worldwide Political Laboratory

Let us start with an affirmative statement about the political essence of the sixties, by examining three key points: the multiplicity, the subjective core and the boundaries. The sixties were a worldwide political mass laboratory composed of an unprecedented range of themes and experimental grounds: experimental politics had never previously involved so many disparate fields of collective life. That multifarious political moment had a singular centre of gravity: the question of the political value of the working-class parties, and the communist parties in particular. This issue, which was the object of intense mass political scrutiny in very various countries, in turn established the boundaries of that political configuration: the consistency of the subjective bodies

---

1   In many cases, the negation starts with the violent defeat of a moment of political invention, but it can occur also with the victory of the latter. In these cases, the new governmental circumstances do not formulate an explicit negation, but strictly limit the recognition of that political moment only as the necessary antecedent of the present order. It was a tumultuous time, it is true, but then there are the real men of government to put things in order.

that composed it positively, or, on the contrary, were extraneous and opposed it.

The core of the sixties was one crucial issue for political invention, the issue of organization. The radical political question that nourished the laboratory concerned the egalitarian value of the organizations that at that time enjoyed the highest credit, and even claimed to guarantee the political existence of the 'proletariat', understood as the condition of ruled labour in the modern social world. An additional complication was that the parties that referred to the 'working class' as their major social basis had made a decisive contribution to twentieth-century state formations.

Despite their differences, in all of them the backbone was a system of parties, or of a single party. Such a system reached full generalization only thanks to the existence of the workers' parties from the second half of the nineteenth century. Before, there were only 'parties of notables' restricted to the medium or higher strata of social hierarchies. Only after the legalization of the workers' organizations could a system of 'parties' comprising all the 'parts' of the social situation be fully established. Nowadays, parties are a shadow of those of the twentieth century; but we can grasp the reasons for their rapid decline over the last decades only by reviewing the political sixties.

In the worldwide laboratory of the sixties, the Communist Party, as Cécile Winter has remarked, 'has not passed the test'. The last political statement of Mao Zedong in 1975 was: 'the bourgeoisie is in the Communist Party'. Claudia Pozzana and I have suggested reading the thesis through a reversal of words, 'the Communist Party is in the bourgeoisie'. If we mean by 'bourgeoisie' the general name of contemporary governmental circumstances, the reversal may help not to constrain the thesis within the straitjacket of the Stalinian tradition of struggles against the 'representatives of the class enemies' infiltrated into the party. The sense of the statement, we believe, is that the Communist Party in general (not just the CCP, to be sure) not only was unable to separate itself from its 'bourgeois' circumstances, but also finally proved to be homogeneous with the dominant subjectivity of the contemporary social world. In this sense, 'it is in the bourgeoisie'. The thesis 'the bourgeoisie is in the Communist Party', or 'the Communist Party is in the bourgeoisie', summarizes the main experimental result of the sixties.

The result came from a variety of forms of political self-organization that extended to virtually all fields of collective life. To say that the core of the sixties was the issue of the Communist Party does not mean that it was exclusively a moment of workers' politics. This was not only the case in factories and work in general, but also in relationships between the sexes and generations, the army, classrooms, prisons and even asylums. In short, everything that involved forms of 'government' of the lives of others was tackled 'politically;' with the term 'politics' meaning all endeavours that aim at deconstructing the ritual hierarchies of the social world and freeing the subjective potential of anyone in any field. A list of examples cannot but be extremely partial, if only in showing their multiplicity.

Some forms of self-organization were present almost everywhere, like the countless student collectives created from nothing, such as those in Berkeley, Beijing, Rome, Berlin and Paris. Some groups were more limited to the national level, and were led by influential people, such as the movement for the closure of psychiatric hospitals initiated by Franco Basaglia in Italy, or the Groupe d'Information sur les Prisons, created by Michel Foucault in Paris. Other groups intervened on particular national issues, such as the various organizations supporting the struggles of African Americans in the United States. There was even a Committee of Concerned Asian Scholars in the American universities, composed of students and young teachers who were strongly critical towards the military aggression in Indochina, as well as towards the theoretical and methodological orientations of US scholarly research on Asia, which they considered shamefully adjacent to the operation of the US government's military-diplomatic apparatuses. Other groups, as I will discuss below in more detail, explored the same crucial political ground in various national contexts, such as the attempts to form independent workers' organizations in China, Italy or Poland. There were also some local experiments that were quite influential, though embryonic, which touched sensitive issues, such as the egalitarian educational inventions of a 'priest against' in a peasant village in Tuscany and an 'anti-authoritarian psychoanalytic kindergarten' in a district of Milan.[2]

There were all sorts of initiatives, which were carried out on quite different social grounds and issues, but proved to be politically contiguous and mutually influential, and were in any case conceived and practised as fully participant in that configuration. What brought all of these experiences together and allowed their unprecedented proximity was the suspension of the values of the hierarchical rituals structuring multiple

---

2   The two leading figures were Lorenzo Milani and Elvio Fachinelli.

forms of social connivance with governmental subjectivities. The basic organizing principle was constituted by the 'any of us' – that is to say, as invoking in principle the right to speak about key issues in every field, regardless of one's 'position', age, belonging to a social circle, and so on. In this sense, they were egalitarian organizational inventions. This was, at least, the main subjective condition that enabled those experiments to exist, and at the same time was the most difficult issue to manage creatively.

At the core of the unlimited multiplicity of the sixties, there was the issue of the political existence of the workers, for reasons that we can conventionally call both 'structural' and 'historical'. The stakes involved both the modern circumstances of the government of labour, and the value of egalitarian politics that for over a century had aimed at radically transforming such circumstances.

If we can acknowledge that equality is always the enigmatic essence of politics, we must also recognize that, in the conditions of wage labour, it represents the crucial difficulty of modern politics. On this point, the discoveries of Marx are not only crucial, but also prove to be especially valuable today, when wage labour is subject to the most rigid, violent and unconditional hierarchical subordination. The kernel of modern communism is the question of workers' political existence, since to invent equality in this field is the most arduous endeavour. How is it possible to subvert the despotic government of industrial labour in a liberating sense? Since the latter moulds the hierarchies that govern the entire collective life of the modern world, this problem was not a novelty in the sixties, but had been at the core of modern politics for over a century.

The main novelty of the sixties was the radical re-examination of solutions that had hitherto appeared to be the most consolidated – namely, the promise that the communist parties and the socialist states guaranteed the political existence of workers. The relationships between the worker centre of gravity and the multiplicity of the sixties was a major element of vitality. On the one hand, a radical reopening of the key point of modern politics mobilized the deployment of egalitarian experiments in every field of social life. On the other hand, the issue at stake was so high that an unlimited multiplicity of political inventions was required. Ultimately, it was the verification of Marx's famous thesis that the proletariat could liberate itself only by liberating the whole of humankind. Only by opening up egalitarian experimentation in every field was it possible to reinvent political organizations for the liberation of wage labour.

The tension between the dense experimental core and the extensive variety of political subjectivities also determined the lines of demarcation. The core of the sixties were forms of self-organization that, though embryonic, fragile and scattered to the four corners of the Earth, were searching for an independent political path in any field, while re-examining the value of the Communist Party at the same time. In other words, with regard to the famous distinction between 'friends and enemies', only those who were able to risk political initiative while questioning existing forms of political organization – especially the 'left' wing – belonged within the scope of 'friends'. By contrast, those who existed exclusively within the parties, especially in the 'communist parties', without openly questioning their value, not only did not belong to the configuration (although they sometimes mimicked its themes and content), but were rather among the ranks of its more resolute enemies. Obviously, intermediate or simply inert positions did exist, but polarization grew in relation to the increase in experimental tension; and conversely, the more experimentation declined, the more this distinction faded into insignificance.

Periodization

This overview of the sixties may also provide reference points for reflecting on the temporality of the events. When did the sixties start and when did they end? I suggest three levels of periodization: a long period that lasted for nearly twenty-five years, from the mid 1950s to the early 1980s; a medium period that lasted for nearly a decade, which includes the central events; and a series of brief moments of intense political activism regarding various national situations, which I will discuss later.

The 'long sixties' began in 1956, with the 'salvoes' of the Sino-Soviet dispute, and ended in 1981 with the coup that suppressed Solidarność in Poland. This first level of periodization highlights that the same crucial issue – the political value of the ideological and organizational apparatuses of the communist parties and socialist states – emerged both at its beginning and its end, and in fact also at every major moment of the long sixties.

The first step in the Sino-Soviet dispute was an editorial in the *People's Daily* entitled: 'On the Historical Experience of the Dictatorship of the Proletariat'. The problem of that 'historical experience' was how to evaluate the forms of organization that promised to guarantee the political existence of the workers and, ultimately, how to assess all modern egalitarian politics since the mid nineteenth century.[3]

The same problem was at the core of the Polish events in the late seventies. Solidarność was primarily the creation of an independent workers' political organization. The turbid interference and manoeuvres of the Vatican and the CIA, and so on, which played on its internal weaknesses and contributed to its annihilation, were secondary to its political novelty. At the time, Alain Badiou wrote that an 'almost chemically pure workers' political thought'[4] had appeared in Poland; except that it was anti-Marxist, or rather it was as far as possible from the horizon of the 'dictatorship of the proletariat' and the Communist Party. In fact, the latter reacted by destroying Solidarność.

In 1975, one of Mao Zedong's last statements, which became the key theme of a decisive political dispute, was a radical questioning concerning the nature of the 'dictatorship of the proletariat'. Mao Zedong stated that it was an unresolved issue that needed to be thoroughly 'clarified', otherwise socialism was almost inevitably doomed to evolve into a new capitalism. The final years of the Cultural Revolution fully resumed the theme that characterized the beginning of the Sino-Soviet dispute, and that the events of the central period of the sixties had obviously made even sharper.

There is a second level of periodization, which is relatively easy to identify, ranging roughly from the mid sixties to the mid seventies, or the decade usually known as 'the sixties', in which both the centre of gravity and the multiplicity became more apparent. There were, moreover, several shorter political moments that require further attention.

The third level of periodization in fact concerns the moments of highest mass political activism in the central sequence of the sixties, which occurred at different times in different countries. For example, the most important events happened in 1966–68 and 1973–75 in China, and in 1968–72 in France and Italy. In the United States, there had already been important moments of political activism in the early sixties, with the great movements for the equality of African Americans. As we have seen, in Poland the central moment of the political sixties occurred in the late seventies and the early eighties. Korea is a special case, since it was (and

---

3   It was not the Twentieth Congress of the CPSU that opened the sixties: Khrushchev's 'Secret Report' initiated the state decline of socialism, but said nothing of the political nature of that decline, reduced to the effects of one 'personality'.

4   Alain Badiou, *Peut-on penser la politique* (Paris: Seuil, 1985), p. 47.

still is) subject to the military effects of the Cold War; but the 1980 Gwangju movement, reviewed in this volume by Yong Soon Seo, also belongs politically to the long sixties.[5]

This periodization cannot contextualize all of the numerous political situations in detail, but it helps to clarify the thesis that the centre of gravity of the sixties was the question of the value of political parties – namely, of those that claimed to be the definitive organization of the working class. The issue was more prominent in countries where there were strong communist parties, such as China, Poland, Italy and France. It was less directly at the core of political experiments in countries lacking communist parties comparable to those present in Europe. In the United States as well, where the political sixties were particularly eventful, the mass political novelties were very far from any communist party model; nor were they consistent with the system of parliamentary parties. Of course, everywhere there have been organizations that imagined being the 'iron nucleus' that aimed at rebuilding the 'working-class party' – but these finally turned into a major internal weakness.

When and How Did the Sixties End?

The closure of the sixties is a quite entangled moment, since it entailed both the entanglement of the three levels of periodization mentioned above and the concentration of their major issues. Its final point was the suppression of Solidarność in 1981. Moreover, workers' intense activism in Poland was particularly against the tide, since in the rest of the world the political configuration had met a number of serious drawbacks from the mid seventies onwards.

These events did not coincide temporally in the various nations and situations, though there was also a process of synchronization that resulted mainly in the events of the Cultural Revolution, which was surely one of the great epicentres of the decade. A first moment of impasse was in 1972, when Lin Biao's obscure 'attempted coup' in China in late 1971 proved a serious obstacle for the Cultural Revolution. The major impasse had actually emerged as early as 1968, with the political exhaustion of the Red Guards; but the 1970–71 clashes, which mainly occurred within the leadership of the party-state, made the political nature of the events very blurred. What, in reality, was the Cultural

---

5   Seo Yong Soon, 'Manifestos without Words: The Idea of Communism in South Korea – The Case of the Gwangju May', paper presented at the Seoul Conference on Communism, 2013.

Revolution? What, at that time, was the meaning of 'right wing', 'left wing' or 'ultra-left wing'?

Significantly, a radical crisis struck the Gauche Prolétarienne, at that time the leading Maoist organization in France, which dissolved itself in a few months. Similarly, in Italy, 1972 marked the beginning of a crisis for the 'extra-parliamentary organizations'. At the same moment, 'terrorist' groups began to form a quantitatively insignificant fraction of petty militarists, with a conspiratorial and ultimately criminal vision of politics, who became easy tools of reactionary manoeuvres by the secret apparatuses of the state. But they represented a strong denial and denigration of the political novelty of 1968.

But the final sequence of the 'long sixties' was not exactly a declining phase, but in fact included plenty of intense political moments. From the mid seventies to the early eighties, there was a long confrontation between political inventions and government manoeuvres.

The main repressive episodes that initiated the final sequence of the sixties turned on events in China – namely the arrest of the Maoist leaders (not only the notorious 'four', but also tens of thousands of others) soon after Mao Zedong's death in 1976. It was in fact an epochal change clearly not confined to China. Moreover, the Chinese 'Thermidor' took place at a time of particular political effervescence – or, rather, great theoretical activism – concerning the above-mentioned 'study of the theory of the dictatorship of the proletariat'. The arrest of the Maoist leaders was aimed at suppressing the long-term political consequences of the independent workers' organizations, which appeared first in Shanghai in 1966–67. The leaders arrested in 1976 had been promoting a series of political experiments in Chinese factories since 1973–74, particularly during a theoretical study movement of 1975, which were suppressed immediately after the 1976 coup.

Another key episode in the final sequence of the sixties was the arrest of Antonio Negri and the other leaders of Autonomia Operaia in Italy in 1979, who were subjected to unfounded and illegal judicial persecution. In this case, too, the target of repression was a series of experiments carried out by independent workers' organizations that had been underway since the early sixties. The arrest of the Maoists and the leaders of Autonomia, as well as the suppression of Solidarność, had a common characteristic: the profound intellectual tension between the protagonists: Negri was the most outstanding Italian political thinker after Gramsci; the Chinese Maoist leaders had a strong theoretical attitude; and the active political friendship between intellectuals and workers in Italy, China and Poland was a decisive feature.

To be sure, the effectiveness of repression was inversely proportional to the internal weaknesses of those attempts. There are always weak points in any experiment, but experimental politics is particularly precarious. It feels its way through the darkness, and no one knows in advance which formulas are required for the organization of equality, least of all in such a brutally hierarchical situation as that of the modern workplace. Egalitarian politics needs to be reinvented each time with the mass mobilization of maximum creativity, which means that an infinite number of weaknesses must be overcome, and risks suppression at every obstacle by the powerful anti-egalitarian automatisms that regulate the government of the historical-social world.

Certainly, more research is required on the specific weaknesses of organizational experiments among Chinese, Italian, French and Polish workers, and on the obstacles they confronted. Moreover, in order to analyze their limitations, we should consider that the stakes not only went beyond the communist parties, but also that they met in them the highest hostilities. Solidarność represented a great and tragic ending, which summed up the ambitions and vulnerabilities of the new political projects of the world's workers in the sixties.

Post-Sixties

The suppression of those egalitarian experiments was meticulous and timely. In addition, since they had targeted the universality ('only freeing the whole of humankind'), the re-establishment of social hierarchies and the extension of inequalities could not but be 'global'. 'Globalization' is obviously not a phenomenon that originated thirty years ago. Marx was able to examine its elementary structure as far back as the middle of the nineteenth century. However, in the contemporary world, the re-establishment of large-scale inequalities has also inverted some characteristics of government policies of the previous decades.

Let us start with the most obvious aspects of the phenomenon. There was a quite visible U-turn in government attitudes in the early eighties. Policies producing widening inequality have prevailed for over three decades, while in the preceding thirty years all forms of government, despite their differences, had adopted systematic measures for reducing inequality. However, the origin of the tendency towards the establishment of policies producing inequality that are prevalent in contemporary governments is not self-evident.

The most reliable analyses of the current economic depression argue that considering it as merely the product of the subprime mortgage crisis of 2007 is misleading, because the latter was the result of a longer process initiated almost three decades earlier. The Nobel Prize–winning economist Joseph Stiglitz argues, with a wealth of documentation, that today's depression is 'the price of inequality'.[6] It has been, he shows, the result of a long series of government policies aimed at widening inequality since the early eighties, rather than an accidental malfunction of the 'market'. We find the same periodization, and essentially the same diagnosis, in the analyses of another Nobel laureate in economics, Paul Krugman,[7] and of the Italian sociologist Luciano Gallino.[8] Other authors agree in tracing the beginning of these processes back to the early eighties.

This periodization, albeit precise, remains not fully explained. Why were the early eighties so momentous? If the origins of the economic downturn were in the nineties, it would be easier to find a possible explanation. In that case, we could assume that the collapse of the Soviet Union and the following fast decline of the European communist parties were responsible for contemporary policies producing inequality. But the turning point had occurred ten years earlier, and in observing the prominent politicians of that time – for example, Ronald Reagan and Margaret Thatcher – one might wonder how they were able to bring about such a decisive change. Reagan was a former radio speaker and a modest movie actor, while Thatcher was most renowned for her ferocity in suppressing the British miners' strike, and for her invariable refrain: 'There is no alternative'. How was it possible that individuals of this kind caused the reversal of government policies worldwide, which brought to a sudden end a trend of reducing inequality that had been ongoing for at least thirty years?

A recent paper by Wang Hui on conceptions of equality gives a valuable insight for the purposes of periodization. He points out that, due to a 'crisis of socialism' in China in the early eighties, the concept of 'equality of opportunities' – at the expense of 'equality', which had been

---

6   Joseph Stiglitz, *The Price of Inequality* (London: Allen Lane, 2012).

7   Paul Krugman, *End this Depression, Now!* (New York: W.W. Norton, 2012).

8   Luciano Gallino, *Finanzcapitalismo. La civiltà del denaro in crisi* ('Financecapitalism: The Civilization of Money in Crisis') (Turin: Einaudi, 2011).

systematically discredited – started to become popular in government discourse, as well as in universities.[9]

The intersection of the conceptual history of 'equality of opportunities' and political events in China is full of implications concerning the transition to the 'post-sixties'. In fact, the former concept was not a novelty of the early eighties. Equality of opportunity had been a typical theme of the American sociology in the fifties – the ideological banner of Talcott Parsons, for example. Even more, it was a founding sociological concept, as one of the categories Auguste Comte would contrast strongly with what he called the 'metaphysical' egalitarianism of the French Revolution.

Equality of opportunity is a congenitally bourgeois value with an explicitly anti-revolutionary polemical aspect. In the fifties, it was a synonym for the 'American dream', according to which even common people could 'freely compete' in order to ascend the social hierarchy and form the middle class. The polemical target of this usage was the 'revolutionary' egalitarianism of the socialist countries, branded as bureaucratic, uniform and oppressive. Moreover, the idea of equality of opportunity proclaimed the egalitarian virtues of the 'free market', albeit through corrective interventions by the government, able to reduce 'ascription' in favour of 'achievement'. The Civil Rights movement and a few moments of critical sociology in the sixties[10] put the egalitarian virtues of 'achievement' seriously into question over the next few years. Finally, the concept lost most of its former appeal in the United States due to the criticisms that had undermined its credibility and the drastic change in government policies.

Since the eighties, this concept has had a paradoxical fate. Just at the origin of the destruction of the middle class in the United States and in Europe – which is to say, when the governments began to reverse their previous policies for reducing inequality that had supported the very idea of equality of opportunity, the concept met with success in China. It became part of the repertoire of a more cosmopolitan university discourse, while, at the same time, government policies identified the widening of inequality as a factor in the 'development of the productive forces'. But the concept also played an 'anti-revolutionary' role in China, discrediting the previous revolutionary priority of reducing inequality, labelled as 'absolute egalitarianism' – presented as a legacy of pre-modern peasant

---

9   Wang Hui, 'Rethinking Equality: The Decline of Representation', forthcoming.
10   For example, the research conducted in Christopher Jencks, *Inequality: A Reassessment of the Effects of Family and Schooling in America* (New York: Basic Books, 1972).

ideologies that no longer corresponded to the most advanced new productive forces and their 'harmonious' development. Do not forget that there is a conceptually 'Marxist' capitalism in China.

In its American 'golden age', however, equality of opportunity did to some extent reduce inequality, and was able to do so because its polemical target was the very existence of the socialist states. In competing with them, the capitalist governments should at least prove to be more authentically 'egalitarian'. Conversely, in present-day China, government policies must not face any comparable 'revolutionary egalitarianism'. Equality of opportunity is a merely reactive discourse with respect to past revolutionary experiences, and thus cannot play any actual role in reducing inequalities. When mass egalitarian political challenges are absent, it is much more difficult for the priority of equality to find a real place in government policy.

Without further examining the twisted phenomenology of this reactive process, let us consider what crucial events occurred in the early eighties that led to the entrenching policies producing inequality. As noted in the periodization outlined above, my hypothesis is that the political sixties ended in the early eighties. Policies promoting inequality emerged at the close of the egalitarian moment. This may only be accidental, however, and the topic requires further research.

A comparison with the major political issues at stake in the last two years of the Cultural Revolution, when 'equality' was one of the main themes of the above-mentioned theoretical debate, may shed some light on the fortunes of equality of opportunity in post-sixties China. The key question disputed at that moment was whether the 'equality' enshrined in the governmental structure of socialism was really so different from the 'equality of opportunity' prioritized by bourgeois governments. This question was not formulated exactly in these terms, but through the Marxist category of 'bourgeois right' – translated into Chinese as 'legal power of the bourgeoisie' (资产阶级法权, *zichanjieji faquan*), as the fulcrum of the system of inequalities in the modern world.

In the Chinese political debates of the mid seventies, and in the wake of classical Marxist theory, the Maoists argued that the sale of labour-power as a commodity was the very source of the bourgeois right, 'equal right for unequal people', and was therefore the main cause of the widening of inequalities, at the same time as masking them. Moreover, despite the different form of ownership, which did not entail the commodification of labour-power, socialism not only structurally 'inherited' the 'bourgeois right', but should necessarily keep it. The system of inequalities protected by the legal system of the socialist government could 'only be limited' (只能加以限制 *zhi neng jiayi xianzhi*). Mao Zedong's political thesis in 1975 was that it was only possible to 'limit the legal power of the bourgeoisie', but that this involved embarking on an entirely original project, since that legal power was intrinsic to the regular functioning of the socialist state.

In fact, the debate pivoted not so much on the opposition between 'equality' and 'equality of opportunity', but on the question, drawn from the classical formulations of Marx and Lenin, of how to make the right 'unequal' in order to make it 'equal' – that is, how to limit the system of 'legally protected' inequalities intrinsic to socialism itself. A crisis of socialism, or rather a deep questioning of its political foundations, was already manifest in China in that debate, which was also the final political confrontation between Mao Zedong and Deng.[11]

The dispute of 1975 opened two roads that immediately proved mutually incompatible. One aimed at limiting the structural inequality inherent to the socialist state (the 'bourgeois right') by means of new political experiments. This would involve mass theoretical commitment with the aim of rebuilding the very concept of the dictatorship of the proletariat. Mao Zedong proposed a fraught road, but it was the only one he deemed to be real. Moreover, he forecasted that, in the absence of that theoretical clarification, the system of inequalities legally guaranteed by socialism would quite probably evolve into capitalism. In 1975 he clearly stated: 'It is quite easy to establish capitalism in China'.

Deng Xiaoping was fully aware of this, but did not see it as a problem. In fact, he immediately strongly opposed those theoretical questions as mere 'disorder' aimed at establishing the anarchy of 'absolute egalitarianism'. Conversely, he proposed the extension of the system of inequalities as a condition of 'development of the productive forces'. Despite the notionally Marxist formulas, the slogan that best expressed the spirit of reforms was: 'To get rich is glorious'.

All those conceptual explorations that Maoists fomented in China in the mid seventies took place amid widely disseminated, publicly debated political experiments aimed at creating egalitarian forms of organization of industrial labour. They maintained that a thorough rethinking of the socialist management of the factories was urgent, since it was structurally quite similar to capitalism. The fact that in the socialist form of ownership

---

11   An analysis of this passage appears in my article, 'How Did the Cultural Revolution End? The Last Dispute between Mao Zedong and Deng Xiaoping, 1975', *Modern China* (May 2013).

the labour force was not a commodity was not a minor difference, but the Maoists maintained it was not definitive either – as is undisputable today.

The re-commodification of the labour force was the inevitable, or rather deliberate, outcome of suppressing those theoretical explorations. Moreover, this happened under the conceptual flag of Marxism. In the 1980s, the piece-wage, which was praised by the Chinese government as the highest expression of the Marxian principle 'to each according to one's own work', became the way to fully restore not only the commodification of labour but also those factory hierarchies whose political values and technical merits had been questioned in previous years.

The turning point in China in the eighties was crucial in defining the tendencies of government policies in the post-sixties period at a worldwide level. The details of Chinese influence on today's globalization require careful research, concerning both geopolitical aspects and the economic and commercial fields. However, the original factor in the growth of China's global influence was the ability of the government to halt political experimentation in Chinese factories. This act of negation, as mentioned above, was also a form of recognition, albeit distorted, of their result. The experiments carried out in the sixties proved the inconsistency of the government discourses on the working class as the historically guaranteed 'base' of socialism. Deng's success was to take utmost account of that outcome, but to direct it not towards new, liberating possibilities, but towards the establishment of a government of labour based entirely on wage dependency. This was one prerequisite of his 'reforms'.

The result of the suppression of those experiments rapidly met with great success worldwide. From the late seventies, the Chinese government declared that any argument to 'limit the legal power of the bourgeoisie' was 'ideological chit-chat', and mocked any attempt to create liberating experiences in the workplace as 'the plots and intrigues' of a small 'gang' of conspirators. The Chinese workers were becoming piecework wage earners, and the full commodification of the workforce was imminent. A turning point of this kind was destined to exercise a globalizing influence. Throughout the world, those who were in the position of controlling waged labour could welcome the removal of a major political obstacle hindering the restoration of the harshest hierarchical subordination of workers, in terms of precariousness, flexibility, impoverishment, and generalized subservience to the 'bourgeois right'. Just as the Cultural Revolution had been the epicentre of the political sixties, Deng's reforms represented instead one major point of reference for the extension of inequality after that period.

Policies promoting inequality in recent decades are the reverse of the experimental egalitarianism of the sixties. But current government policies aim not only at 'negating' the last great worldwide political moment, but also at annihilating all the changes that egalitarian inventions had produced in the conditions of subaltern labour for 150 years. In other words, they firmly intend to remove all of the limitations on the structural despotism that dominates waged labour in the modern world – limitations achieved at the cost of harsh political battles sustained for generations. When you read Pun Ngai's survey of the factory dormitory regime of Foxconn, they resonate, even in their details, with Marx and Engels's analyses of the conditions of the big industry of their time, which contemporary technological innovations only make even more despotic.

The peculiar logic of current circumstances – a set of governmental subjectivities fed by reaction against not only the sixties but also a long epoch of political experimentation – depends on the fact that the centre of gravity of the sixties concerned the political value of the whole 'historical experience of the dictatorship of the proletariat'. The new governmental circumstances proclaimed that all egalitarian politics were doomed to failure, that nothing could limit the 'bourgeois right', and that everything that attempted to do so was pure evil: the 'Evil Empire', as the US president used to say.

In fact, the socialist states and communist parties, far from being the monsters that their classic bourgeois competitors often described, were actually key components of the governmental forms of the twentieth century, which all state regimes had to consider carefully, and even draw inspiration from. Founded on the promise of the political recognition of workers, the socialist states had long been a force of moderation of unconditional capitalist despotism. The fact that, in principle, the socialist states did not oversee the commodification of labour force had produced an anomaly limiting the harshness of the general system of wage slavery worldwide, which also strongly influenced capitalist-parliamentary governments. In short, Stalin's five-year plans were a major incentive behind Roosevelt's New Deal; likewise, the expansion of the welfare state following World War II was a response to the challenge of the socialist regimes across half of Europe and half of Asia. A complicated interdependence between such different and even mutually antagonistic state regimes temporarily produced a limitation of inequalities inherent in the bourgeois societies of the modern world.

However, that limitation, far from corresponding to historical progress, which those parties and governments claimed to represent politically, was actually an exceptional and precarious result. It entailed a relationship between peculiar governmental circumstances and the working class, which passed through the existence of communist parties.

In the sixties, the emergence of independent workers' organizations quickly destroyed that equilibrium, leading first to the collapse of the major communist parties and then to the irreversible decline of the entire party system of the twentieth century. The Polish workers' laboratory of the late seventies and early eighties was the experimental demonstration that any claim of an alternative political essence of the socialist states in respect to the capitalist-parliamentary ones was groundless, to say nothing of their historically founded superiority. Although the USSR collapsed only a decade later, the rise and subsequent suppression of Solidarność was the point of no return in the process that led to its end.

The decline and fall of the USSR and its satellites had inevitable repercussions on the capitalist-parliamentary states. For example, in Italy the self-destruction of the Italian Communist Party began literally the day after the fall of the Berlin Wall, despite its much-vaunted independence from the USSR. It is even more remarkable that the collapse of Christian Democracy and the entire party system of the First Republic came shortly after. Those parties that pretended to be archenemies imploded pathetically in unison. I fully agree with Wang Hui that the decline of the entire party system of the twentieth century was due to the decline of the communist parties.

Of course, there is the exception of China, which had the most enigmatic of all contemporary forms of government. The most intense political experiments had been carried out in China, and, conversely, it was there that, in a more prompt and effective way, a dominant subjectivity was reconstituted, capable not only of interrupting egalitarian experiments, but also of taking from their results the maximum advantage for establishing new governmental circumstances.

A hypothesis that I have advanced elsewhere is that Deng's faction proved successful and became hegemonic because it was able to strike at the internal weaknesses of these experiments.[12] However, the main force

---

12   Ibid.

that allowed for the reconstitution of a dominant governmental subjectivity in China was not simply its repressive *force de frappe*, which was certainly quite strong, but the ability to depoliticize radically any reference to the 'working class', while at the same time formally retaining its name among the state insignia. Even today, the dominant governmental subjectivity proclaims itself as being the 'vanguard of the working class', and it will not give this formula up easily. In fact, the preservation of this name, which is devoid of any political value, is one major guarantee of governmental stability in China today. In short, one deep source of the subjective strength of the CCP is its status as the vanguard of the de-politicization of the concept of the 'working class'.

Egalitarian Inventions and Governmental Circumstances

The main obstacle to the theoretical description and periodization of the sixties is that the categories of 'class' and 'class struggle' are not only inadequate, but also obscure their political singularity. The sixties are unreadable with classist categories because they were actually a great political test of classism. This theoretical difficulty is, in its turn, one of the main factors in the efficacy of 'negation'.

The prolonged experimental investigation of the sixties about the political value of the Communist Party surely did not merely concern an organizational technique, but involved a whole framework of cultural references of modern egalitarian politics. Socialism, according to such a system of political knowledge, was to be the culmination of the 'history of class struggles', and the Communist Party and the 'dictatorship of the proletariat' were not only institutional forms, but also fundamental concepts of a well-structured system, including, besides politics, also history, economics, philosophy, and virtually the whole space of modern knowledge.

Since the entire encyclopaedia of classist political culture (in both its revolutionary and reformist variants), together with the Communist Party that was its fulcrum, 'did not pass the test', we must find new categories in order to reflect on all moments of egalitarian politics. The fact that the last major political moment is not legible in terms of 'class struggle' has a retroactive effect on the possibility of contemplating all modern political inventions (not only the modern ones). They are in effect today subject to a radical devaluation. What do we think today of the political novelty of the October Revolution, the people's war in China, or the partisan warfare in Italy during the Nazi occupation? Moreover, the issue is not limited to twentieth-century politics. Did there not appear at the end of the seventies a historiographical current that denied the political value of the French Revolution, taking advantage of the discrediting of the classist categories that influential French Marxist historians had adopted in the previous decades?

The most entangled issue is that of so-called 'class antagonism', and the whole system of concepts that pivoted around it. We do not have an alternative theoretical vision as systematic as 'classism', and anyhow our aim is not to reject classism but to rethink it politically. I will try here to summarize some assumptions of a research path working towards an understanding of 'class antagonism' not as a sort of unmoved mover of a general theory of history, but from the point of view of the singularity of the moments of egalitarian politics. From this angle, the concept of 'class antagonism', rather than the omnipresent link between history and politics ('all history is history of'), appears to have held a true political value only in peculiar moments – namely, when it was a resource for dealing with the crucial issue of modern egalitarian politics, which is that of how to articulate the separation between organizational inventions and governmental circumstances.

We should examine egalitarian inventions and governmental circumstances from two different angles. When considering egalitarian inventions, we have to determine which political novelties have opened up new paths and consider them one by one – as well as their internal limits, the impasses that they encountered, and the vital problems that they left unresolved. In short, due to their exceptional nature, we should carry out a unique analysis of each of them.

Conversely, we will assume that an automatism, or general matrix repeated with minor variations, regulates governmental circumstances. It obviously takes different forms, as we can see in the incessant changes occurring at the various historical junctures. However, these variations are 'reactive', in the sense that they ultimately depend on the existence of the egalitarian inventions.[13] They react to the latter through the peculiar mechanism of negation, mentioned above.

Governmental circumstances are the set of subjectivities engaged in exercising the functions of government over the lives of others, or aspiring to do so, at the various levels of the hierarchical rituals of a certain

---

13   This point draws great support from the concept of 'reactive subject' proposed by Alain Badiou in *Logiques des mondes* (Paris: Seuil, 2006).

historical-social world. In fact, egalitarian inventions have to face different forms and levels of governmental circumstances. This became a
decisive issue in the sixties, since the multiplicity of the inventions emphasized the need to deal with the peculiar modes of operation of the various
governmental subjectivities.[14] Moreover, every political experiment needs
to identify the dominant subjectivity of an historical-social world,[15] in
order to separate from it effectively.

As for the relationships between the set of governmental subjectivities
and the dominant one, I will argue later that only the labouring of the
egalitarian inventions for existing independently can actually grasp their
peculiar logic. I would like first to outline a general hypothesis about their
automatism. My assumption is that the dominant subjectivity plays the
role of a kind of 'ideal ego', which inspires all of the governmental subjectivities of a social world. In other words, since all of them wish to take the
place of the 'Master', the dominant subjectivity, the self-proclaimed guarantor of all the ritual hierarchies, becomes the model for identification. Of
course, a dominant subjectivity keeps its place and its role until it is able
to ensure the functioning of the system of hierarchies in that world.
Otherwise, competitors are always ready to overthrow it.

We still need to clarify the functions and objectives, or rather the
compass, which guide the actions of governmental subjectivities – how
governmental circumstances operate in a dynamic sense, to use the sociological jargon. Since we consider them an automatism, we can say that a
peculiar 'drive' regulates governmental subjectivities. The debt to

---

14   A remark on the traces left by that political moment on a renowned theoretical itinerary. It is
because of having been himself a participant in the political sixties that Foucault has addressed his
theoretical attention to the multiple forms of 'governmentality'. See *Sécurité, territoire, population. Cours
au Collège de France, 1977–78* (Paris: Gallimard, 2004), Lesson of February 1, 1978. In early 1978, on
the trailing edge of the sixties, Foucault is looking for an alternative route to the 'worn-out concepts
of ideology of class', (Lesson of March 1, 1978). But he does not disclose the source of the concept of
'governmentality', presenting it as a mere result of scholarly research. He is said to have derived the
concept from studying of the Christian 'pastorate', which he cited as the major source that allowed
him to overcome a vision of the state centred on the notion of 'sovereignty'. If we do not take the
declared source too literally, we can more accurately see the concept of 'governmentality' as record-
ing, and at the same time erasing, what the egalitarian experiments of the sixties had discovered,
though it had been unsystematically theorized. Because of their multiplicity, they had to deal with the
specific character of the forms of government in different sites: school, hospital, factory, asylum,
prison, army, and so on. In each of them, peculiar forms of organization were needed, capable of
effectively separating themselves from the localized government circumstances. Foucault himself had
been committed, as mentioned above, in the Groupe d'Information sur les Prisons'.
15   Emphasis on the subjective nature of the governmental circumstances is not a novelty. In
Weber's theory, the three types of *Herrschaft* – charismatic, traditional, bureaucratic – are forms of
dominant subjectivity. Obviously, for Weber, the existence of political subjectivities heterogeneous to
these forms of *Herrschaft* is inconceivable.

Freudian theories is obvious, but we must not forget that Freud refused to acknowledge 'drives' (*Triebe*, often [mis]translated as 'instincts') other than Eros and Death, especially in the field of collective life.[16] We should also determine whether the 'governmental drive' is consistent with the dualism of the drives in classical psychoanalytic theory.

The main 'instinctual aim' of the governmental subjectivities is easily recognizable: putting themselves on the top of at a given level of the ritual hierarchies, while claiming to be the guarantee of their stability. In doing so, each governmental subjectivity proclaims itself entrusted with the task of assigning a positive (or negative) value to the good (or bad) performers of the hierarchic rituals. However, this is only the imaginary side of their existence: is the imagination that the identity of rulers consists in assigning degrees of identities to the ruled. Instead, the real existential condition of the governmental subjectivities must meet two requirements, which are ubiquitous at all levels, but particularly manifest in the dominant subjectivity: (i) to compete in order to occupy the top position of a hierarchy, and (ii) to impede the existence of egalitarian subjectivities. Let us examine this more closely.

Any governmental subjectivity automatically aims at placing itself at the top of a certain subset of governmental circumstances or, in the case of the dominant subjectivity, at being at the summit of all the instances of government of a social-historical world, which roughly corresponds to the 'government of the state' (though not necessarily in the ordinary form). It would be superfluous to give examples of the competition – often fierce and certainly more violent at the higher levels – between the rulers and/or aspiring rulers to occupy the highest rank in the ritual hierarchy at various levels. From the highest head of state to the lowliest self-important bureaucrat, the supreme enjoyment is to occupy a place at a higher hierarchical level from which to make decisions concerning the lives of the others.

The other automatism of the governmental drive is to frustrate the emergence and functioning of organized egalitarian subjectivities. When an element of organization of egalitarian subjectivities appears, albeit in embryonic form, it constitutes an impasse of the governmental circumstances – or, rather, its very existence reveals the fictitious character of the ritual hierarchies of a particular world. One of the main tasks of any governmental subjectivity is therefore to prevent the existence of anything

---

16   Freud rejects the concept of 'gregarious instinct' of the social psychology of the time. Sigmund Freud, *Group Psychology and the Analysis of the Ego* (Empire, 2014).

that exposes the inner inconsistency of such rituals, and consequently of its position at the top of them.

The very nature of 'equality' is at stake – an issue that will always be a challenge for thought. A 'classic' response may provide valuable insight. Saint Just wrote that the spirit of equality does not consist in being able to tell someone else, 'I've got the same power as you' (*je suis aussi puissant que toi*), since 'there is no legitimate power' (*puissance légitime*). Equality means, 'Every individual is an equal portion of sovereignty' (*que chaque individu soit une égale portion de la souveraineté*).[17] From this perspective, the existence of organized egalitarian subjectivity places not just on 'sovereignty', but also governmental circumstances at every level, at an impasse.

It is for this reason that those in government are so zealous in denying any political value to egalitarian subjectivities. In some cases, in the face of important mass political events, it is also possible that the dominant subjectivity is forced temporarily to admit some of the goals of egalitarian politics, and even to take measures to limit inequality. In any case, confronting egalitarian inventions, governmental subjectivities automatically react as a rule in terms of 'negation'. Invariably they label such developments as absolute disorder, anarchy, fanaticism doomed to catastrophe, and so on. Alternatively, when they are not able to do this openly due to strong egalitarian pressure, they do their utmost to distort the real issues at stake, and to direct those inventions towards a dead end or failure.

These two elements of the governmental drive – to occupy the highest possible position within the structures of government, and to prevent the emergence of egalitarian impulses – are consistent with each other. By exercising their hostility in order to eliminate rivals, every governmental subjectivity glorifies the hierarchical structure of a social world. At the same time, it must do everything it can to destroy any tendencies towards collective existence, irrespective of ritual hierarchies, because an egalitarian intention of this kind disrupts the consistency of a prevailing hierarichy.

Therefore, the governmental drive can be traced back to the original 'two drives', which are interwoven in a peculiar form of enjoyment:

---

17   Louis Antoine Léon de Saint-Just, *L'esprit de la révolution et de la constitution de la France* (Paris: Editions 10/18, 2003 [1791]). 'L'esprit de l'égalité n'est point que l'homme puisse dire à l'homme : je suis aussi puissant que toi. Il n'y a point de puissance légitime ; ni les lois ni Dieu même ne sont des puissances, mais seulement la théorie de ce qui est bien. L'esprit de l'égalité est que chaque individu soit une portion égale de la souveraineté' (p. 25).

autoerotic narcissist omnipotence and deadly destructiveness. The latter is targeted both at rivals competing for government posts, and especially for the egalitarian subjectivities. As the great analyst of governmental drives, William Shakespeare, wrote: '. . . within the hollow crown / That rounds the mortal temples of a king / Keeps Death his Court'.[18]

Classism and Political Invention

Bearing in mind the factors discussed above, let us question what role the conceptual device composed of 'class analysis', 'class struggle', 'class antagonism', 'class party', and so on has played as a political resource. The hypothesis, as I have suggested, is that the conceptual framework of classism played a crucial role in important modern egalitarian experiments, but that the essence of those moments was always a singular organizational invention.

Of course, the protagonists of those political moments, such as the October Revolution or the prolonged people's war in China, described and theorized them according to a class-based vision of politics. However, the conceptual and organizational device of classism was not an 'ideal type', nor a 'theoretical model' that Marxist revolutionaries had put into practice, perhaps by making some tactical adjustments. In respect of the creation of original forms of organization, classism was, rather, a topographic instrument for clarifying and refining experimental politics.

Classism certainly played an important role in tracing the lines of demarcation with 'enemies', as well as in spreading political activism among 'friends'. However, whenever the concept of 'class antagonism' had a real political value – which is not always the case, since it has also played an anti-political role – it actually indicated an egalitarian organizational invention affirmed as such, in the sense of the 'affirmative dialectic' proposed by Badiou.[19] That is to say, let us agree to organize ourselves independently from governmental circumstances.

For instance, Mao Zedong's class analysis enabled the Chinese revolutionaries to answer the question: 'Who are our friends and who are our enemies?', as he asked in the first sentence of his famous 1926 essay, 'Analysis of the Classes in Chinese Society'. However, 'friends' and 'enemies' are distinguishable primarily for their attitude towards political

---

18   William Shakespeare, *Richard II*, Act II, Scene 2.
19   Alain Badiou, 'The Affirmative Dialectics', in this volume.

invention.[20] 'Friends' are those who support organizational invention, and may be involved in it. Conversely, 'enemies' are those who position themselves in the sphere of dominant governmental subjectivity, or in its wake, and work to prevent and suppress the emergence of organized egalitarian subjectivities.

A clarification on this point, to which the category of Carl Schmitt, the couple 'amicus/hostis', taken as the quintessence of the 'political', has introduced some equivocation. The fortunes of this category have been surprising, especially after the end of the sixties and in left milieus. The fact that Mao Zedong had formulated the question, 'Who are our friends, who are our enemies?' was also a pretext for a re-evaluation of Schmitt from the left. The perspective I would suggest is instead that, during a moment of egalitarian invention, friendship and enmity are the result of an experimental process, rather than constituting an a priori that determines subjective choices. On the contrary, the couple amicus/hostis definitely determines a priori the incessant competition within governing circles to acquire the dominant position, nothing being at stake other than victory over competitors.

As for the arguments that, in the revolutionary classist vision, seem to converge in Schmitt's dualism, it is out of the question that the division between friends and enemies passes also through the 'parts' of the social situation. It is also true that, in their turn, all sorts of historical, economic and cultural conditions, and especially the effects of governmental circumstances, mould those 'parts', or 'classes', of a social world. However, the entire revolutionary classist conceptual apparatus, including 'class analysis', 'class antagonism', 'class party', 'class alliances', and so on, far from being a permanent, indisputable and objective frame of reference for egalitarian politics, have real political value only at specific, peculiar moments – moments favouring a separation between invention and circumstances.

In such moments, class analysis has uncovered a number of subtleties that have enabled the refining of that separation. For example, the various governmental subjectivities – namely the objective of governing the lives, bodies, desires and thoughts of others at various levels of the social hierarchy – are not always firmly associated with the dominant subjectivity. We assume that the latter is a certain 'ideal' with which all the other governmental subjectivities tend to identify themselves, but which cannot

---

20   The title of the original version of this famous text by Mao is 'Analysis of the Classes in Chinese Society and their Attitude towards the Revolution'. See Minoru Takeuchi, ed., 毛泽东集 *Mao Zedong Zedong ji* (Tokyo: Hokubosha, 1970–72), vol. 1.

permanently regulate the entire operation. In inventive egalitarian moments, 'class analysis', when put at the service of experimental politics, has favoured the initiatives of revolutionaries to accentuate the instability of such relationships.

In addition, the set of egalitarian subjectivities does not necessarily constitute a unitary body. In fact, the latter has existed only when it was able to organize forms of political alliance among whoever is willing to share the risks of invention. 'Class analysis', therefore, has helped not only to distinguish between 'friends' and 'enemies', but also to limit the range of hostility and expand the scope of the friendship. The true value of the 'we' implied here, beyond any imaginary formation that it might nourish, did not relate in any way to an historical, economic or even cultural 'identity' in respect to which 'our friends' resemble 'us' more closely than do 'our enemies'. The value of 'friendship' depended on the political experimentation that the 'we' had initiated and was conducting.

'People's War' and 'Class Analysis'

The contribution of class analysis to fostering organizational invention was thus not that of an 'objective', let alone 'value-free', analytical device. In fact, it worked as a political resource only by asserting itself through intense disputes with other positions which, by means of equally 'classist' arguments, denied any value in those experiments. Mao's aforementioned 'Analysis of the Classes in Chinese Society' is the first in the canonical *Selected Works*, because it is considered his first 'Marxist' essay. However, as Wang Hui has remarked, from the twenties to the forties, Mao's main political invention was the 'protracted people's war'.[21] The 'party' was a political space at the service of that invention, but was not its real nucleus – even less was 'class analysis' a model for the political choices that the people's war had implemented.

An oppressive militarization, following the collapse of the imperial regime, dominated China in that moment. The activity of various warlords, Chiang Kai-shek's reactionary volte-face, the Japanese invasion, the interference of foreign states, and so on, were all phenomenal forms of the militarized dominant subjectivity that governed China in reality. The people's war aimed at launching forms of unprecedented political exist-ence of ordinary people, namely the vast majority of poor peasants, and

---

21   Wang Hui, 'The Crisis of Representativeness and Post-Party Politics', in this volume.

putting a halt to the unlimited destructiveness of those governmental circumstances.

As is well known, Mao's analysis was far from uncontested within the CCP. Those who denied or underestimated the political capacity of the peasants argued, in accordance with an established class-based vision, that peasants would never become a truly 'revolutionary class' for specific economic, historical and cultural reasons. Mao's class analysis only prevailed thanks to the indisputable political and military results of the people's war.[22] His vision was also grounded on detailed investigations, rich in sociological and anthropological subtleties, that explored the different subjective attitudes of the various characters of the rural world (landlords, and peasants who were rich, medium, medium-poor and poor), as well as the circumstances that dominated the peasants' lives. Remarkably, those governmental circumstances also included the power of the 'spirits', and even 'marital power' for women.[23]

The analysis of the 'ruling classes' was also quite subtle: the target was not the bourgeoisie as a whole, but the 'comprador bourgeoisie' distinguished from the 'national bourgeoisie', by means of which Mao was able to develop a conceptual framework for identifying the dominant subjectivity in China at that time as 'semi-feudal and semi-colonial'. He made a series of distinctions that allowed an extension of the scope of political experimentation and, at the same time, increased the instability of governmental circumstances and their internal discontinuities.

Moreover, the classist framework allowed the experimental forms of the peasants' organization to confront the most difficult issues of modern egalitarian politics. The fact that a major strategic point was the 'alliance with the proletariat', and that the latter was even declared the 'leading class' of the entire revolutionary enterprise, has been considered – and never more so than today – proof of the dogmatic and substantially imaginary nature of Mao's classism. It is 'obvious' that the quantitative consistency of the Chinese working class was minimal. Nevertheless, the reference to the proletariat indicated that the guiding principle of peasant mobilization was to cope with the peculiar forms of government of the modern world. In this sense, 'bourgeoisie', with all the above-mentioned distinctions, was the general name for contemporary governmental

---

22   A problem of periodization: 'Analysis of the classes in Chinese Society' was written before the start of the 'protracted people's war', but its goal was to localize the chances for organizing the political activism of peasants.

23   In *Investigation on the Hunan Peasant Movement* (1927).

circumstances, while 'proletariat' designated the most advanced political experiments in which the Chinese communists encouraged the peasants to participate.

The analytical apparatus Mao elaborated from the late twenties to the forties constituted an immense resource for the peculiar invention of people's war. In fact, it rose and faded with it. After 1949, the political invention to which those concepts owed their existence had expired, and Mao's class analysis was never again able to play a comparable political role.

The October Revolution and the Party

The October Revolution is another political moment that needs to be considered from a new perspective. What remains today of any political assessment of the October Revolution in terms of class struggle? As a tentative path for reflection, I would suggest a reconsideration of the October Revolution focusing on the separation between invention and circumstances. At the time of the October Revolution, the European war, and not only the 'ruling classes', constituted the governmental circumstances. War was the road that all European dominant subjectivities took with equal conviction – their mutual hostility was secondary – in order to prevent and hinder organizational invention which presented an increasing threat to established power. The only way of stabilizing the latter was to turn the European populations into cannon fodder, with the active help of the 'patriotism' of most of the socialist parties of the time. War was the true government of Europe from 1914 onwards.

What about organizational invention? At that time, the 'class party' of course played an important role, but was not the key locus of organizational invention. Why did Lenin say that he was prepared to leave the party unless it approved the insurrection? Because insurrection, I would argue, was the core of organizational invention at that time. We could view that insurrection as, rather than a general tool in a momentous period in the 'history of class struggle', the original organizational experiment through which, in those conditions, the egalitarian subjectivities separated them from the overall militarization of Europe. Lenin stated that only revolution could put an end to the war. 'Revolution', beyond its political-historical associations, designated primarily the ability to stop the overwhelming death-drive that dominated Europe at that time.[24]

---

24   Freud's theory of instinctual dualism came to maturity precisely in the circumstances of that war.

The Class Struggles from Guizot to Marx

The inescapable problem in rethinking classism is how to assess Marx's own position, since the equation Marxism = classism is so 'self-evident' that Marx is usually credited with holding the copyright on the vision of politics as 'class struggle'. In fact, Marx stated clearly that he had not discovered the existence of 'classes' and 'class struggles', since before him 'bourgeois historians and economists' had already elaborated those concepts. His own original contribution, he wrote, was the principle of communist political organization aimed at the abolition of classism, the 'dictatorship of the proletariat'.[25]

We have now reached the origin of the key concept of revolutionary classism, which moreover was the main experimental terrain of the sixties. In the middle of the nineteenth century, Marx's concept identified the exceptional political existence of the 'proletariat', as distinguished from 'bourgeois' governmental circumstances. The political laboratory of the sixties, instead, proved that the main obstacle to egalitarian politics was that, under the 'dictatorship of the proletariat', organizational invention had become indistinguishable from the governmental circumstances. Would we come to any conclusion if we asked ourselves whether social-ism had 'betrayed' the original inspiration of Marx? Rather, we should question the political value of Marx's classism. What were the govern-mental circumstances from which Marx's political endeavour intended to draw a firm line of separation?

The complication is that, at the core of the main governmental novelties of the 'bourgeoisie', there was 'classism' itself. Not surprisingly, Marx cited François Guizot as one of his main sources concerning the concepts of 'class' and 'class struggles', despite the barbs of sarcasm he launched against him at the opening of the *Manifesto* as being haunted by the 'spec-tre of communism', together with Metternich, the pope and the tsar, as it was actually happening in 1848. In fact, Guizot was not the only historian who first conceived the history of France and Europe as the 'history of class struggles'. But he was the author of the formula, and the man who reorganized the French government according to classist criteria from the 1830s onwards.

As for the historiographical position of Guizot, for him as for other so-called 'liberals of the Restoration', such as Thierry and Mignet – all

---

25   Karl Marx, 'Letter to Weydemeyer', 5 March 1852, at marxists.org.

carefully studied by Marx – a class-based vision of politics and history operated primarily as a 'selective negation' of the French Revolution. They judged as very positive the sequence of events during 1789–91, led by the middle class, but as entirely negative those of 1792–94 – the work of the 'multitude', as they termed it. Guizot expanded the concept of class struggle to the entire history of France from the Middle Ages until the French Revolution. It was, he maintained, a 'history of class struggles' in the precise sense of a series of struggles of the middle class to succeed against the rule of the aristocracy, and at the same time to defend themselves from the plebeian multitude.[26]

As a man of government, Guizot mainly adopted a series of measures in favour of the middle classes, who thereby gained access to bureaucratic positions.[27] But his ministerial career ended abruptly when the 'multitudes' of workers burst on the scene in 1848, not as a 'spectrum' but as embryos of political organization. Nevertheless, Guizot had initiated a form of government that all of the post-revolutionary states had to adopt once it became clear that a simple 'restoration' of the pre-1789 regime could have no effect. 'Classism' was therefore primarily the result of a reorganization of the technologies of government that the bourgeoisie operated following the French Revolution, in place of a government based on 'orders'.

A new perspective on this entangled issue comes from Badiou's theorization of the 'state' as the 'meta-structure' that 'holds', or more precisely 'prevents the delinking' of, the parts of a 'historical-social situation'. This thesis, which explores, we might say, the ontological status of the state, opens a promising path for reflecting on the nature of classism politically. Without being able to report here all of the mathematical argument, which is quite dense in this key passage of *L'être et l'événement*, the main point is that any 'state of situation', and the 'state of the socio-historical situation' in particular, is the special set to which all the subsets, or parts, of the situation 'belong'.[28]

The 'state of the situation' applies particularly (and exclusively) to the subsets, or the compositions of multiple elements, and not to the multiple elements as such, since the latter fully 'belong' to the situation. Any situation, as Badiou writes, is able to 'present' all its elements as fully

26   See Ceri Crossley, *French Historians and Romanticism* (London: Routledge, 1993).

27   See Pierre Rosanvallon, *Le moment Guizot* (Paris: Gallimard, 1985).

28   See Alain Badiou, *L'être et l'événement, Meditation*, "L'état de la situation historico-sociale", pp. 121–8 (Paris Sevil, 1988). (Paris: Gallimard, 1985).

structured. A key theorem of set theory proves, however, that it is not the same for the composition of elements, or subsets. All of them are 'included' in the situation but not all 'belong' to it. At least one of them, although 'included' in the situation, can be proved not to 'belong' to it. Such a subset, or part, therefore localizes a 'void' – a possible source of inconsistency that exceeds the capacity of representation of the structure of the situation.

To address this inconsistency, is therefore necessary to posit a peculiar 'set of all the subsets', able to 'structure the structure' of the situation. The 'subsets', even if not all 'belonging' to the situation, nonetheless fully 'belong' to such a 'meta-structure', or the 'state of the situation'. Such is, Badiou argues, the role played also by the 'state of the historical-social situation'. In this sense, the state, rather than linking the parts of a social situation, is what prevents their delinking. Just to mention one of the most fascinating results of this entanglement of concepts ('destined however to simplify choices', wrote the author on one occasion), the 'formula' of the 'state' is astonishingly simple. It can be written $p\,(\alpha)$, which is simply the mathematical way of expressing 'the set of all the subsets', or p, of a given situation α. Being able to write the state as an ordinary $p\,(\alpha)$ is quite helpful in dissolving many of the surrounding 'ideological nebulae'.

Let us return, from this perspective, to the passage of the French Revolution. In the ontological circumstances outlined above, I would argue, a radical perturbation occurred. Post-revolutionary governments could no longer ensure the 'belonging' of the 'parts' of society in the terms of 'orders', conceived as being fixed and immutable, based on an allegedly natural or theologically guaranteed hierarchy. Or, rather, they could not take for granted any equivalence between 'belonging' and 'inclusion', of which the dominant subjectivity would be the 'natural guarantor'. Such had been, so to say, the spontaneous form of all the previous '$p\,(\alpha)$'s of the historical-social situation, as in the case of the Three States in France before 1789, or the hierarchy of 'scholars, farmers, artisans and merchants' in the Chinese Empire.

The irruption of the principle of equality of the French Revolution, as a desire for an 'equal portion of sovereignty', introduces an alteration that the circumstances of the *ancien régime* cannot fully metabolize. In fact, the political innovations of the French Revolution allowed the emergence on the national scene a principle of reality that was already effective in the bourgeois social world. In the age of the 'market', which is the age of the bourgeoisie, the subjective existence of individuals is delinked from pre-established communities. Belonging to an 'order' (*Stand*) no longer predetermines the destiny of its 'elements'. As Marx and Engels wrote, such destinies result from the highest 'randomness of the conditions of life' (*Zufälligkeit der Lebensbedingungen*). [29]

The new forms of bourgeois government, like the *ancien régime*, necessarily (ontologically) aimed to guarantee the 'inclusion' of all the 'parts' of the historical-social situation. Following the French Revolution, however, no dominant governmental subjectivity could exist simply by assuming that elements were naturally destined to belong to established parts of the situation, which in their turn were stable subsets belonging to the 'state of the situation'. The allegedly spontaneous equivalence between belonging (to the situation) and inclusion (in the state of the situation) proved to be radically inconsistent. New technologies of government were necessary. The 'classes' were therefore the result of the perturbation that the principle of equality had introduced into the ontological consistency of the state – or, rather, of the appearance of a principle of the reality of its inconsistency, which in its turn induced a necessary change in the attitudes of the dominant governmental subjectivities.

The newly conceptualized 'classes' were similarly conceived of as 'parts' 'belonging' to the 'state meta-structure', but they nonetheless involved a peculiar novelty. Unlike the immutable *Stande* of the old regime, *Klassen* referred to much more unstable 'subsets', both quantitatively and qualitatively, affected by changing and contingent factors such as technological, physical, natural or demographic conditions, interests, desires and conflicting passions.

In short, 'classism' represents the new 'rules of the game' – to quote a helpful remark by Rosalind Morris[30] – of the government of the 'bourgeois' social world. Classes are a realistic readjustment that suppresses what the French Revolution had proved to be imaginary: the assumption that the destinies of elements belonged to presupposed communities and at the same title included in the state meta-structure. In order to take hold on the 'parts', the new dominant subjectivities must adopt new concepts for identifying them. New criteria of classification are necessary for 'preventing the delinking' of 'parts' of the situation much more unstable, and to which the 'elements' belong much more randomly.

---

29   See Karl Marx, Friedrich Engles, *Die Deutsche* Ideologie, m/werke/me/me03/me03_009.htm.
30   At the workshop Capital, Class and Culture in Asia, Columbia University, New York, Department of Anthropology, 21–26 May 2012.

A key thesis of *The German Ideology* states that class 'is a product of the bourgeoisie' (*ein Produkt der Bourgeoisie ist*). In the bourgeois world, Marx and Engels argue, where the worker is governed as a 'seller' of labour-power to be exchanged 'freely' as a 'commodity' with others, it skips any equivalence between the conditions of individuals at birth and the position they occupy in the division of labour. For the proletarians, in the bourgeois social world the set of conditions of existence becomes *etwas Zufälligem* – something random – and this 'randomness' is precisely the foundation of the difference between *Stand* and *Klasse*.

In the *Manifesto*, however, Marx and Engels glossed over this point, and argued, 'All history is the history of class struggles', which maybe was intended to cut with some previous philosophical intonation, but finally was also a radicalization of Guizot's thesis. They radicalized the 'bourgeois discovery', to be sure, with the aim of abolishing its inner logic: the class struggle to eliminate the classes. However, if they were searching for the existence of a form of political organization independent of 'classism', how to distinguish the 'dictatorship of the proletariat' from the prevailing governmental circumstances of the modern world?

Marx was quite aware of this problem, as we can see in the controversy he engaged with in his *Critique of the Gotha Program*, where he argued against the idea that the aim was to establish a form of 'state' ('and do not say that this is a state of the future', he thundered). Is it not the case that his criticism was so harsh since it related to the fate of his own discovery? Marx had a premonition that it was quite possible that the 'dictatorship of the proletariat' would become the name of one of the variations of modern government.

The *Critique of the Gotha Program*, I would argue, with all its *vis polemica* against the 'spirit of servile faith in the state typical of the Lassallean sect', marked a theoretical and political predicament, which was to resurface at every great political moment. Lenin highlighted the issues of Marx's polemic in *State and Revolution*, maintaining that the socialist state was still a 'bourgeois state without the bourgeoisie', and that revolutionaries should reduce it to a 'half state'. Mao, in his turn, quoted Marx and Lenin's misgivings about the issue as a crucial reference in 1975, emphasizing that the concept of the dictatorship of the proletariat needed to be 'clarified', since it marked 'not such a great difference' with capitalism, other than the form of ownership.

A final tentative remark on Marx's theoretical legacy. All politics that it has inspired have inherited from it a symptomatic aporia. The goal is to create a form of political organization independent of classist governmental circumstances: communism = the end of classism. At the same time, the analytical equipment for implementing this separation relies on the radicalization of classism. However, classism = government of the modern social world. Therefore, despite the stubbornness of the great Marxist revolutionaries, from Marx to Mao, in maintaining the 'dictatorship of the proletariat' as the decisive operator of the separation, the annihilation of organizational invention under the effects of governmental circumstances that bore this very name has haunted every decisive political moment.

Metaclassism/Hyperclassism

This detour through one of Marx's original dilemmas may help us to return with some new resources to the initial problem: What do we have in common with the sixties, and what should we take care not to repeat? Or, rather, what issues should we rethink in order to refine our subjective fidelity to the sixties, while at a same time looking beyond the impasse of that political configuration? One key point concerns, I believe, the oscillation between what I would call 'metaclassism' and 'hyperclassism', which are both rooted in the Marxist tradition.

As noted above, within classist revolutionary politics have always been intertwined, on the one hand, attempts to undo the ritual hierarchies of the social world – that is to say, to conceive of egalitarian politics beyond classism – and, on the other hand, the radicalization of classist categories, which, in their turn, have been congenitally embedded in modern forms of government. This oscillation began in fact with Marx himself, who was, however, also the first to reflect on the decisive internal obstacles that his political invention had to face. We could say the same of Lenin and Mao. The idea of the 'dictatorship of the proletariat', as the alleged balance between organizational invention and governmental circumstances, has always caused much anxiety to the great Marxist revolutionaries.

At the core of the sixties, there was a political re-examination of all that 'historical experience', and therefore of a key point of the entire classist revolutionary tradition. We should therefore evaluate its results primarily on this terrain. However, there is an element of the political discourses of the sixties – a recurrent feature of the 'language of the situation', as Badiou would say – that deserves particular scrutiny. In the sixties, the oscillation between metaclassism and hyperclassism was so intense that we should make some extra effort to discern its logic.

That oscillation, I would argue, and the subsequent shattering of the conceptual framework of classism, was the symptom of a peculiar predicament, as well as of an effort to overcome it. Let us follow therefore the path of a 'symptomatic reading', in the wake of Althusser's seminal concept. In the sixties, I would argue, the prolonged discord between experimental egalitarian invention and the cultural space of classist revolutionary politics was an aggravating factor in that symptomatic oscillation.

The most novel experiments of the sixties explored disparate political innovations that exceeded the conceptual and organizational framework of revolutionary classism, while putting its political value to the test. The sixties in China are paradigmatic as one of the points of most intense oscillation. One first clue to the symptom is the very name 'Cultural Revolution', which designated the rethinking, from the bottom up, of 'revolutionary culture'. This rethinking targeted a well-articulated system of knowledge, which in its turn claimed indisputable mastery over the entire battery of revolutionary political concepts, and in fact reacted as if ejecting a foreign body.

When fresh inventions emerged in the political arena, and started to interrogate the egalitarian values of that cultural system, as well as of the governmental circumstances with which it was intimately coextensive, the entire ideological and organizational space of the Communist Party proved to be strongly refractory. A dramatic face-off then occurred between, on the one hand, those attempting to promote new experiments and, on the other, a compact conceptual system that considered them a symptom of intolerable disorder. The former, in order to declare their own existence, had necessarily to test the political value of that cultural space; while the latter, ultimately impervious to any political testing, did its best to hinder all of the possible self-organized egalitarian subjectivities.

The new experiments placed under scrutiny the political culture embodied by the Communist Party, aspiring to regenerate it critically, but met the most formidable obstacles from within the party itself. In this sense, it was also true that the 'bourgeoisie' – the enemies of egalitarian invention – were in the party. Moreover, since those experiments shared essential points of reference with the conceptual and organizational framework of politics in China, they had to make huge efforts to draw a line of separation from the dominant discourses, and to make principled arguments of their own. In the most intense disputes of the time, it became necessary to find a hearing for the project of identifying a dividing line, overcoming the impression that both 'friends' and 'enemies' spoke the same 'language of the situation'. Alertness to this issue remains indispensable when interpreting those events today.

In order to exist, political inventions were in urgent need of new conceptual tools, which nonetheless could only be fragmentary results of an ongoing process. The revolutionaries actually created several new concepts that facilitated a clear demarcation with the political discourses of the time – for example, the declaration of one of the first great documents of the Cultural Revolution that the 'masses can be liberated only by themselves and nobody can act on their behalf', or Mao's last theses about the urgent need for a thorough rethinking of the 'dictatorship of the proletariat', quoted above.

In other cases, when the inventions lacked original theoretical elaboration, resort to the framework of previous political concepts was almost inevitable. But the classist conceptual framework, as embodied by the party, was itself hostile to those inventions, and when it was not able to suppress them, tended to metabolize them as a set of ritual activities in glorification of governmental harmony. Therefore, when the revolutionaries borrowed the old concepts, they often emphasized an even more radical class standpoint, in order to defend their inventions from prevailing political discourses, and to avoid being confused with them. However, the more the arguments became hyperclassist, the more they lacked distinction from the cultural framework that operated to annihilate experimental politics.

On this point, the 'symptomatic reading' of the oscillation between metaclassism and hyperclassism in the sixties gives a result quite different from Althusser's original reading of Marx. Althusser maintains that, when Marx was not able to formulate new concepts, old concepts took the place of the new ones – which, although 'essential in thought' were 'absent from discourse'. This thesis has important implications, since it emphasizes that the thought is in excess on the discourse.

However, in the sixties that excess and conceptual substitution produced unique effects. It was not only that the new metaclassist concepts, 'absent in the discourse', were disguised in the clothes of the old concepts. Since the political laboratory of the sixties was questioning the foundations of the classist conceptual system, it was not at all simple to use the old concepts as substitutes for the new ones, which still lacked a discursive formulation. Indeed, the old concepts returned to the scene, but they symptomatically assumed a more imperative form – not only because the experimental process was making their political value uncertain, but because the cultural revolutionaries were also trying to stress their singular political intention towards the established revolutionary culture. Therefore, in the sixties there was an unnerving oscillation between metaclassism and an even more adamant hyperclassism.

Take for example the remarkable oscillations of Mao himself. In 1957, in 'On the Correct Handling of Contradictions among the People', he proposed a political category that we can consider the first expression of a new political vision, at the very beginning of the 'long sixties'. The 'contradictions among the people' are not 'class contradictions' in principle. Mao argued that class antagonism alone was not sufficient to define revolutionary politics, and that communist organization needed to deal with a huge range of contradictions that were not dependent on the categories of class and class struggle. These contradictions did not involve class antagonism, but an infinite multiplicity of non-antagonistic relations. In this sense, we can say that Mao assigned metaclassist tasks to communist politics.

However, a few years later, in 1962, he declared: 'Never forget class struggle.' In this case, class struggle was synonymous with politics. He surely meant that egalitarian inventions were essential, and was opposed to those who insisted that the task of the Communist Party was to govern the 'development of the productive forces'. However, for the purpose of fighting de-politicization, he resorted fully to a classist perspective, declaring even more peremptorily: 'Never forget.'

A similar oscillation occurred during the Cultural Revolution. In 1966, when Mao said, 'Bombard the headquarters', he meant, 'Let us test thoroughly the political value of the Communist Party'. In this sense, he was metaclassist. However, in January 1967, a famous editorial in the *People's Daily*, which he had personally inspired, declared that the Shanghai 'January Storm' was a 'seizure of power' – a term he used to imply that a 'revolutionary class' had overturned a 'reactionary class'. Mao thereby conceptualized those events in a hyperclassist manner. He did so, it is true, by way of offering unconditional support to the Shanghai workers who had created independent organizations; but those events in fact exceeded the conceptual space of 'class struggle' and 'seizure of power'. The very existence of organized workers outside the Communist Party was the radical novelty that caused the power structure in Shanghai to collapse. For this reason, in merely classist terms, the Shanghai events are strictly unintelligible, and Mao's statement did not clarify the situation.[31]

One can observe other examples of the same oscillation in the central years of the sixties in Europe. May 1968 in France certainly exceeded the parameters of classism; but in the following years the main organization was named Gauche Prolétarienne, which evidently claimed to be even more 'classist' than the proletariat itself, trying to position itself to its left. Significantly, in a few years their hyperclassism turned in the opposite direction, leading to a sudden self-disbanding whose causes were unknown to even its protagonists. In Italy, there was an organization called Lotta Continua, invoking the 'perpetual continuation' of the 'class struggle'. It echoed Mao's appeal to 'never forget', but also disbanded itself after only a few years.

The same pattern was expressed in the name of Potere Operaio. A metaclassist perspective, I would argue, has characterized Negri's entire political career ever since the early sixties, even though he probably would not agree at all with this definition. Negri had anticipated with great foresight a theme that would emerge fully only in the following years: the search for a form of political existence for workers independent of the Communist Party. But the name 'Workers' Power' allowed the classist conceptual system to resurface in the strongest terms: the concept of 'power' designated the workers as a political class that aimed at the seizure of power. In this sense, Negri's swing towards hyperclassism had much in common with Mao's position – and here perhaps he would agree more – including his sincere and unreserved support for the search for a new workers' political organization.

A great problem for all of 'us' – meaning anyone who searches for the possibility of new, inventive politics as a key resource for thought – is how to find a way out of the oscillation that still constitutes one major legacy of the sixties. For instance, when Michael Hardt and Negri theorize the concepts of 'empire' and 'multitude', which denote not only the conflict between the bourgeoisie and the proletariat, they look beyond the framework of class. On the other hand, when they theorize the novelty of a 'cognitariat' – i.e. a 'proletariat of knowledge' – their pitch becomes

---

31   A more detailed discussion of this episode can be found in my article, 'Theoretical Problems in the Study of the Cultural Revolution'.

hyperclassist. We can find many other examples, since all of 'us' experience this oscillation in one way or another. Everyone who welcomes new possibilities of egalitarian politics must cultivate a subjective proximity to the sixties – but this oscillation also represents the inner limit of such loyalty.

A last example of this phenomenon concerns some discussions with Pun Ngai. She has for some years been carrying out studies of Chinese factories, which offer in-depth analysis of the new forms of wage labour in China. Moreover, her investigations into the 'dormitory labour regime' reveal a general trend towards factory despotism today that goes far beyond China and Foxconn, encompassing the whole of contemporary labour relations. Present conditions in China differ greatly from those of thirty years ago, and are not legible through the 'classist' lens of the socialist era.[32]

One question that seems to recur in Pun's enquiries is which obstacles prevent these new workers from organizing themselves in terms of class, while all of the social conditions for such a development seem fully mature. Surely, Pun acknowledges the need for political inventions for organizing the singular subjectivities of the new Chinese workers. But what might be the role of classist concepts today? To mention once again a problem that is not only lexical, the most recent Statute of the Communist Party of China confirms in its very first sentence that it is 'the vanguard of the working class'. Obviously, it does so in order to prevent the emergence of independent workers' organizations.

The Current Circumstances and Us

In China today, as everywhere else, the answer to the questions of who rules, and how, are not self-evident. The Communist Party? Five thousand years of Chinese culture? Large groups holding financial and media power? We find the same difficulty in identifying the governmental circumstances in Europe. Certainly, they no longer depend on the party system established after World War II. At present, the main governmental circumstance is most probably the economic crisis, besides the decisive role the euro has played for some years. To have a currency as a 'government' certainly muddies the waters, but such opacity is 'normal'. As a rule, a peculiar governmental mistiness prevails – 'ideological nebulae', in Marx's words – that only inventive political skills might clarify. The

---

32   Pun Ngai, 'Another Cultural Revolution is Inevitable: Bottom-Up: The Chinese Working Class in Its Making', paper presented at the conference, The Idea of Communism, Seoul, 2013.

weaker such skills are, the thicker is the mist. 'The evil mist is back again', Mao wrote in a poem in which he reflected on the political impasse he faced in the early sixties.

The comprehension of the functioning of the government in a social world is under condition of political invention. A pure analytics of 'governmentality' is university imagination. It is fully possible to answer the questions of who rules, and how, only by carrying out new egalitarian experiments. Only from the point of view of inventive politics can one face questions such as: How do the government instances work? Where is the dominant subjectivity situated and what relationship does it have with the other governmental subjectivities? Most importantly, how is it possible to establish a rational distance from the governmental drive, in order to limit its destructiveness and open a path to new egalitarian experiments?

Only political invention can dissolve the 'governmental mist', for the basic materialist reason that, in order to understand the essence of the circumstances you need to alter their 'regular' functioning – just as in Mao's aphorism that 'to know the taste of a pear you must transform it by eating it'. In order to discover the logic that drives governmental subjectivities, they must be perturbed by egalitarian invention. One could also recall here Machiavelli's aphorism that, just as, to draw the mountains, one should watch them staying 'lower in the plain', similarly, 'one must be popular to know the nature of the princes'. The Florentine secretary was not able to theorize equality, but he grasped the need for a peculiar distance from the government in order to decipher it.

But it is not enough to be 'popular'. We must also be organized, and we have to recognize that this is the weak point that we must overcome. Having this concern in mind, I will try to summarize three final issues, in particular: the intricate relationship between our organizational inadequacies and the current governmental mist; the likely consequences of the continuation of this obscurity; and some inescapable tasks before us today in our quest to find a new political path.

1. A general assumption of these final remarks is that the obscurity of the present circumstances is the result of our organizational inadequacy. This is an intricate matter indeed: the current 'evil mist' increases the efficacy of governmental circumstances, because it increases the obstacles to egalitarian politics; but, in the last analysis, the fragility of a new political configuration is a major aspect of that obscurity. All those who are impatient to overcome this weakness, 'anyone of us', blunder along, make

a few uncertain steps, and just stammer something new. This helps us to go on – we 'must go on' – and not resign ourselves to the destructiveness of the present state of things; but there is still a lot of work to do if we want to organize ourselves inventively. Until we have acquired these skills, the present circumstances will be impervious to rational knowledge, and will sink further into the obscure effects of the governmental drive.

The process opens up a confused scenario that requires us to sharpen our powers of observation. To understand the government circumstances as the 'hollow imprint' of previous egalitarian inventions, as I have done so far, does not entail considering them as a stable form, or a process of stabilization. They in fact constitute a process, whose energy is essentially parasitic upon past moments of significant political invention; they represent the 'hollowing out' of its subjective value through the peculiar mechanism of negation described above.

Moreover, this process is not limitless, since the 'emptying out' has a sort of physiological boundary. In the current situation of the after 'post-sixties', two generations after the events, 'negation' is much less effective. When, let us say two decades ago, it was able to induce the 'self-negation' of mass egalitarian subjectivities, it played the role of stabilizing governmental circumstances, but how would this be possible today? The 'negation' of the sixties is not able to make a strong impression on a young person for whom half a century seems to measure a span of geological time.

2. The 'hollow imprint' is no longer an effective stabilization process, since the 'negation' of a previous political moment can no longer provide the dominant subjectivities with enough energy to annihilate new potential egalitarian subjectivities. Once this essential resource is exhausted, what energy can governmental circumstances rely on? All of them, especially the dominant subjectivity where 'keeps Death his court', are always guided by a powerful desire for annihilation, both against competitors and against egalitarian subjectivities. We could also assume that, as long as their consistency is still 'reactive', it comprises an element of moderation of that desire, but that, when it is no longer possible to parasitize inventive energies reactively, the destructive component of governmental circumstances becomes unlimited.[33]

The US financial crisis and its lasting effects are examples of blind

---

33   Badiou calls it the 'obscure subject'.

destruction, in which it would be futile to search not only for a 'bureaucratic rationality', but even for the failure of such a rationality. The financial crisis is now the architrave of the governmental circumstances in Europe, and the dominant subjectivity will hardly give it up without replacing it with something even more deadly.

Evidently, war is always among the available options, but the men of government consider it with some caution – not for the sake of pacifism, but because a generalized state of war could not effectively suppress the egalitarian organized subjectivities, and, on the contrary, might even risk providing a powerful stimulus for their existence, echoing developments in the twentieth century. A more likely scenario is the militarization of large areas, as in North Africa in the past few years, and more recently in Eastern Europe. Militarization favours the governmental desire for annihilation and, at the same time, enables tight control over large populations.

3. Finally, there are some tasks, or rather some operational issues, that any one of us may have to deal with. Firstly, we need to watch very carefully for the appearance of possible egalitarian organizations, taking into account that, in each case, something unpredictable and uncertain is at stake, and it is difficult to identify political invention in its embryonic forms. Each novelty might be 'the spark that sets fire to the prairie' or a 'flash in the pan'. Alternatively – even worse – it might be an intense and durable fire, which, however, only results in the passing of the baton from one governmental faction to another.

Special vigilance is required towards mass riots. Given the increasing destructiveness of current circumstances, mass disturbances that manifest disgust for such nihilism are likely to become endemic. 'Do not be afraid of the riots', said a famous directive. That is to say, deal with them by searching for possible political inventions, and not from the point of view of anti-riot technologies. The problem is that tumult is a ubiquitous element in the social world, but is not immediately convertible into egalitarian subjectivities, although it is certainly intertwined with them.

Our difficult task is therefore how to discern egalitarian inventions from the rest of the tumult, and favour their independent growth. In the tumult, there is always a component of egalitarian subjectivity that should be carefully analyzed; but is not the only one, and neither is it pre-emptively distinct as such. Alongside it, there is also an important subjective component, which despite its urge to reject the brutality of prevailing circumstances is ultimately consistent with them. The separation between these two components is often invisible at first sight. In-depth investigation is required in order to distinguish indignation against the nihilism of government from mere hooliganism, and challenges to hierarchical rituals from arbitrary abuse. If the egalitarian subjectivities are not capable of creating a process of separation from governmental drive, the tumult stands ready to be at the service of the destructiveness of prevailing circumstances, becoming a tool by which one dominant subjectivity settles scores with its competitors, placing new obstacles in the way of egalitarian invention.

8 Manifestos without Words: The Idea of Communism in South Korea – The Case of the Gwangju May

Yong Soon Seo

The Gwangju May and South Korea in the 1980s: The Event and Its Aftermath

In what follows I will examine the political event that took place at Gwangju in May 1980, named officially by the Korean government in 1996 the Gwangju Democratization Movement.[1] This event constitutes a decisive moment in the contemporary history of South Korea. At the same time, the event is very complex. It served to determine the course of Korean social movements during the 1980s, as well as the macro-political process of democratization. Moreover, when viewed from outside the frame of democracy (due of course to its status as a popular uprising), an entirely different question emerges: the idea of communism. My main focus regarding the Gwangju event resides in this problematic idea. In order to understand it, I shall first of all summarize the event itself.

The protest and revolt of Gwangju began with a demonstration on the morning of 18 May 1980 against, and in defiance of, the martial law proclaimed by General Chun Doo-Hwan and his political supporters, who had taken control of the state by means of a military coup in the preceding months. The demand of the people of Gwangju was very simple: to establish a democratic regime. Obviously, there was nothing revolutionary about it.

The response was ruthless state violence, which was exceptional at the time in its severity and scope. Under martial law, airborne troops were called in to quash demonstrations by unarmed citizens with deadly force. This violent reaction enraged the people of Gwangju, who overcame their fear and rose up in revolt. The participants in the protests were ordinary citizens, and their demands were modest and not exceptional: liberal democracy, political reform and the end of martial law. But what they

1   My special thanks are due to Jason Barker for helping me to express my argument in English, and for our stimulating discussions.

received instead was extreme violence; ineffable violence beyond words; violence unprecedented in peacetime in the modern history of Korea. In the end, with fear dispelled, almost every citizen stood up to the army's repression. The military forces opened fire at protesting crowds, causing large numbers of casualties. These ordinary people raided the armouries and police stations in nearby towns, and, armed with guns and grenades, spontaneously defended themselves. After intense gunfights lasting until the night of 21 May, the improvised civilian militia corps succeeded in pushing the army out of the city, thus transforming it into a temporarily liberated space. A great majority of those who joined the civilian militias were from the lower classes. Although intending to continue their resistance to the point of victory, the 'resolution committee', composed of prominent local figures – such as religious leaders, lawyers and professors – tried to calm down and normalize the situation in order to save civilian lives, and negotiate terms with the army for the people's safety once they had disarmed. But the army already had a plan to quell the resistance ruthlessly, which led to its prolongation, with civilians prepared to risk their own safety in the pursuit of their struggle.

Despite the fact that this impasse was engineered by the army, the spontaneous courage of the people of Gwangju provided space for them to resist its repression, which they succeeded in doing by capturing armouries in nearby towns, and forcing the army's temporary retreat, following which a liberated space was created. Finally, confronted by the army's final assault, a life-or-death struggle became necessary to justify the legitimacy of the Gwangju resistance.

Before daybreak on 27 May, the resistance was suppressed by the army in its enforcement of martial law, and this totally changed the configuration of the social movement in South Korea. By then, what was at stake for the movement was to overcome military autocracy and establish the institutions of formal democracy. But this unprecedented event revealed the violence of the state-form. Under the control of the new military regime of General Chun, the state denounced and oppressed its own people as mobs, before placing them in the firing line. In the end, instead of a naive idea of democratization, the vision of the democratization movement was transformed into a revolutionary one aiming to overthrow the military regime. The most tenacious of the subjects faithful to this event began to conceive a 'revolution' aiming at the overthrow of the state's power, which, within two or three years, was crystallized in the enterprise of the revolutionary labour movement. Shortly after the

Gwangju event, myriad factions were established and sought their own versions of revolutionary projects, although they commonly adopted Marxism-Leninism as their basic political line. In other words, in those days, Marxism-Leninism enjoyed a strong revival in South Korea, while simultaneously heading towards decline and termination in Europe. Many among the intelligentsia delved into this old-fashioned mode of political thinking – essentially Stalinist – with a conviction of its potential for changing dominant realities.[2] That was what traversed the intellectual configuration of South Korea in the 1980s, albeit with insufficient durability to survive the collapse of the socialist bloc, which dealt a fatal blow to political militants. Large swathes of them were swallowed up by the tide of parliamentary capitalism, and entered into the opposition parties of institutionalized politics. Some of them even converted to the far right.[3] The rest set up left-wing parties, attempting to enter the national assembly. They might have chosen to pursue revolutionary goals, but instead made a U-turn in the direction of institutional democracy.

The remains of what displaced the events of 18 May are the ruins of its fidelity, in the Badiouian sense of the word. Parliamentary capitalism absorbed the name of that event, and confined it within the framework of institutional democracy. In the 1990s, as formal democracy began to paper over the cracks of the event, the state politics of South Korea came to adopt of an obscure and all too limited title, namely the Gwangju Democratization Movement.

Political Subjectivity Subtracted from Democracy

My goal is to examine this event in relation to communism. This is certainly paradoxical, for this movement's demands were solely democratic. The people of Gwangju demonstrated for the establishment of formal or liberal democracy. But during the course of its development,

---

2   For example, Park Hyun Chae, an economist, tried early on to analyze the economic structure of Korean society at the time from a Marxist point of view. See Park Hyun Chae, *Minjok Kyungjae'ron* ('Treatise on the National Economy') (Seoul: Hangilsa, 1980). This work was completed before the Gwangju event, though it owed its success to it. Lee Jin Kyung, a sociologist, developed a Marxist-Leninist theory of social formation for the Korean context. See Lee Jin Kyung, *Sahoe'kusungchae'ronkwa Sahoekwahak Bangbeop'ron* ('The Theory of Social Formation and the Method of Social Science') (Seoul: Achim, 1987).

3   For example, Kim Moon Soo was a remarkable leader of the workers' movement in the 1980s in Korea, who completely changed his convictions and became a right-wing politician. Kim Young Hwan, a political leader of the pro-North faction, converted to become a propagandist of the extreme right.

unexpected things happened at the level of subjectivity. In order to grasp the event's singular character, it is necessary to take note of its subjective dimension. The passage from democracy to communism in the social movement in the 1980s precisely indicates a radical transformation of political subjectivity. Communist subjectivity is herein derived from an event in excess of democratic ideology. But this excess is not the simple consequence of the Gwangju event. There was already communist subjectivity latent within it, albeit in inconsistent form. In its post-evental practice, this subjectivity appeared under the name of 'revolution'. Afterwards, when fidelity to the event declined, communist subjectivity disappeared. From start to finish, throughout its entire sequence, what was at stake here was therefore political subjectivity itself.

Of course, it is true that the event contains diverse elements: the democratization movement, problems of regional discrimination, the insurrection's 'revolutionary' dimension, and so on. Various studies have attempted to respond to questions raised by its unprecedented nature.[4] But almost all of them have focused on objective analyses: causes, effects, the role of the various parts of the citizenry, and so on. In the last instance, almost all studies have conceived its role in terms of institutional democratization, as if there had never been any attempt to reach beyond democracy.[5] But Gwangju's uprising is not something to be contained within the narrow framework of democracy, or democratization. Of course, it is not possible to say that the people of Gwangju had 'revolutionary consciousness' at the time. As a recent study by Kim Jung Han shows, democracy was, by definition, the prevailing ideology animating people in Gwangju.[6] At any rate, whether 'democracy' was predominant as ideology or not, this mere fact carries no weight in my analysis. What matters is the novelty that emerged in the course of the people's uprising, and not what they thought in reality.

---

4   There are many collective works, essentially objective studies, on the Gwangju event: *Gwangju Gwang'yoksi 5·18 Saryo Pyon'chan Wiwonhoe* ('Commission of Historiography on 18 May in Gwangju Metropolitan City'), ed., *5·18 Minjung Hangjengsa* ('History of the 18 May Popular Resistance') (Gwangju: *5·18 Saryo Pyon'chan Wiwonhoe*, 2001); *5·18 Ki'nyumjaedan* ('The 18 May Memorial Foundation'), ed., *5·18 Minjung Hangjeng'kwa Jeongchi, Yeoksa, Sahoe* ('The 18 May Popular Resistance and Politics, History and Society') (Gwangju: *5·18 Saryo Pyon'chan Wiwonhoe*, 2007).

5   A remarkable exception is a study by a Korean political scientist, Choi Jeong Woon, *Owol'ŭi Sahoe Kwahak* ('The Social Science of May') (Seoul: Owol'ŭi Bom, 1999). His pioneering research, based on the testimonies of participants, strongly influenced studies published later on. His insights on the subjectivity of this event are highly praiseworthy. However, I do not agree with him concerning the nature of the subjectivity in question. I shall address this point further below.

6   Kim Jeong Han, *1980 Daejung Bonggi'ŭi Minjuju'ŭi* ('Insurrection of the Masses and Its Democracy in 1980') (Seoul: Somyeong, 2013), pp. 79–82.

In fact, demonstrations in the early phase started with students' claims for democratization and protests against the illegitimate enforcement of martial law by the new military regime. As time went by, however, their demand for democratization was relegated to a secondary position. What really counts in such circumstances is the rage and courage of ordinary people in taking a stand against violence instigated by the state. Overcoming their fear, the common crowds of Gwangju inadvertently emerged into the space opened up by the politics of emancipation.

What I am attempting to do in my summary of this event is to highlight some basic ideas from which the elements of the idea of communism can be established – some old political values which, in the context of South Korea, might even be deemed novel: freedom, equality and justice. Evidently, these ideas characterize the collective courage of people during uprising; but, as we see all too often, they are rare and not readily visible. In the case of the Gwangju May, this is especially the case, since those ideas were manifested by acts and not words. The movement of Gwangju exhibited several paradoxical characteristics. First, it did not declare a revolution, but the moment was truly revolutionary in the sense of subtracting itself from state power. Second, it did not proclaim the politics of emancipation, but belonged to its dimension. Today, what is important for us to grasp is the idea of emancipation – that is, the 'idea of the commune'.

Various aspects of the old ideas of freedom, equality and justice are inconceivable from within the scope of prevailing, so-called democratic values. Those old ideas, neglected or deemed unthinkable today, are building blocks for constructing 'the idea of the commune'. Based on this observation, the thesis I want to develop concerns a certain idea of communism as an abstract possibility divorced from the old one. On my definition, the idea of the commune is the subjective element for constructing the idea of communism, and thus that which is at stake is the dimension of political subjectivity connected to emancipation.

The Idea of the Commune Part 1: Freedom from Violence – Resistance by Logics

In the course of the events from 18–20 May, deliberations on human atrocities were made under the most exceptional circumstances. The people of Gwangju, having faced down the army's atrocities, fled in fear for their lives. What such deliberations encompassed was the nature and limits of what they were capable of enduring as human beings. They deliberated in the face of real atrocities and, according to eyewitness testimony, felt shame at their own helplessness when faced with such overwhelming violence.[7]

In the event's early phase, on 18–19 May, after being dispersed by military forces, the people came back to participate in demonstrations right away. They first fled and then gathered to protest, without any loss in their numbers. On the contrary, the increase in the crowds caused the army confusion. The more the numbers of the protesters increased, the more enraged they became at the murderous violence of the army. This stubborn tenacity amounted to a desire to overcome a natural instinct for self-preservation. Nevertheless, it would be misleading to imagine that it derived from a determination simply to restore 'human dignity'.[8] Although this deliberation began in a sense of astonishment at such barbarity, ultimately this was a process aiming beyond human dignity. That is to say, these people thought in terms of protest as much as they participated in it. It was imperative for them to stand against the atrocities of the army of the new military regime. In order to exceed the limit of the existing struggle, there was no alternative but to fight. This event was a 'resistance based on logics' – in other words, a 'resistance by logics', as Badiou puts it,[9] in the sense that people reached the necessary conclusion to 'resist and rise up' by crossing the limit of self-preservation characteristic of human animals, through an axiomatic procedure of deliberative thinking.

Meanwhile, these individual deliberations were collective. In other words, the determination to resist through individual deliberation raised to the collective plane provided the initial momentum to create the 'politics' of the Gwangju May. In any case, we should not restrict this politics to the domain of structural causality, or to that of ethics. Indeed, in the course of overcoming their fear of state violence, the people of Gwangju advanced to practising radical political action – somewhat 'fanatically', one might say, without knowing it. The proof of this exists in the firebombing of local public offices that took place from the evening of 20 May. According to many witnesses, these arson attacks were organized and carried out with purpose, after an exhaustive debate on whether to

---

7   Institute of Documents of Korean Contemporary History, ed., *Gwangju Owol Minjung Hangjaeng Saryo Jeonjip* ('Collected Edition of Documents on Gwangju's Mass Resistance in May') (Seoul: Pullbit, 1990), p. 313.

8   Choi, *Owol'ŭi Sahoe Kwahak*, pp. 92–4.

9   See Alain Badiou, *Metapolitics*, transl. Jason Barker (London: Verso, 2005), p. 4.

do so or not. As Choi Jeong-woon has pointed out, such acts were carried out with the deliberate intention of bringing the people of Gwangju out onto the streets.[10] And it is no exaggeration to say they amounted to a declaration of war, affirming in no uncertain terms that the struggle would not end peacefully. At the same time, they constituted immediate retaliation against state apparatuses, such as the local broadcasting stations that had remained silent in the face of the army's despicable acts, and tax offices diverting tax income to the army.[11] In the early phase, it was this incendiary attack that provoked the people of Gwangju to confront the state in the political domain. In this way, the deliberation and determination against state violence amounted to a political declaration; an *active* declaration rather than the reasoned judgment of a spectator, such as Kant famously exercises when he draws out the moral consequences of the French Revolution. A declaration, in other words, which takes the *immediate* form of *an act*.

The Idea of the Commune Part 2: The Idea of Subjective Equality and the 'Absolute Commune'

From the evening of 20 May, the resistance of Gwangju was elevated to another level in both its extent and intensity. While the intensity of the popular protests increased, there was a street procession of many large buses and trucks, and several hundred taxis, with their headlights illuminated, heading towards the provincial office of Cheonnam Province, in which the army headquarters were located. On the morning of 21 May, people started gathering on the main street from everywhere in the city. Gwangju effectively underwent a leviathan-like transformation into a single body composed of the masses. Many people voluntarily contributed money and provided protesters with drinks and rice balls. There was confrontation between people and the army, and while negotiation over the terms of the army's retreat was going on between civilian representatives and commanding officers, the provincial office was completely surrounded by the crowd of 300,000 people. Almost everyone who could take part had come out to encircle the building, because the population of Gwangju in those days was estimated at around 730,000. Such was the scale of what we are entitled to name an 'absolute form of collective subjectivity'.

10   Choi, *Owol'ŭi Sahoe Kwahak*, pp. 133–4.
11   Institute of Documents of Korean Contemporary History, *Gwangju Owol Minjung Hangjaeng Saryo Jeonjip*, pp. 3,066: 677.

In the most important study, Choi Jeong-woon describes this collective subjectivity as 'absolute community' and 'life shared in common'[12] in which personal life comes to be inseparable from the life of the community. Social difference, the motivations of traditional community, the rule of hierarchy and prejudice, and so on, are rendered completely meaningless. The people of Gwangju, in overcoming the fear ingrained in social mores and graces, constitute 'one community' without divisions. Choi considers 'absolute community' as emerging from collective struggle in the face of extreme violence. According to his explanation, the absolute community 'fused each and every citizen and made them identify their own lives with other people's'.[13] He goes on to say that the absolute community is considered as 'what is established through the fusion of citizens, who overcome their fear, with a large number of colleagues [when] all constituents find their own conviction in themselves'.[14] In the final analysis, he defines the absolute community as something that appeared at the moment when all forms of social division disappeared. Meanwhile, the absolute community, as Choi interprets it, was transformed into another state from the moment weapons appeared or negotiation was entered into with the army – a transformation that permits us to think the true characteristics of politics. For Choi, at the moment when the absolute community proceeds to politics, the community starts to be disrupted. This is how Choi removes the absolute community from the horizon of politics. But his assessment appears to be incorrect.

While keeping his profound insight in mind, I would focus on what he hardly notes – or, rather, what his analysis chooses not to see. It is evident that there were acts of sharing among people in Gwangju; they voluntarily distributed free meals among protesters who were exhausted by hunger and lack of sleep, and voluntarily donated their own blood for transfusions to injured comrades. On that account, Choi describes sharing life as an essential characteristic of the absolute community.[15] In Korea, sharing meals with other people at the same table has a meaning that surpasses polite hospitality; simply put, if you share food with somebody else it means he or she is no longer a stranger to you. Sharing blood is more profound, and unambiguously universal in meaning. When

---

12   Choi, *Owol'ŭi Sahoe Kwahak*, p. 142.

13   Choi Jeong-woon, 'Jeoldae Gongdongche'ŭi Hyongsung'kwa Haeche' ('Formation and Dismantling of Absolute Community'), in Commission of Historiography on 5·18 in Gwangju Metropolitan City, ed., *5·18 Minjung Hangjengsa*, pp. 324–5.

14   Choi, *Owol'ŭi Sahoe Kwahak*, p. 151.

15   Ibid., pp. 139–42.

somebody is wounded and their life is threatened, blood donation erases all forms of social separation and hierarchy. Needless to say, it is an egalitarian act with egalitarian consequences. In the space opened up by the absolute community in Gwangju, the division between 'my property' and 'your property' disappears; my life and your life henceforth become identified as one. In that community, we see the advent of a certain kind of non-separation. On that account, the absolute community must be called 'the community of subjective equality', and the acts of sharing food and blood declarative acts. The declaration of the equality of everyone here and now is manifested through concrete acts of the people. It shows that the Gwangju event crossed over from moral kinship, and finally proceeded to the politics of subjective equality, traversing the ethical horizon of respect for differences. Thus, subjective equality takes its place as the second idea of this event.

In line with what Choi suggests, when it comes down to the political acts (requisition of cars and fuel, negotiation with the army, distribution of arms, and so on), a rupture in the absolute community occurred.[16] However, in my view, it may have occurred as a result of the collective subjectivity that traversed all kinds of differences. From there onwards, the politics of the new 'commune' emerged as an immediate consequence. Therefore, I suggest we name this collective subjectivity the 'absolute commune' rather than the 'absolute community'.

The Idea of the Commune Part 3: The Declaration of Justice

'The absolute commune' of Gwangju inevitably opted for political acts. 'Commune-effect' is an apt designation for what enabled people to exercise state-like power or effective dual power, to negotiate with the army (as one would with foreign enemies), and, finally, to arm themselves.

On the morning of 21 May, negotiation between civilian representatives and the army was broken off. At one o'clock, the army opened fire on protesters and inflicted large numbers of casualties. Immediately, people came down to local armouries and police stations in order to equip themselves with captured weapons. Shortly following an exchange of fire, the troops pulled back from the provincial office building, using this strategy as a delaying tactic to create the conditions for a forceful re-entry

---

16   Ibid., pp. 169–81. Choi explains the division of absolute community in terms of a division between armed citizens and non-armed citizens. He therefore considers the use of arms as the political act that destroyed the absolute community.

after a temporary period of calm. On the evening of the same day, on entering the provincial office building, the civilian militias discovered that the troops had retreated to suburban areas of the city, thereby transforming the city centre into a liberated space.

But this was a commune enacted without any form of premeditated organization, and installed through people's voluntary will, pure and simple. There was no revolutionary organization and no model of leaders commissioned to lead a revolt. The absolute commune established in Gwangju showed its potential for collective subjectivity, albeit one that failed to develop into a popular organization and concentrate that potential. Ultimately, its militants were destined to perish under fire from the army.

After 22 May a process of intensification of political opposition was followed by the Commune's decline. In the five days from 22 to 26 May, prominent local figures attempted to disarm civilian militias and to calm the situation down. At this point the Gwangju commune began to suffer political division. Without any central organization to direct their struggle, activists divided into two camps: hawks, insisting on the continuation of armed struggle; and doves, preferring to find ways of giving up their weapons safely and achieving a peaceful resolution. The opposition between these two sides was aggravated to the point at which the hawks threatened the doves at gunpoint, and expelled them from the provincial office building.[17]

The hawks were mainly composed of the lower classes, who held arms as civilian militias. The doves, on the other hand, were composed of distinguished local figures and Catholic priests, who had participated in the democratization movement of the 1970s. It was the doves who led the Citizens' Resolution Committee, and who negotiated with the army, without being able to placate the hawks, who called for the continuation of armed struggle. Most of the doves had no direct links with the uprising, and were somewhat incongruous figureheads for a commune that had come into being through the taking up of arms. In contrast, the hawks, or the group of civilian militias, were frustrated at the prospect of their struggle coming to nothing, their sacrifices denigrated as the rioting of violent mobs. Division was of course inevitable. If the doves had agreed to initiate the immediate return of arms and to allow the re-entry of the army and its enforcement of martial law, for the civilian militia corps this

---

17   Institute of Documents of Korean Contemporary History, *Gwangju Owol Minjung Hangjaeng Saryo Jeonjip*, p. 310.

would have meant nothing less than yielding to the illegitimate violence of the new military regime – downright betrayal of popular justice in Gwangju, in other words. Some of the militias left the provincial office building, but many decided to remain, resisting until they were felled by army fire. It was four o'clock in the morning, just before dawn, on 27 May when the civilian militia corps, consisting of 500 people standing their ground, was decimated by superior fire power. Some 200 people were arrested, and between 200 and 300 were killed in the fighting.

What counted for the people of Gwangju, who had been faithful to the spirit of a seemingly impossible and misguided endeavour, was resistance at all costs, and the thought *in actu* of a 'fight to the end', which in this case signified a standing of one's ground, a death-defying confrontation with state power. Choosing struggle over self-preservation, the politics supporting the people's uprising amounted to an unspoken manifesto or declaration of their self-imposed fidelity to popular justice.

Let us note the last words of a deceased militiaman – one of its leading figures, Youn Sang-Won, who defended his post to the last:

We have to face them down mercilessly. If we leave the provincial office building, the struggle will have been in vain, and we will have sinned against history and against the souls of the departed. Let's resist and not be afraid of death. Even if we are killed, that's how we lived. We must fight to the last for this country's democracy. Let's leave a proud record of what we stood for. After this night, a new morning will surely come.[18]

What remains of the commune is nothing less than the fidelity demonstrated by the civilian militia. What was at stake was not objective victory; the situation at the time dictated the final defeat of the commune. Nevertheless, a great number of militia members, these faithful subjects, stood their ground without renunciation. There was, objectively, no victory. But equally, the militias did not lose. If there was a victory, it was a subjective one: their fidelity to the popular justice invented by their acts amounted to subjective victory. And this subjective victory produced hope: hope as 'enduring fidelity', as Badiou says.[19] They defended the

---

18 Cheon'nam Research Centre for Social Problems, *Deul'bul'ŭi Chosang: Youn Sang Won Pyeongjeon* ('Portrait of Wildfire: Critical Biography of Youn Sang Won') (Seoul: Pullbit, 1991), p. 321.
19 Alain Badiou, *Saint Paul: The Foundation of Universalism*, transl. Ray Brassier (Stanford, CA: Stanford University Press, 2003), p. 95.

popular justice of the commune without renunciation, and finally became immortal subjects.

A Task Bequeathed by the Commune

As we know, the subjectivity necessarily constituting the politics of emancipation in this context is threefold, consisting of freedom from the state, subjective equality, and the prevalence of the idea of justice. These universal ideas were all manifested in the Gwangju event of May 1980. Bequeathing us the ideas of the commune, through declarations without words, or rather manifestos *in actu*, this unclassifiable event has left its trace behind in the form of an intellectual puzzle. Language typically fails to capture such ideas, owing to its formal and abstract nature, so it is not an easy task to revitalize them. The Gwangju May has been re-established to a certain extent, albeit by way of the limited designation of the so-called 'democratization movement', although nowadays even the status of this name is at risk. The prospect of a novel designation of Gwangju beyond the mandate of 'actually existing democracy' looks bleak. Gwangju today has been relegated to the status of a purely intimate act – one with no bearing on the state of the situation save a kind of morbid nostalgia for times past. It is as if Antigone's desire to put a loved one to rest had no meaning or consequence other than a mere familial obligation.

Recently, the Gwangju uprising has come to serve a useful function for the liberal establishment, in being stigmatized and denounced as a rebellion serving the interests of the North by lazy peddlers of demagogic propaganda. What we have to defend, however, are precisely these kinds of novelties, or 'new old' ideas, and the practices based on them. Our task is to save the event of the Gwangju May through reinvention – a reinvention extending beyond its limited denomination as a 'democratization movement' – and reimagine the ideas or principles upon which its commune was based. These ideas are beyond the reach of institutionalized democracy.

I dare say that reacquainting ourselves with the obscure and soon-to-be-forgotten ideas of Gwangju might be a first step towards the advent of a new communism. A struggle without return. A struggle through reinvention.

9   Stairs of Metaphor: The Vernacular Substitution-Supplements of South Korean Communism

Ho Duk Hwang

Is this your face?
Mr Pak, could this really be your face?
Like a dead visage in an alcohol bottle,
Your gaunt cheeks like a swollen sponge
Your dry, wispy hair exposing your skull,
Oh! Could this truly be you?

The Pak I knew before, strong as an ox
Sitting across from me, wielding his pen in C Co.,
Under harsh beating his guts all skewered,
Now food for the crows.

On a dark, dank night in Shanghai,
Windy and rain-soaked,
Together in some underground cellar, fists clenched,
Your eyes wide open when they broke you,
You have emerged from the prison gate a walking corpse.

Pak, Oh Pak, XX!
Your loving wife has embraced your ruins,
Your surviving comrades grasp you by the hand,
Gritting your teeth, as if cursing heaven
The tears flow from your eyes.
Oh, Mr Pak! I can read your face.

Yes, Mr Pak
Repay an eye for an eye,
Repay a tooth for a tooth
Until I forget all the X together,
Until both of our hearts stop beating.

Sim Hun, 'Mr Pak's Face'[1]

---

1   In *Chosŏn Ilbo*, 2 December 1927.

Communism: Infinite Generic Concepts or the Unspeakable Name

The people's sentiment towards communism in South Korea is one of fear – namely, fear of the fear that is embodied in politics. The reactionary, overwhelming forces that attack every symbol of community external to the existing state system still control the law and the state. With the Korean War under suspension and still without a peace treaty, a post-colonial, divided Korea exists in a perpetual state of emergency. The name 'commie' (*ppalgaengi*) immediately brings to mind the 'other' war in which 5 million people, or one quarter of the entire population of the Korean Peninsula, were either killed or injured by periodical ideological purges and other means of the South Korean anti-communist system. In this system no one could utter the phrase 'I am a communist' without the fear of being arrested. The original law regulating all thoughts and actions – especially the express display of communist affiliation – that posed a threat to the body politic and national security was the colonial-era Maintenance of Public Order Act. This was followed by the Cold War-era Anti-Communist Law, which was in turn succeeded by the National Security Law that still exists today.

The most severe sentence for violating any of these laws has always been death. If the subject is the position of potentiality to which signifiers may connect, then the advent of the signifiers 'communism' and 'social-ism' in this position marks the moment when the subject's 'mortality' is attested. Although journalistic freedom and freedom of conscience are protected by the constitution, a gathering of more than two like-minded people is deemed a 'conspiracy'. Any long-term meetings that foster imag-inings of a new community (commune) are enough to invoke the National Security Law over and against the principles governing the common law. When we say that speech signifies empathy/conspiracy between two or more individuals, and possesses performativity through articulation, no one can claim that declaring oneself a communist is equivalent to Communist Party membership without violation of this law. Those who are found to be merely aware of assemblies associated with communism are considered to be complicit, and can be punished under the National Security Law. No one remains safe from the National Security Law.

An explanation of the National Security Law by the current South Korean minister of justice – an expert on defence against North Korea's Communist Party – sums up what is implied by communism in today's Korea: 'National Security Law is defined as the entire legal system that ensures national security and guarantees the life and freedom of the people.'[2] In fact, then, anti-communism forms the very foundation of the law. South Korea's legal system, which is based on national division and anti-communism, represents without exception the *exceptio* legal convention, a political concept that determines an enemy whose function is both to create and to perpetuate the rationale of national security.

Of course, this does not mean that the state of South Korean politics is devoid of the idea of communism. The sense of community in the Korean term *uri* ('we') retains a communistic philosophy that has remained with us. If, as Alain Badiou says, 'the communist Idea is the imaginary operation whereby an individual subjectivization projects a fragment of the political real into the symbolic narrative of History',[3] this operation is one that cannot be suspended. However, when we examine the period from Korea's colonial past, through the subsequent years of developmental dictatorship, to contemporary South Korea, the fact that the state is based on the implied exclusion or prohibition of the symbol of communism is clear. If the Idea is an immutable constant that exists outside of history and the Concept is a linguistic unit that projects the universal treatment of objects and events onto the symbolic narrative of history, the history of the concept of Korean communism in Korea is one that cannot be written, or must be written differently.

When we attempt to construct a history of the concept of communism in South Korea by connecting ideologies with events, we encounter four difficulties. First is the problem of concept-substitution, or supplementation. In South Korea, communism has been replaced by a 'different' signifier and a 'different' symbol. In a divided nation where the national policy is centred on anti-communism, and North Korean sympathizers are threatened politically and bodily, the concepts employed by critical political forces can only be severely restricted. Freedom, democracy,

---

2   Hwang Kyo-an, *Kukka poanpŏb* (National Security Law), (Seoul: Pak Yŏng-sa, 2011), p. 3. Suspicions of interference by the National Intelligence Service in the South Korean presidential election of 2012 through psychological warfare against the North, or some broader concept of national security, have been denied. Anti-North psychological warfare is claimed to be a form of defence against actions of the North Korean Communist Party. As long as the domain of security encompasses human 'psychology', this law has no exteriority. In fact, the National Security Law was promulgated in 1948, five years before the actual criminal law. Article 1 of the law, referring to 'those who violate the constitution, assume government authority, or form organizations or associations whose purpose is to rebel against the state' is nearly equal in its range of application to the colonial-era Maintenance of Public Order Act, Article 1 of which referred to 'those who organize associations whose purpose is national revolution'.

3   Alain Badiou, 'The Idea of Communism', in Costas Douzinas and Slavoj Žižek, eds, *The Idea of Communism* (London: Verso, 2010), p. 3.

liberal democracy, nationalism, populism, citizenship, *demos* and commu-nity are terms that have been ineluctably caught within a conflict of interpretations or within a conflict of moral criticism. Thus, it has been difficult to break these terms free from the political romanticism over authenticity and purity of will. (Even in the campaigns directed at subverting state control, these terms have necessarily possessed an inter-pretational disparity of denotation within the same concept.)

The struggle of the South Korean 'communist' is, then, without an adequate signifier, without a proper name. Where the autoregressive/ lucid does not possess a symbol – namely, an act without concept – the act becomes stranded in the interstices between the real and the imaginary. Those who are susceptible to dangerous substitution, supplementation and proxy signifiers are given to arrive at a different point. Through a prohibition of the symbolic and the *signifie*, the movement struggles within 'the real' deprived of any mediation. In this divided nation, not even adjectives are safe. When the law is applied in such a way as to 'lay bare to the public the plot of these impure factions to command plausible-sounding adjectives like "progressive", "novel" and "innovative", in order to deceive the people, all the while shaking hands with the enemy and eventually selling out our country to the [North Korean] puppets',[4] even within the limit of descriptive words alone, this is a disquieting division. Democracy, the *volk* (*minjok*), the *demos*, the worker, the populace – all are considered dangerous. Through a 'creative' and enforceable interpreta-tion of symbols, those who monopolize both the laws of the state and the laws of grammar, the 'masters' of South Korean communist ideology, are ironically the heads of the Bureau of National Information.[5] Regardless of its claim to support democratization and social reform, the state can interpret these tendencies as a 'subterfuge for social revolution', and judge them to be anti-state organizations, which is in fact what has happened.

Second, there is the problem of negation, or rather the negation of negation. South Korea was one of the few countries to retain the

---

4   The Supreme Council for National Reconstruction, ed., *Han'guk kunsa hyŏngmyŏngsa* ('A Revolutionary History of the Korean Military'), vol. 1-1, (Seoul: Han'guk kunsa hyŏngmyŏngsa Pyon'chan Wiwonhoe, 1963), p. 272.

5   From the founding of a separate government in South Korea until the autocratic Revitalizing Reform (*Yusin*) government based on 'Korean-style democracy' began in 1972, the most comprehen-sive, systematic and substantial work on communism was Kim Hyŏng-uk, *Kongsan chuŭi ŭi hwaldongkwa silchae* ('The Activities and Reality of Communism') (Kwangmyŏng ch'ulpansa, December, 1972). Known as the J. Edgar Hoover of South Korea, he was, from 1963, the longest-serving head of the Korean Central Intelligence Agency, for six years and three months.

'Anti-Communist Law' until 1980. Since then, the law has not disappeared, but lives on as a dimension of the current National Security Law. Disavowal of the national policy of anti-communism was considered dangerous in the past, and it still remains so today.[6] Discourse or campaigns critical of the regime of anti-communism necessarily meant the disavowal of anti-communism in its systemic manifestation. Such absolute negation of communism creates a dialectical problem of its creating only its own negation – the double negative of communism: *anti-anti-communism* – that is different from communism in the positive.[7] In one of the few lawful channels for knowledge about communism – material critical of communism – there are two courses through which the representative space of anti-communist negation can be penetrated. First, the symbols (i.e. X, asterisk, circle) used in place of redacted text, namely, the effaced negativity which is visualized as the traces '*XXXX*'. For instance, consider the effect of the following erasure: 'The capitalist class monopolizes private property, manages the workers, uses surplus value in production, and XX politically, ruling by XXXX'. The symbol 'X' is of minimal symbolic value, but maximal imaginative value. The second course was the negation of prohibition, or the movement for double negativity in which the emergence of the position 'anti-anti-communism' was the inevitable result. Social movements under a system of anti-communism had to begin from a position removed from criticism of an anti-communism that was superior to and transcended the legal system itself. Prefixes such as 'anti-', 'de-' and 'over-' , as well as the term 'pro-North' (denoting a North Korea sympathizer), mentioned above, are themselves heads grafted onto a regime, and within this limitation they are headings without contents. Anti-communism – the stronghold of South Korean conservatism – is the dwelling place of substanceless individuals, where distraction is carried out only by the creation of enemies and disavowal of the Other. Without

---

6   To quote one Korean prime minister's reply to the National Assembly, 'The national Policy of [South] Korea is not democracy but anti-communism' (Kim Chong-p'il, 21 September 1971, National Assembly Reply). Roughly fifteen years later, when an opposition party assembly member pronounced that 'the national policy of Korea must be liberation, not anti-communism', he was arrested during the assembly session (15 October 1986).

7   The National Security Law System that protects against direct and indirect infiltration by the North Korean Communist Party is based on a constitution that prescribes that all territory on the Korean Peninsula is national (South Korean) territory, stipulates that the political system north of the truce line is an anti-state organization, and considers the communist ideology that directs the North's system and related organization membership, meetings, communications and utterances to be instances of 'giving aid/comfort to the enemy', or 'sympathizing with the enemy', and punishable. The Anti-Communism Law and the anti-system and system critique 'communist affiliation' which it regulates have both at once acted as the categorizing 'generic singular'.

renewed uncertainty of the regime's prefixes (anti-, de-, over-), the regime of anti-communism is something that cannot be transcended. Indeed, anti-anti-communism is the history of South Korean social movements itself. Of course, the effect of blank space caused by hyphens and censorship symbols is clear. While the censored remains on the frontier of the symbolic realm, it incites through imagination that exceeds the symbolic. The hyphen, through the negative 'movement' itself, approaches the real. However, we cannot say that the opposite of the opposite of communism is communism in the affirmative. Under communism's prohibition, anti-anti-communism shares the same ideological poverty as anti-communism. Moreover, the double negative as a positive – those who oppose anti-communism are communists – is the logic of the Republic of Korea's regime. Because, according to *The Communist Manifesto*, 'Communists everywhere support every revolutionary movement against the existing social and political order of things', the double negative has become inculpatory evidence of conspiracy with enemies outside the purview of the law. In South Korea, communism is not an ideology but an anti-state organization, an epithet for North Korea. The pattern of manipulation, torture, propaganda, repulsion of the North, alignment with the North, or directives from the North – often via Japan, the United States or Europe – is often judged definitively in terms such as: 'A certain event XXX claiming the charge fabricated, in league with the propagandistic activities of the North puppet regime, benefited the anti-state organization.'

Even while taking the critique of the double negative as a starting point, only when the interpretation of those exceptional 'masters' was disavowed has the idea of communism been able to be rescued. It follows that this rescuing excludes communism and any of its attendant conceptualizations and conceptual histories. At the moment when these critiques and progressive movements fall prey to the legal clutches of the concept, the object X is on the one hand sacred, and its existence is free of guilt despite its being killed in this state of exception. At the same time that the concept of communism is enforced, capital punishment – the law enforcement of the anti-communist state – is presented. The connection to communist culpability was even connected to destiny through its succession in the system of punishing the families of the guilty. South Korean communism (at times forged through torture) is visualized through the interrogation reports that constitute 'spy' accounts, sentencing and eventual statements, and biographical rehabilitation of the communists involved is impossible without blood-drenched 'confessions' and 'affidavits'. This is the reason that fictional 'family histories', or epic natural history allegories such as the *roman-fleuve*, came to replace the ideological and conceptual histories of South Korean communism.

Third is the regional and spatial limitation of historical development stage theory. Historically, spatial modifiers were always attached to 'our' concepts – the concept of 'our' by definition sharing an inevitable connection with communist ideology.[8] For example, there is the difficulty that arises with the determinacy or indeterminacy possessed by regional limitations such as the Asiatic Mode of Production. However, adjectives such as Asiatic, East Asian, national, Chinese, Korean, Japanese and international are all primarily modifiers that spatialize the temporal. Through the superimposition of time-space continuum as revolutionary stages, the regional or local limitations of the international communist movement (such as the Comintern's issues on Asiatic, national and colonial questions) and the actual sources of this limitation, historical development stage theory, have limited the movements based on the principles of real underdevelopment and restriction. The time for revolution was always too soon (until the Chinese communist revolution, at least). Korean liberation discourse that included the communist movement (despite its being based on the inevitable premises of 'movement/action') could not break free from the discursive matrix overwhelmed with discussions of Korean and Asian historical stages, the determining of the subject of history, and social formation. Moreover, the struggle over the redirection of historical consciousness and for securing the subject of popularization and revolution, locutions like communism or socialism were continually economized. Concept finally withdrew, and was subliminalized into ideology. In an active sense, the communist movement established the combination of

---

8   I will define the relationship between Idea and Concept in the following way: if Concept is a linguistic unit that projects comprehensive capacity for the universal treatment of matter into the symbolic narrative of History, then Idea can be termed an immutable constant that exists beyond historical context. According to Hegel, there is real unification between living truth and concept that is ideology, and it is here that concept always has negative meaning. As the negativity of concept appears as force, this is able to become the logic of existence. In the best instance, concept is the 'shape' of idea. If Idea is regulative, Concept is reflective. According to Alain Badiou, 'We will say that an Idea is the possibility for an individual to understand that his or her participation in a singular political process (his or her entry into a body of truth) is also, in a certain way, a *historical* decision' (Badiou, 'Idea of Communism', p. 3). On the other hand, concept refers to the diverse linguistic practices of particular speakers performed within the concrete context of a certain era – in short, both the element of a symbolic narrative and the leading language in a given situation. Concept, becoming the 'expressions' of an individual and recorded as historical symbol, should be understood as regulative rather than reflective.

regional limitations and the limits of historical stage theory itself as the strategies and tactics for grasping the reins of state power. Within the ideological dimension, communism was always hidden or extremely minimized.

Fourth is the problem of the public and the private – the antimony between theoretical openness and the underground movement; or, the ethics of South Korean communism. The history of South Korean communism is a blood-soaked body, the ground littered with letters, diaries and documents. Rather than in the language of media and the streets, Korean communism existed only within legal pronouncements and as a transgraphical practice. Rhetorical communism existed only as censorship symbols or proxy signifiers. Even short memos were deemed to be *'preliminary* activities in the aiding of the enemy' and triggered punishment. Actions and speech by communists existed 'underground'. The moment they surfaced into the public eye, these 'excavated' creeds were captured by the legal system. The brutalized bodies of private individuals evoked the existence of the idea of that which is common: the eye of the incarcerated, the disordered face, the broken frame, the blood-spattered prison uniform; aphasia, incoherent babbling, mental derangement. The state/legal exhibition in the form of violence often utilized the making of *córpus delícti* ('bodies of crime'), their illocutionary presentation, and this conspicuous publicity itself became both the dynamic force of the anti-communist system and communism's historical representation – the source of the double negative imaginative force. The real of South Korean communism is underground, in the mind, but also inscribed into bloody flesh. Korean communism, in which 'public' is founded not on the commune but always in the most private forms – confessions and testimony, the ground littered with sincerity, the corporeal – exists as an exceptional rupture of these forms, and remains now in the ashes of archives, the ethics of the witness, and the iconographies of those who suffered.

The conceptual history of South Korean communism cannot be captured in an historical progression by keywords. We must examine not only the 'concept' (con-cept: inclusion as one) but also the 'exception' (ex-cept-ion: inclusive exclusion). Such conceptual history is a conceptualization of concepts – namely, the unity in multiplicity that is contained by the generic. To quote Quentin Skinner, in order to evaluate the conceptual history of communism, 'We need . . . to be ready to take as our province nothing less than the whole of what Cornelius Castoriadis has described as the social imaginary, the complete range of the inherited

symbols and representations that constitute the subjectivity of an age.'[9]
Histories that do not belong to a given 'thing' can indeed be histories of
that 'thing' after all. When communism itself is defined not as a state or an
idea, but as 'the movement which abolishes the present state of things',[10]
this 'Korean' difficulty is an exceptional one, and can even be understood
as the governing rule of communism's infinite difficulties.

The four difficulties that limit communism, or rather form it into infinite generic concepts – the concept substitution-supplements of
communism; negative negation (the double negative); the regional and
spatial limitations of historical stage theory; and the antimony between
the public and the private (confession, conscious, corpus) – shall here be
called simply substitution-supplementation. The history of Korean
communism is not the history of communist movements, concepts or lexi-
cons, but the history of 'the real', which surpassed but never reached
communism.

Liberation, the Propagation of Democracy, and Limitations:
Multitude and Individuum

In practical terms, communists do not necessarily exist where the name
communism is invoked.[11] If they are present wherever there is criticism
of ownership and political grounds and action for the common, then as a
movement and as an idea, they exist everywhere. Rather, the question we
must ask is the following: Up to what point is an action with no name or
under a different name possible?

It is important to note that, even when the prohibition was lifted,
numerous concept substitutions were produced at the point of suture
between historical time and spatial restrictions and the requisite subjectivization. For example, during the only time when communism was able
to become 'public illocution', the two or three years after the liberation of
15 August 1945, the communist ideology and movement had already been
formed. The unfolding of Korean communism at the point of liberation

---

9   Quentin Skinner, *Vision of Politics, Volume 1: Regarding Method* (Cambridge: Cambridge
University Press, 2002), p. 102.
10   'Communism is for us not a *state of affairs* which is to be established as an ideal to which reality
will have to adjust itself. We call communism the real movement which abolishes the present state of
things. The conditions of this movement result from the premises now in existence.' Karl Marx, *The
German Ideology* (1845–46), at marxists.org.
11   'On the Common, Universality, and Communism: A Conversation between Étienne Balibar
and Antonio Negri', *Rethinking Marxism* 22: 3 (July 2010), transl. Arianna Bove, p. 326.

was determined and substituted under the conditions of the following three limitations: the temporal limitation of historical stage, the spatial limitation of post-colonial Korea positioned in Asia, and the communal-national (*inmin-minjok*) limitation of the Korean people. From these limitations arose the conceptual removal of communism and the proletarian revolution itself, the refusal to distinguish between nationalism and communism, and the political exclusion of traitors to the nation and pro-Japanese affiliates.

With these limitations and exclusions, the concept of communism was replaced by democracy. Strategic and tactical concepts began to appear panoramically: the critical approval of 'bourgeois democracy' that sprung from the French and American revolutions, the referencing of Soviet and Chinese 'New Democracy' or 'General Democracy', and the absorption of 'coalitional' or 'ethnic democracy' signalled by the possibility of left–right political conciliation. Moreover, these types of bounded concepts gradually converged upon the interest of the protection of 'progressive democracy' through the removal of liberal democracy and, at the present stage, the monopoly of the proletariat. The 'greatest limitation' on Korea's so-called 'ethno-nationalist rebirth'[12] was the concept of 'progressive democracy'. The Korean communist movement leader and internationalist of the post-liberation era, Pak Hŏn-yŏng, acclaimed this concept as groundbreaking, asserting that 'the Communist Party of Korea is at the forefront of fulfilling progressive democracy'.[13] He stated in 1945:

The core of the Chosŏn [Korea] problem lies with the achievement of complete independence and the establishment of a democratic state. Here, the most important issue is the question of who is the enemy. Our enemy remains the forces of Japanese imperialism, and its close connections through the pro-Japanese factions . . . Today, widespread misunderstandings about 'proletarian revolution' and 'the construction of a socialist system' stem from the ignorance of those who have heard nothing and know nothing of the Communist Party of Korea's opinions

---

12   Sin Nam-ch'ŏl, 'Minchu chuŭi wa hyumanijŭm – Chosŏn sasang munhwa ŭi tangmyŏn chŏngse wa kŭkŏs ŭi kŭmhu panghyang e taehayŏ' ('Democracy and Humanism: On Current Thought and Culture of Chosŏn and its Future Direction') (April, 1946), in Chŏng Chong-hyŏn, ed., *Sin Nam-ch'ŏl munchang sŏnjip II* ('The Writings of Sin Nam-ch'ŏl, Vol. 2') (Seoul: Sŏngkyunkwan University Press, 2013), p. 220.

13   Pak Hŏn-yŏng, 'Chosŏn minjok t'ongil chŏnsŏn kyŏlsŏng e taehayŏ' ('On the Founding of the Korean National United Front') (20 October 1945), in *Chosŏn inmin ege tŭrim* ('To the People of Korea') (Seoul: Pŏmusa, 2008), p. 20. This work was presented under the title Communist Party of Korea's Central Committee representative, Pak Hŏn-yŏng.

and policy lines. Whether our party emerges in an era of unlawfulness or in a lawful manner, it supports the bourgeois democratic class and the construction of democracy.[14]

Amid the turbulence of colonial experience and the spatial restriction of ideology, relationships between land-owner/capitalists and the pro-Japanese, democracy and popular sovereignty, ethnicity and the people, equality and distribution, and exclusion and unification had to be 'strategically' and 'tactically' confused. In particular, the National United Front of Korea, which was deemed to be developing a 'domestic revolutionary force', was divided over the policy of 'excluding pro-Japanese traitors to the nation and unifying progressive democratic elements'.[15] 'The working people' were substituted for the revolutionary proletariat class, and they were considered the 'pure people's front', the 'multitude' with abundant potential power. 'Bourgeois land owners' were called 'pro-Japanese traitors to the nation'. The dissolution of ownership relations was accomplished through the proxy social agendas of 'land reform' and 'nationalization'.

The issue of ownership – the central thesis of *The Communist Manifesto* – has been described by Karl Marx in the following way: 'In all these movements, they bring to the front, as the leading question in each, the property question, no matter what its degree of development at the time.'[16] Thus it is described as the core principle of democracy over the exclusion of pro-Japanese traitors and ultra-nationalists. Pak Hŏn-yŏng likewise summarizes the fundamental nature of ownership in the communist movement: 'If land reform were to be carried out across the country, this would establish the foundation of democratic development in Korea.'[17]

The South Korea in which the United States was stationed became a sphere of much propaganda and contention regarding 'democracy'. Everyone was in principle a supporter of democracy. In a country where, 'not only did every last person consider themselves democrats but . . . quite a few non-democrats insisted that they be acknowledged as democrats',[18] how could communist ideology be effectively substituted

14 Ibid., p. 21.
15 Yi Kang-guk, *Minchu chuŭi Chosŏn ŭi kŏnsŏl* ('The Construction of Democratic Chosŏn') (Seoul: Pŏmusa, 2006), p 87.
16 Karl Marx and Friedrich Engels, *Manifesto of the Communist Party* (1848), at marxists.org.
17 Pak Hŏn-yŏng, *Chosŏn inmin ege tŭrim*, p. 73.
18 Pak Ch'i-u, 'Minchu chuŭi ŭi chinjja wa kajja' ('Democracy, the Real and the Fake'), in Yun Tae-sŏk and Yun Mi-ran, eds, *Pak Ch'i-u sŏnjip* (The Collected Writings of Pak Ch'i-u), (Incheon: Inha University Press, 2010), p. 577.

through democracy? The difficulty with the articulation of the term 'democracy' is evidenced by the multitude of derivative terms appearing in one liberation-era dictionary: 'progressive democracy', 'American-style democracy', 'Soviet democracy', 'liberal democracy', 'New Democracy', 'working people democracy', and many others. If it was claimed that 'the so-called democracy advocated by both the communists and the opposing anti-communist camp is nothing more than camouflage meant to conceal the fascist nature of political ideologies of colluding monopolistic capital',[19] why did the signifier 'democracy' continue to demand advocacy from the leaders?

The man who ideologically formalized the 'progressive' character of democracy was the partisan philosopher Pak Ch'i-u. As a hidden ideologue of the Communist Party of Korea, he conceived of a redistribution that permitted 'true one-to-one, actual one-to-one, realistic equality' as an inherently democratic campaign. If we say that totalitarianism relies on the indivisible principles of organic theory of the state or nation, then democracy was based on infinite divisions until it reached to the individual level, in accordance with formal logic. As the atom and the individuum are established by the Law of Identity (Subject who claims, 'I am me') and the Law of Contradiction (Other who claims, 'I am not you'), the one-to-one principle and the association among these indivisible singularities form the principle of majority vote by representatives that drives democracy:

> With the hope of moving inevitably towards a society in which each individual works according to his ability without condition or exception, and distribution is based on work, only now has equality begun to become a reality in Korea. Therefore when Korea achieves the majority demand for one-to-one equality this will be a great, inevitable leap forward towards democracy . . . This is why not only should we not sink to the level of bourgeois democracy, but progress towards a democracy of the workers that can firmly ensure the demand of the workers for actual one-to-one equality, which is in fact a natural course.[20]

---

19   Paek Nam-un, 'Ilbanjŏk minchu chuŭi, kongsan chuŭi, Chosŏn kuse chuŭi', ('Common Democracy, Communism, and Chosŏn Salvationism'), *Chosŏn minjok ŭi chillon chaeron* ('The Chosŏn Nation's Truth Review'), (Seoul: Pŏmusa, 2007), p. 131.

20   Pak Ch'i-u, 'Chŏnch'e chuŭi wa minchu chuŭi: Sinsaeng Chosŏn ŭi minchu chuŭi rŭl wihayŏ' ('Totalitarianism and Democracy: For the Rebirth of Chosŏn Democracy')) *Pak Ch'i-u sŏnjip* (The Collected Writings of Pak Ch'i-u), (Incheon: Inha University Press, 2010), p. 207.

Actual progressive democracy meant a transition from bourgeois democracy by means of the workers (and therefore socialism or its preceding stage). However, this sort of transition has historically faced continued setbacks. As is well known, democracy is not a procedure of truth, but a procedure through authority and arbitration, in which various authorities contend for ownership over the term 'democracy'. However, there were too many different forms of democracy, and 'ethnic-national' limitations that continually adhered to these forms.

But who were the common people? Mostly, they were a set complementary to the pro-Japanese, traitors to the nation. The concept of democracy, itself a stand-in for communism, was again employed this time as a proxy for pro-Japanese/anti-nationalist antagonism. The method of this removal was in reality lucid, but ideologically and conceptually opaque. The construction of socialism or the demand for the actualization of communist ideology slipped into a strategy of organizational self-purification as 'the construction of an independent nation-state', or perhaps a 'subjective' state formation. Because of the demand to be 'progressive' that was imposed by historical stage theory, active efforts to differentiate the self resulted in the spatial exclusion of the precedence of liberal democracy-as-propertied class and the temporal removal of Soviet-style proletarian dictatorship democracy and classless communistic democracy. In that process, the dual status of the 'nation' (*minjok*) as both subject and object of conquest was continually evoked.

Here, Mao Zedong's strategy of excluding traitors to the country (漢奸) as part of the New Democracy Movement was seen as the model for progressive democracy and its exclusion of pro-Japanese elements. For example, Sin Nam-ch'ŏl understood the subject of democratic construction to be the 'political/economic human, the national human'.

The democracy we now speak of is 'New Democracy'. It is a democracy endowed with a new meaning. It is progressive democracy. As Mao Zedong stated in his speech before the Yenan Association for the Promotion of Constitutional Government on 20 February 1940, 'New Democratic government, the constitutional government of New Democracy. This is not the outmoded democracy of the past, the bourgeois dictatorship practised in Europe and America, nor is it the new Soviet-style dictatorship of the proletariat.' This is a New Democracy joined with the global current and the affairs of the Korean state. In short, as Mao stated, this is democratic governance through the alliance of various revolutionary classes excluding the impure elements of traitors to the nation (漢奸反動派) . . . The realization of democracy through the exclusion of pro-Japanese and traitors to the country and nation and the formation of a true popular front are what we have been hoping for. This we can again ordain as the 'path toward progressive democracy'.[21]

If this was a central moment in the Korean communist movement, in which the potential power of the concept of nation was re-evaluated, was this, then, nationalistic or communistic? Under national (*minjok*) communism, even though nationalism could be disavowed, the nation could not be. What would remain as a configurable political subject if 'nation' were removed in opposition to 'traitor to the nation'? For instance, the construction of national culture was re-evaluated under the conditions of 'a struggle against imperialism and fascism, and a struggle to clean up feudal vestiges'. In short, the construction of national culture based on the condition of 'the shared joy and delight of production' was positively appraised through 'historical-social limitations of a world culture in which everyone could share a genuine, intimate communal sense'.[22] Under the global nature of the international communist movement that posited Asia as a regional mediation unit, this practice was retro-fitted and re-presented as 'the national'. However, despite the appealing force of negative expressions like 'pro-Japanese' and 'traitor to the nation', this sort of removal engendered the propagation of multiple symbols for the representation of all that 'remained' after the negative forces were removed. Eventually, the Communist Party became the proletarian party or the people's worker party, and the term communism faded away until it was unutterable. Negation of negation is indeed powerful, but it is a passion without substance.

The principle of progressive democracy was above all a form of realism based on ideological plurality in the division of the Korean Peninsula by the US–Soviet occupation. In this process, the three vectors of history, region and subjectivity were considered. First is the theory of the five

21   Sin Nam-ch'ŏl, 'Minchu chuŭi wa humanijŭm – Chosŏn sasang munhwa ŭi tangmyŏn chŏngse wa kŭkŏsŭi kŭmhu panghyang e taehayŏ' (April 1946), in Chŏng Chong-hyŏn, ed., *Sin Nam-ch'ŏl munjang sŏnjip II*, (The Collected Writings of Sin Nam-ch'ŏl), (Seoul: Sŏnggyunkwan University Press, 2013), pp. 221–2.
22   Sin Nam-ch'ŏl, 'Minjok munhwaron' ('The Theory of National [Korean] Culture') *Sin Nam-ch'ŏl munjang sŏnjip II*, (The Collected Writings of Sin Nam-ch'ŏl), (Seoul: Sŏnggyunkwan University Press, 2013), pp. 186–7.

stages of history by which the Comintern or Soviet's international campaign assigned the post-liberation Korea to a 'stage' of bourgeois democracy. Second is Asia as a regional limitation. Mao's move towards New Democracy Theory was a shift away from the so-called historical develop-ment limitations and regional conditions of Asia, which were, for Marx, a conundrum in his theories of Asian stagnation and the Asiatic Mode of Production. Asia, considered as an instance of the fine-tuning of the global communist movement for regional mediations, utilized 'situation analysis' and 'strategies and tactics' while applying the problem of 'the *minjok*' under the de-/post-colonization sequence. Third is the nation (*minjok*). The inter-national tasks of overcoming imperialism and fascism, as well as the domestic tasks of dissolving colonial and feudal vestiges, brought about the development of multiple revolutionary classes for the establishment of a democratic state. The all-encompassing name for such classes was the nation, which was equated with compatriots and the working masses.

In the achievement of mass organization and subject formation, the latent power of the nation was of the greatest consideration. In post-liber-ation South Korea, the liquidation of pro-Japanese elements and traitors to the nation was presented as the core task in this communist opportu-nity. Although changes occurred by way of the three elements of world history, Asia, and the *minjok*, all were based on 'democracy', and despite the subject formation of the people, the workers and the masses were built within a framework of *minjok* liberation. Democracy became the fodder of the enemy, and along with discourse on state construction, it was reduced to a liberal democracy marked by electoralism. This was not a strategic failure, but rather a failure of concept and symbol.

Communism/Democracy/Nationalism: From Double Negative to Double Alternative

An idea always requires a concept. Concepts mediate between lofty abstractions and practical campaigns. The communist 'frugality' displayed by the liberation-era Asian communist movement displayed the impossi-bility of rapid communist evolution outside Europe, due to regional or local limitations and historical stage theory. Asian communism remained floundering in that notorious net of the Asiatic Mode of Production until the Chinese Communist Revolution, in certain cases even until the 1960s, only to continue in altered form as 'semi-feudalism' during the apotheosis of the South Korean social movements of the 1980s. What state are we in now? Looking back at the theses of the Comintern, this question relates to the approvals and oppositions to important decisions after 1942 by the 'communist fatherland' – the Soviet Union. Pak Hŏn-yŏng's claim, 'Whether the Communist Party of Korea emerges in an era of unlawfulness or lawfully, it supports the bourgeois democratic class and the construction of democracy', was true both internationally and locally.

Between vernacular communism and communistic vernacularism – or, more exactly, national communism and communistic nationalism – there were numerous stages, each of which required the 'idea of communism' to be concealed in order for the struggle to ensue. Under such a restriction, the discourse and theories concerning South Korean communism's social formation and political circumstances have relegated the ideology of communism to a state of immaturity, in which it is always 'too early' for implementation. The difficulty of this indeterminable signifier was induced not by the essential issue of the common or property question, but rather by the imposition of stage theory. Stage theory that calculates the extent of temporal delay, that produces numerous metaphors about communism, metaphorical stages, still lie in our path. Presented in a schema à la Roman Jacobson, South Korean communism is composed of metaphors in the impulse for similarity while in a state of suppressed impulse for contiguity, for metonymy. ('Communism [is] . . . progressive democracy . . . populism . . . labour centrism . . . national liberation . . . Third Worldism . . . and an extreme categorization under the regime of national division which includes all of these would be "commie" or "red".') Therefore, this communism (through stages of broad yet tightly woven metaphors) can never be gathered into a history of expressions. When the conditions of history are stages and its divisions are prohibitions, what it reaches is the indeterminateness of communist ideology.

What results from multiple democracies – including controlled official democracies – with the adjectival metaphors of locally bounded concepts is obvious. If, according to conceptual history and speech theory, essential and inevitable relationships exist between speech acts and movement, no matter what we take up as 'Idea', we will at some point end up fighting for supplementation or proxy ideology. For instance, this eventual fighting for democracy, what will it look like, you ask?

The essential difficulties lie in democracy. As Slavoj Žižek claims, 'In democracy, one can fight for truth, but not decide what IS truth.'[23] As for

---

23   Slavoj Žižek, *Organs Without Bodies* (London: Routledge, 2007), p. 197.

South Korean democracy, upon what is it founded? What sort of truth does it desire? What type of decisions has it made? In a society that demands democracy itself as absolute truth, this is an inevitable problem possessing the actual practice of the concept of democracy. As an example of a state in which the primary factors of realistic constraints, although removed, still remain connected to the 'concept', the adjectival limitations that result from substantive absence have arguably accomplished nothing in the end. Reclaiming a concept from the enemy is always more difficult than fighting for one's own concept. The same can be said of Asia or *minjok*. Asian communities, irrigation cultivation communes, the Asiatic Mode of Production, Asian identity, and other negative limitations – after their dissolution by the strong growth of Korean and other Asian economies, these may be converted to positive limitations, or even competencies.

Things like democracy with Asian values and Korean-style democracy are examples of this. When concepts such as 'Our Socialism', Chinese-style socialism, and conversely Korean-style democracy and Asian-style capitalism emerged, these local limitations were construed as exclusively conservative by both ends of the spectrum. On the other hand, although there were attempts to recapture this type of limitation in a manner similar to Christianity's fulfilment theory (for example, the claim of 'global democracy' by Kim Dae-jung that the tradition of democracy had existed in Korea and Asia also, and was fulfilled by the [re]arrival of the [Western] institution, argued against Singaporean 'patriarch' Lee Kuan Yew's outlook on Cultural Destiny and Asian Values[24]), the fact that this logic is advantageous to the logic of tradition/democracy is certain. The conceptualization of regional limitation that included official, state-directed nationalism and resistance nationalism (Korean nationalism ≠ populist nationalism, *minjok* restoration ≠ *minjok* liberation) was endlessly propagated, and in fact as long as this was accepted, animosity often vanished. (As long as one's subjectivation process is aligned with the nation, anyone could say that they lived for the nation.)

The course proceeds on and on, up to those Muslims who dream about a specific Arab modernity that would magically bypass the destructive aspects of Western global capitalism . . . The recourse to multitude is

---

24   Fareed Zakaria, 'Culture is Destiny: A Conversation with Lee Kwan Yew', *Foreign Affairs* 73: 2 (March–April 1994); Kim Dae-Jung, 'Is Culture Destiny? The Myth of Asia's Anti-Democratic Values', *Foreign Affairs* 73: 6 (November–December 1994).

false not because it does not recognize a unique fixed 'essence' of modernity but because multiplication functions as the disavowal of antagonism that inheres to the notion of modernity as such.[25]

The history of South Korean communism displays the dynamics of a process that is marked by the inosculations of locally limited yet disparate and alternative adjectives on the one hand, and the disavowal of hostilities internal to society by exclusion, on the other. The man who appropriated national liberation and progress in the name of national restoration, autonomy, and Korean-style democracy is Pak Chŏng-hŭi, known for his theory of the defeat of communism through unification of the peninsula, the successor to Japanophilism, and bulldozer-style high modernism, all for the sake of *minjok* revival.

Communism has fought an extended battle in the name of democracy and the nation. However, the true propaganda of capitalism was always democracy, and 'today the enemy is not called Empire or Capital. It's called Democracy.'[26] It is claimed that all capital is international 'national capital'. After struggling for liberation from state domination and authority by daily gatherings at the public square, only to continue the suffering of incomparably arduous, inevitable political existence, it is difficult to deny the empty, though earnest, signifier that is democracy. In South Korea, where non-democratic signifiers of liberation are prohibited, Žižek's question, 'Do those who want to distinguish another ("radical") democracy from its existing form and thereby cut off its links with capitalism, not commit the same mistake?'[27] is unavoidable and demands attention.

The history of the historical concept of democracy as substitution for the ideology of communism, as laid out in this chapter, suggests a particular conundrum for Korean communist history. This is the question of whether ideologies existing only as proxy concepts can arrive at their intended target of their own volition. Have we fought using the 'concept' of communism? Through the process of deducing the truth of the 'idea' of communism, could we have established it as a sequence of subjectivation

---

25   Žižek, *Organs Without Bodies*, p. 186.
26   Alberto Toscano, 'From State to the World: Badiou and Anti-Capitalism', *Communication and Cognition* 37: 3–4 (2004), p. 200.
27   Žižek, *Organs without Bodies*, pp. 186–7. The battle between the adjectives 'original or cosmopolis' and 'indigenous or vernacular' is the perennial debate between 'Democracy' and 'Asian Values'. Does there remain anything to obtain from the contraposing of the original/radical democracy in our style, Chinese-characteristic, Asian, Korean and Japanese-style democracy?

while thinking of its place in history? Could the Idea of communism or the Real of communism still exist without communistic practices or speech acts? There 'were' four methods of reading about, writing about, and acting towards communism in South Korea: 1) On communism, speaking about something other than communism. Where the conceptual development and ideological outlook of communism were stymied, substituting symbols and imaginations for communism were inevitably produced. Things like progressi··e democracy, new democracy, coalitional democracy, and democracy of the working masses appeared as proxy metaphors in a non-metonymic development. Periodically, the names of 'places' (Cheju, Yŏsun, Puma, Kwangju!), 'events' (3 April, 18 May 1987, June!), or 'objects' (barricades, Molotov cocktails, candlelight!) themselves would also become metaphors. 2) Conceptualization through regional/local limitations. While spatial limitations in categories such as 'Asian' or 'national' expressed the vernacularity of South Korean communism, they also produced endless temporal stages (stage theories). Not where, but 'when' are we, and who are we with? As proxy concepts and restrictions of spatialized historical time came together, 'vernacular communism', which cannot be called communism, emerged. I call this a 'step of metaphor'. 3) The practice of negative negation. The third method of reading and writing about, or acting toward communism is 'removing and reading' negated adjectives and prefixes like the 'anti-' in anti-communism, or 'writing in double negatives', such as in anti–anti-communism. Removal and hyphenation became serialized in the negative 'movement' and ideological imagination. Yet the lack of philosophical content resulted in encounters with the Real. 4) The 'letters' of communism that cover the ground and capture the mind. This was where the method of writing and reading what was prohibited may be found. However, the ideology of the common – because it was the language of communism – could not be made public. This reading and writing lingered in the ethics of the mind, or was substituted by a ravaged body that represented the vestiges of the movement. The 'treasured documents' of a dead person littering the ground are but one symbol of the South Korean communist movement.[28] At times these situations came to be viewed as the exclusion of the development of concept, hostility towards theory, and the establishment of the real as absolute. The combination of the last two difficulties, 3 and 4, was deemed to constitute 'imagination without symbols'. This is because

---

28   Im Kyŏng-sŏk, *Ijŏl ˌsu ŏmnŭn hyŏngmyŏnggaˌdŭl ŭi taehan kirok* ('The Unforgettable Records of the Revolutionaries'), (Seoul: Yŏksa pipy'ongsa, 2008), p. 229.

negative negation, such as the opposition to anti-communism, resembles 'object a' as an indeterminable concept, or perhaps the symbol X as the redacted, the erased, a purely negative concept of limitation (*grenzbegriff*).

Of course, if there was a history to the debate, then a fierce public debate also raged on the issue of the common. In particular, I have not yet mentioned another sequence in the 1980s, the exception to an exception. At any rate, it is impossible to write off the ideology of communism without speaking in terms of inequality, reading and conversion, demonstration, exile and asylum, arrest and imprisonment, escape and border-crossing (and sometimes betrayal or secession), reinstatement, campaigning and holocaust. The horror within the real appeared in the form of deranged symbols. Korean communism? The 'Korean communism' or 'Korean communist' I speak of today is in fact an impossible signifier that functions as the subject (of a sentence). Historically, 'Korean communism' has been an underground language, a void signifier. As soon as the signifiers that substitute for 'communist', such as the nation, the *demos*, the populace and the workers, connected with an event, become personalized, the impulse for public safety to drive the entire social movement into 'commies' and 'spies' continues. Despite the void and substitution-supplementation, the categorization of the 'communism' imagined by the regime operates omnidirectionally. On the other hand, the idea of communism is infinite. If the seemingly unlimited analytic ability of the regime is an artificial infinitude within the bounds of its anti-communist manifestation, then the Idea of South Korean communism is a sublime infinitude. If we say that modern philosophy can begin from the fixedness of the subject, then the communism that could not be located in 'subject', 'actor', and 'clear-cut identification' was not the object of philosophical inquiry in South Korea, but rather the 'object a', the very wellspring of truth and desire.

Reading the linguistic landscape is akin to ascending an endless metaphorical staircase. Between the steps or stages of this metaphorical staircase is the negation of negation, and it is on this point that I shall conclude. According to Balibar, when considering the bankruptcy of twentieth-century real socialism, communism must be formulated in terms of *an alternative to the alternative*, as it was historically realized.[29] But we cannot simply interpret this as asking: 'Do you have an alternative?' In searching for infinite truth within limitless possibility, we must enter in

---

29   Balibar and Negri, 'On the Common, Universality, and Communism', p. 321.

through portals of events. Metonymy realizing communism – eventualizing the unfolding of the conceptual movement through revolt – desire without yielding.

The question of whether we have ever had a performative understanding of communism has always encountered the predetermined task of the negation of negation. This is its limitation, but also its potentiality. The void of 'ideology' between metaphors and negatives also means infinity. Although paradoxical, there is some truth in the violence of the expression 'tin-can commie' (*kkangt'ong ppalgaengi*). The history of South Korean communism is really the history of the tin-can commie. When a can is filled, a prison is completed. However, at the point when the can overflows, the idea becomes both an 'alternative' and an 'alternative to an alternative'. Let us refrain from just filling the can of the enemy with substance. Filling the enemy's can (liberal democracy) with our substance is the very cause of our current tragedy. Between the historical and current sequence of the negation of negation (anti-anti-communism) and the practical question of an alternative to the alternative (alt-communism), South Korean communism remains an ideological hypothesis. The day when communist ideologies are not replaced by broken faces and substitution supplementations will soon come. Think in the standstill.

10 Unpopular Politics: The Collective, the Communist and the Popular in Recent Thai History

Rosalind C. Morris

They call it a 'democratic coup d'état' *see. You have to have a lot of* coups d'état. *Otherwise it isn't democracy.*

Khamsing Srinawk, *The Politician*

When Yingluck Shinawatra was removed from prime-ministerial office in a coup in May 2014, political theorists, historians of the state in Thailand and scholars of tragedy could all imagine, if only on the basis of an antiquated formalism, that they were watching the tale of Antigone play itself out in a Siamese mode.[1] Here was a sister, apparently sacrificing herself to her brother's cause, facing off against the generals, and bearing the banner of blood on the staff of duty. The leader of a party founded by her brother, Thaksin Shinawatra (who was himself ousted from the prime minister's office in a 2006 coup), was formally charged with corruption and negligence in relation to both political appointments and a rice-subsidy programme that had transferred billions of baht to the rural periphery. Her opponents claimed that this latter policy was a mere extension of her brother's rule and, to that extent, she appears for them to be as guilty of privileging familial bonds over national interests as of any particular crime. In this sense, her error redoubles her brother's, for it

---

1   The essay was written in 2014 and finally revised in 2015. History does not share the tempo of book production and, inevitably, the events, persons and offices to which this essay makes reference have been followed by others. New developments and configurations of influence have emerged and others have receded. Some issues, such as the plight of the Rohingya immigrants fleeing Myanmar had become more visible. But these were not new phenomena, except insofar as visibility constitutes a particular dimension of eventfulness. Moreover, in early 2016, there was still no House of Representatives in Thailand and government was in the hands of a body appointed by the 2014 coup group that called itself the National Council for Peace and Order. I have not attempted to revise the essay to keep up with the constant and often microscopic re-alignments of power and personal interest. What is written here remains my assessment of the scene as it appeared in 2014, and it is my belief and hope that the political logics that I observed and have attempted to analyze in these pages remains silent.

was his confusion of family and economy that had led to his own conviction for corruption when, in 2006, he was found guilty of illegally
transferring shares and other assets to kin and members of his household
staff as a means of evading taxes.[2]

The Hegelian formula of tragedy based in the reading of Antigone
famously characterizes the opposition between the state and family as a
function of the contradiction between ethical life in its 'spiritual *univeral-
ity*' and its 'natural' state. These forms of life ought otherwise to be in
harmony, but under certain circumstances, writes Hegel, their contradic-
toriness is brought into active relief. The pathos of that situation, however,
is not a function of the opposition but of the fact that the characters who
find themselves cleaving to one or other of the ethical structures are also,
and at the same time, under the sway of what they oppose, so that,
together, they constitute what Hegel refers to as a totality in concrete
existence. If there is an element of Antigonal tragedy in the plot of
Yingluck's rise and fall (for now) from power, then, it would derive from
the fact that an opposition between state and family, as ethical universality and natural ethics, has been historically produced as a dimension of
political actuality in Thailand today. Under such conditions, Yingluck
would be as compelled by state law as by a sense of personal duty, even if
and when she acts on the basis of the latter.[3] That such an understanding
dominates the political scene in Thailand today is evidenced by the fact
that the ruling junta lifted the ban on her movements and granted her
permission to travel to France in July 2014, on the occasion of her brother's birthday, with the calm assurance that she had confirmed her
willingness to return and submit to their investigations.

While the spectre of Antigone and Hegel's return hovers uncannily

---

2   Rosalind C. Morris, 'Intimacy and Corruption in Thailand's Age of Transparency', in Andrew
Shryock, ed., *Off Stage, On Display: Intimacy and Ethnography in the Age of Public Culture* (Stanford, CA:
Stanford University Press, 2004), pp. 225–43.

3   It goes without saying that this rendition of the Antigone story is a Hegelian one, far from the
more radical narrative of a sublime avowal of death that Lacan discerns in the play. For Lacan,
Antigone's determination towards death, made even before Polynices' burial has been forbidden by
Creon, signals her transcendence-in-transgression of the opposition between family and state, social
obligation and personal will. In his analysis, she defies both norm and reason in her singular pursuit
of her own (radically asocial) *jouissance*. See Jacques Lacan, *Seminar VII: The Ethics of Psychoanalysis*,
ed. Jacques-Alain Miller, transl. Dennis Porter (New York: Norton, 1993). There is, of course, nothing of this radicality in Yingluck Shinawatra's political self-sacrifice, but the paucity of narrative
figurations with which to think what Paul Allen Miller has translated as the 'same womb-ed' in a
drama pitting bureaucratic formalism against dynastic competition makes the Sophocles play seem
relevant for Thailand today. All the more so because an implicitly neo-Hegelian understanding of the
state underwrites the insistent sacralization of the Thai state today. See Paul Allen Miller, 'The
Sublime Object and the Ethics of Interpretation', *Phoenix* 61: 1–2 (Spring 2007), p. 4.

above Thailand with the ghosts of speculative fantasies killed in the financial crises of the last two decades, it does so in the shadow of a vociferous
and nearly uninterrupted insurrectionary practice. Such insurrection is
testimony not to the paradigmatic opposition described by Hegel, but to
a set of circumstances both unprecedented and misrecognized as mere
repetitions. What the Antigone scheme hides is the place of capital in
governance, and in the debate about what the state ought to be, what
form it should take, and what role it should play in mediating between
capital and the population at large. On the other hand, what the Thaksin/
Yingluck drama reveals is that the manifold contradictions which today
structure the social field can appear to be reconciled in a totality bearing
the name of the people. In Thailand today, the name under which that
internally differentiated totality acquires its seeming coherence vacillates
between the monarch and the leader, Bhumipol Adulyadej and Thaksin
Shinawatra. It is determined by the conflict between communism and
populism, and by the displacement of the former by the latter. To begin to
understand this situation, we will want to historicize what otherwise
appears as a simple cycle of governmental destruction and restoration in
popular uprisings and military coups.[4] Doing so requires an analysis of
the trajectory of communism within the country, not because it is the only
alternative to the contemporary impasse but because it reveals so much
about the contradictions that have yet to be surpassed. It also requires an
analysis of the forces and ideas that conspired to negate the communist
hypothesis and the goal of radical equality. Let us then consider them.

Accusation, Contradiction, Symptom: Speaking of Thaksin

It is a remarkable fact that, today, one of the wealthiest families in the
history of Thailand, a family whose capital has been accumulated across
the space of only four generations, can be accused simultaneously of illegitimate accumulation and illegitimate dispensation; of playing the market
and betraying the market; of monarchical, or at least king-making ambitions and communist tendencies; of authoritarianism and populism. But

---

4   There is a certain resemblance between this description of a recursive destruction of Thai
governments and the formal continuity in resurrection that Marx once claimed was the hallmark of
the Asiatic Mode of Production. I want to be clear, therefore, that the not-so-strange phenomenon of
apparent crisis and perduring stability is not here attributed to any Asiatic, or Siamese, cultural principle. To the contrary, it is a function of specifically material conditions, and of the valorization of
stability that has been produced, in Thailand, in the interest and under the imagistic sway of the
military–monarchical alliance.

these are precisely the accusations that have been brought to bear against the Shinawatra family, and most especially the brother-and-sister team of Thaksin and Yingluck, over the last decade and a half. From the itiner-ant-farmer patriarch who emigrated from Guangdong in 1860 and married a Siamese woman, to his son, the investor in bus-routes and petrol stations, to his grandson, the architect of Thailand's massive silk industry, and his great-grandson, the dominant figure in its telecommuni-cations networks, the Shinawatra family appears to incarnate the principles of an economy that has, at last, relinquished the feudal logic that underwrote the polity well into the twentieth century. With no basis in land, except as a commodity for speculation, the Shinawatra family's power stands as testimony to an historical transformation in the nature of the economy – one that pits industrial capital, agricultural capital and a residually feudal aristocracy against each other. However, the accusations against Thaksin and Yingluck are not only a product of the tension between these economic forces and forms (schematizable as such only from within the mode-of-production narrative). They are also evidence of a discontinuity and a dissonance between transformations in the economic domain, on one hand, and changes that have unevenly and with different intensities afflicted the political realm, on the other. In this sense, as Hamlet would have it, the time of Thai contemporaneity is out of joint – not with the rest of the world, but with itself.

The accusations against the Shinawatras are not all of the same order. Indeed, they can be divided into two distinct, if related, sets of contradic-tory claims. The first (of illegitimate accumulation and illegitimate dispensation, of playing the market and betraying the market) are organ-ized according to economic axioms. The second (king-making ambitions and communist tendencies, authoritarianism and populism) are struc-tured by political axioms. To a significant degree, the latter two couplets are accorded an autonomous status, with the former being read as the mere instruments and forms of appearance of the latter. This occurs every time Thaksin, Yingluck and the *Pheua Thai* ('For Thais') party are accused of vote-buying and parliamentary dictatorship – of manipulating the economy and bureaucratic procedure to secure power. However, the apparent autonomization of the political effaces the inverse process, which occurs simultaneously and on its basis – namely, the subordination of political life to economic imperatives. Only under the conditions in which economic power dictates law can someone like Thaksin be said to 'buy' the appearance of representativeness. And this is true despite the fact that, since the 1980s, electoral office has been necessary to secure authority in areas where, previously, economic power and the threat of force could suffice.[5]

Together, the linked sequence of contradictory accusations condenses the political crisis now afflicting the Thai nation. Part of that crisis is linked to the fragile nature of the constituted authority in a nation where coups (twelve since 1932) regularly entail the suspension, invalidation and rewriting of the constitution, as well as the recurrent dissolution of the institutions of governance. Part of it derives from the ambiguous status of the monarchy, conceived as head of state in an electoral democracy (about which more will be said). And still another part derives from the more general and still unresolved conflict over state form that first began to appear at the end of the 1980s[6] – in the very moment that the communist hypothesis of radical equality was finally severed from the governmental project of the party-state.[7] By then, most of Thailand's own communists had relinquished armed struggle, returned from the jungle, and, in not inconsiderable numbers, embraced the culture concept and the idea of socially meaningful inequality in place of class contradiction as a description of Thai society.[8]

In another time, speaking in another idiom, we might have said that

---

5   On the emergence of the 'electrocats' (*nak leuktang*), see Kasian Tejapira, 'Toppling Thaksin', *New Left Review* II:39 (May–June 2006), pp. 13–14.

6   Kevin Hewison, 'Of Regimes, State and Pluralities: Thai Politics Enters the 1990s', in Kevin Hewison, Richard Robison and Gary Rodan, eds, *Southeast Asia in the 1990s: Authoritarianism, Democracy and Capitalism* (Melbourne: Unwin & Allen, 1993).

7   This severance has, of course, not been performed everywhere. The possibility of a dictatorship of the proletariat, administered by a party-state, remains a powerful ambition for significant numbers of people in African states, and in some Latin American ones. There, too, one sees the recurrent devolution of communism into populism, organized around the figure of one or another leader. Achille Mbembe has read this phenomenon in the idiom of the fetish, but that concept seems most appropriate in contexts where the party-state and the ideology of representativeness are least developed. In the present situation, I am persuaded by Badiou's argument that the personality cult expresses the desire for a singular guarantee of an otherwise ungroundable claim to representation – a structure that is ubiquitously attested by the obsession with 'leadership' as a panacea for institutional failure. Achille Mbembe, 'The Aesthetics of Vulgarity', transl. Janet Roitman and Murray Last, in *On the Postcolony* (Berkeley, CA: University of California Press, 2001).

8   The party's membership was always very small relative to the estimated number of sympathizers. Less than 20,000 can be counted among the party's armed forces, though more than a million people were thought to have shared its ideological project. The first defections were from the intellectuals who had joined the party following the massacre of students in 1976, and they did so on one of two bases: either the Maoist strategy of peasant insurrection was seen to be inappropriate to an increasingly industrialized economy, as Thailand's was becoming in the 1970s and '80s, or Marxism-Leninism was said to be culturally foreign to the logic of patron–clientship inscribed in so-called traditional culture. On the cultural turn and the end of communism, see Rosalind Morris, 'Populist Politics in Asian Networks: Positions for Rethinking the Question of Political Subjectivity', special twentieth anniversary issue of *Positions: East Asia Cultures Critique* 20: 1(2012), ed. Tani Barlow. See also Kasian, 'Toppling Thaksin'.

the current crisis consists in the blockage of crisis, in the failure to achieve the destructive precipitation of the new. For every eruption of mass protest during the past twenty-five years, there has been a corollary moment of negation and re-encompassment. The present situation is marked by a stuttering, repetitive quality, with the military defence of both capital and the monarchy providing the leitmotif of constant resta-bilization. Its current slogan, coined by the ruling military junta and turned into a romantic pop song, is 'return to happiness' (*kheun khwamsuk*).[9] The rhetoric of return cannot, however, conceal the fact that there has also emerged a new set of dynamics that both open onto a criti-cal horizon and threaten to undermine it by reabsorbing egalitarian energies into populist forms.

In this chapter I am interested in how and why populism and communism can appear, from a certain perspective – namely, the perspective of contem-porary financial capital in a monarchist state – to be indistinguishable in a manner that forecloses rather than refutes the division and the difference that communism would entail. That this perspective should be disputed is without question, but its vulnerability to critique does not make it any less powerful in the discursively constituted reality of the contemporary Thai world. Nonetheless, my concern here is not with the particular content of any accusation – Is Thaksin a populist? Is Yingluck? Rather, I am interested in what populism signifies, what antagonism it encodes and conceals.[10] And I

9   See the official statement of the Thai government at: thaigov.go.th/en/program-1en/item/83780-national-council-for-peace-and-order-ncpo-program-bring-back-happiness-to-the-nation.html.   The song and its accompanying music video is available on embassy websites (for example, 'Thailand in Focus: "Returning Happiness to the Thai Kingdom" song', at thaiembassy.org). It features images of a cavalcade bearing yellow flags followed by shots of the king and queen in various activities associated with the king's so-called subsistence-economy policy – planting and examining rice. Most of the video is, however, devoted to the army in various peace-keeping and emergency-service provision roles. It is doubtful that any state has ever produced a more salubrious anthem, nor one more likely to be confused with a love song. Interestingly, the edited version of the video released on Youtube focuses on ethnic inclusiveness and professional diversity, but does not include any images of the royal couple, perhaps to immunize them against appropriations that might then be vulnerable to defacement by one of the many anonymous anti-military and anti-royalist blogs operated by expatriate Thais (youtube.com/watch?v=2Yo8BOVyOqk). Inevitably, and despite these precautions, a sharp parody, with inserted frames of violent clashes and the army shooting directly into protesting crowds, is also now available online: 'Thai Army Happiness', at youtube.com/watch?v=oQZvVAZrNYI.

10   I agree with Žižek that populism is typically characterized by a gesture that reifies an existing social antagonism and gives it not only a false content but an ontological one, in the form of an enemy. I agree further that it entails an analogous reification and subordination of the governing political Idea to a nameable figure, and thereby eliminates what Adorno insisted was the essence of dialectical materialism, namely a recognition of the simultaneous difference and co-extensiveness of Concept and actuality. Having said as much, I do not believe that Stalinism or Maoism escape the accusation of a comparable reification. On the latter point alone, it seems to me, Laclau's critique of Žižek's analysis can be admitted. But I side with Žižek in believing that the danger of populist movements

am interested in what may be foreclosed but also promised under the prohibited name of communism as a result of this conflation.

But, first, a brief survey of the scene.

A Popular Scene, a Populist Triangle

On almost any given day in Thailand, one can find people protesting. In many instances, the protestors are making claims on the state for the amelioration of economic injustices. Often, this entails the demand for subsidies, or fixed commodity prices. In other instances, however, the protests are directly addressed to questions concerning the representativeness and legitimacy of the current government – though not of the state per se. Thus, yellow-shirted protestors associated with the People's Alliance for Democracy (PAD) protested against the legitimacy of Thaksin's reign in 2006 on the grounds of his corruption and market interventionism. They protested against Yingluck's regime for extending subsidies (and thus violating free-market principles), and because she was said to be the means by which Thaksin continued to exercise power despite having been banned from office (the accusation of shadow governmentality is almost always coupled with one of vote-buying). In contrapuntal opposition to the yellow-shirted protestors are the red-shirted members of the United Front for Democracy against Dictatorship (UDD) and their supporters, who defend the representativeness of Thaksin, Yingluck and the Pheua Thai party on the grounds of its overwhelming electoral majority, as well as the moral legitimacy of their policies aimed at the mitigation of inequality and the attenuation of rural–urban disparities in particular.

Swollen with the bodies that bear their affiliations in a reduced totemism of colour, the streets of Bangkok appear, from afar, as spectacles of a desire for the political. Protests, marches and rallies regularly interrupt the flows of traffic and the rhythms of commerce, even as they are

---

lies in their structurally overdetermined incapacity to provide the terms of their self-limitation. In the absence of such a principle, populism seems invariably to drive towards identitarian nationalism and the absolutization of enmity, for which Schmitt's political ontology provides the ideological rationalization. See Slavoj Žižek, 'Against the Populist Temptation', *Critical Inquiry* 32: 3 (Spring 2006); Ernesto Laclau, 'Why Constructing a People is the Main Task of Radical Politics Today', *Critical Inquiry* 32: 4 (Summer 2006). See also Laclau, *On Populist Reason* (London/New York: Verso, 2005). On dialectical materialism, see Theodor Adorno, *Negative Dialectics*, transl. E.B. Ashton (New York: Continuum, 1973). But see, on the difficulties with this translation, Fredric Jameson, *Late Marxism: Adorno, or, the Persistence of the Dialectic* (New York/London: Verso, 1990). Schmitt's theory of the enemy as the essence of the political appears in Carl Schimtt, *The Concept of the Political*, transl. George Schwab (Chicago: University of Chicago Press, 1996).

absorbed into it. Food stalls and merchandize kiosks crust the periphery of the streets or the edges of parks around the protests, as vendors offer T-shirts, buttons, flags and other insignia of affiliation, as well as CDs and DVDs featuring the musicians who perform for one or other of the political assemblages.[11] Patronized by the police as well as by the protestors and those not insignificant numbers who come to watch this political theatre without ideological commitment, these spontaneous and ephemeral markets are the symptoms of a social intensity that the protests and rallies both constitute, and that their organizers attempt to structure towards political ends.[12] Yet, as anyone familiar with Thailand knows, the spectrum of political sayability is remarkably narrow, constrained by a prohibition on communism, an increasingly prosecuted *lèse-majesté* law, and a threat of force that repeatedly exercises itself in the name of order.[13] Nor do the protestors entirely disavow this containment; most are avowed anti-communists and staunchly monarchist.

The UDD claims to act largely in the interest of poor farmers (but see below), and has a logo reminiscent of the workerist aesthetics of the 1930s. While it is sometimes impugned for Maoism because its membership includes former members of the Communist Party of Thailand (CPT), its rank and file are generally reticent to avow revolutionary politics.[14] There are also former CPT members among the leaders of the

---

11   For a detailed ethnographic account of the place of music and the market in the red-shirt protests, see Benjamin Tausig, 'Bangkok is Ringing', PhD dissertation, New York University, 2013. See also Benjamin Tausig, 'Neoliberalism's Moral Overtones: Music, Money, and Morality at Thailand's Red Shirt Protests', *Culture, Theory and Critique* 55: 2 (2014).

12   I have discussed the significance of the ideologically uncommitted members in producing the image of the mass and the basis for mass-mediated political subjectivation in Rosalind C. Morris, 'Surviving Pleasure at the Periphery: Chiang Mai and the Photographies of Political Trauma in Thailand, 1976–1992', *Public Culture* 10: 2 (1998).

13   The tradition of using *lèse-majesté* to mitigate political opposition is long-standing in Thailand, but its increasing prosecution in the last decade can be variously read as a symptom of growing anxiety within the ruling military–monarchical alliance about the possibility of real republicanism, as the last gasp of an ageing monarch whose heir lacks popular support, or as a recognition of the increasingly significant role of ideological contest in the public sphere. On the history of the legal category and its political instrumentalization, see David Streckfuss, 'Kings in the Age of Nations: The Paradox of Lèse-Majesté as Political Crime in Thailand', *Comparative Studies in Society and History* 37: 3 (July 1995); and *Truth on Trial in Thailand: Defamation, Treason, and Lèse-Majesté* (London: Routledge, 2011). On recent cases, see Pavin Chachavalpongpun, 'Thailand tightens Lese-Majeste Screws', *Asia Sentinel*, 8 May 2013, available at asiasentinel.com. The most recent charge, brought in July 2014, accuses the former Pheua Thai MP and one-time UDD co-leader Colonel Apiwan Wiriyachai of making statements offensive to the monarchy during a rally speech in Petchaburi, in June 2011.

14   In an article published in *Asia Times* in May 2013, William Barnes made the assertion that the UDD was not only communist but actively avowing a violent overthrow of the government. He cited former CPT member Therdpoum Chaidee on the Maoist inspiration of the tactics following the grenade attacks that marred a 10 April protest rally, leading to twenty-five deaths and more than 800

yellow-shirted PAD, who similarly shirk the kind of radical negation (destruction of the state and appropriation of its apparatus) that a previous generation of Mao-inspired revolutionaries insisted was the precondition of liberation. There is, in fact, no correlation between previous affiliation and current ideological sympathies. In Thailand, former CPT members are as likely to speak of their revolutionary past as youthful delusion as they are to avow it in the form of nostalgic attachment. All the more remarkable, then, are the constantly resurgent crowds of people clamouring at the gates of power, calling for more representative government and, in the very presencing of their bodies, demonstrating their distrust of representation. Their materialization in the already-crowded streets is something like a short-circuiting of the representational process – a drive to access the political apparatus immediately.

Able neither to reconcile these contradictory forces nor to heal over the gap in the Symbolic where competing ideological commitments have sundered but not entirely replaced a fantasy of national unity, both groups hold fast to the idea of the monarchy as a force that can guarantee what otherwise seems destined to fracture irreparably: a singularity to stand in for the lack of either group's capacity to achieve universality. Yet, even as it avows its fidelity to the monarchy, the UDD and its supporters gravitate around the figure of Thaksin Shinawatra. Their cultic adoration of his person constitutes both a shadow of the royal cult and a throwback to those personality cults that were associated with the kind of class-party whose demise on the international stage made Thaksin's rise to power possible.

In those contexts where the working classes are putatively represented

---

injuries. According to Barnes, Therdpoum explains the red-shirt movement's adulation of Thaksin as a temporary but affectively necessary stage in the longer-term movement towards socialism. But he also quotes Jaran Dittapichai as saying that the protest group had adopted 'Mao Zedong's method of thinking' and some of his techniques, including the establishment of a united front'. He continues: 'I was a communist and several leaders were former communists . . . but the red shirt people don't like communism or socialism.' See William Barnes, 'Thai Power Grows from the Barrel of a Gun', *Asia Times*, 13 May 2010, available at atimes.com. For a stinging rebuttal of Barnes and Therdpoum, see the anonymous blog of the Political Prisoners of Thailand, wherein its authors both question the degree to which red-shirt members actually desired the return of Thaksin (in 2010) and cast aspersions on Therdpoum's own analysis of Maoism: 'Mao's main revolutionary strategy was countryside encircling the cities and peasant revolution. The current actions look more like the Paris Commune than a rural-based armed revolution.' See Political Prisoners of Thailand, 'Red Shirts as Communists', 18 May 2010, at thaipoliticalprisoners.wordpress.com. At the time, Yingluck Shinawatra had not yet entered the scene as heir and proxy for her brother, and it was possible to imagine that the movement would evade the populist temptations of the cult of personality. Since then, it is possible to discern both an ideological maturation in the movement's leadership, which takes its distance from Thaksinism, and a hardening of Thaksin loyalism among ordinary members.

by a class-party, the accusation of the cult of personality derives from the presumption that the party and the people are one, that there is a perfect adequacy between its rule and their desire. In such cases, claims Alain Badiou, a popular attachment to a single figure is at once an acknowledgment of the non-identity between class and party (whether because of bureaucratism or hierarchization) and the expression of a need to guarantee the legitimacy of that party – a need whose only satisfaction comes in the form of a 'representation of the representation'. Badiou refers to this as a singularity, for which the name of the leader, the figure of a single person, comes to function as both displacement and image.[15]

Now, Thailand has never had anything like a class-party of the sort experienced in China – that phenomenon 'brought to a point of paroxysm' in the Cultural Revolution. Political parties in Thailand have long been recognized for their fundamentally factional orientation.[16] The fact that parties are often dissolved and reconstituted under different names but with the same personnel and membership suggests the ephemerality of the form. Thus, for example, the Liberal Democratic Party merged with the Thai Rak Thai Party in 1998, which became the People's Power Party, itself banned along with its founder and leader, Thaksin Shinawatra, and supplanted by the Pheua Thai Party, for which Thaksin remains the titular head in exile. At the time of writing, there are six parties in the coalition government, five in opposition, six with no parliamentary representation, and five that are banned. Of the latter, all but the Communist Party of Thailand, which was banned in 1948, have been banned since 2007, all for ostensibly violating electoral laws. Almost all, it will be noted, have monikers of an emphatically populist sort: Thai Rak Thai ('Thais love Thais'), Pheua Thai ('For Thais'), Palang Prachachon ('People's Power'), Rak Prathet Thai ('Love Thailand Party'), Chart Pattana Pheua Phaendin ('National Development for the Homeland Party'), Mathubhum ('Motherland').

If, Thaksin can function as a singularity that claims to guarantee an otherwise impossible identity, then it is not one of party and class, but of party and people. This is not a function of his personal charisma, his vote-buying, his access to media, or even his pro-poor policies, though all play their roles in his popularity. It is, rather, overdetermined by the conditions in which class and party cannot function as a unity, not least because

---

15   Alain Badiou, 'The Cultural Revolution: The Last Revolution', transl. Bruno Bosteels, *Positions: East Asia Cultures Critique* 13: 3 (Winter 2005), p. 505.
16   Kasian, 'Toppling Thaksin'.

extraneous forces – mainly those of global financial capital – dictate who wins an election and what policies will be tolerated, how much the national dividend will be socialized, and so forth. Nonetheless, the postulation of an identity between Thaksin and his supporters has to encompass the extravagant disparities of wealth and power that separate him, his family and his wealthy allies from the rural poor. To the extent that he can do so, he assumes a position that directly competes with that of the king – not because he aims to be king, or even a king-maker, as the cruder accusations would have it, but because of this capacity to serve as the representation of the representation. The very desire for such a figure testifies to the failure of the electoral system to produce an adequate representation of the interests of the complexly stratified populace in whose name the government governs, but especially those of the poor.

Sometimes, the groups of protestors are as small as a few hundred people, who assemble before a government office and present themselves to representative authorities as those who wish to be heard. On other occasions, these groups swell to several hundreds of thousands, as during the protests against the military coup of 1991, in the period preceding Thaksin's overthrow in 2006, or during the prolonged period between 2008 and 2010, when opponents and supporters of another military coup offer themselves to be seen within the international media circuitry that today confers objectivity without recognition. The same vacillation between small activist protests and large-scale demonstrative strikes, to use Rosa Luxemburg's typology, could be seen during the brief period following Yingluck Shinawatra's electoral victory.[17] Since her dismissal on 22 May 2014 by the military junta that refers to itself as the National Council of Peace and Order (NCPO, Thai: Khana Raksa Khwam Sangop Haeng Chat, or คสช), the prohibition on such assemblages, partially justified by recourse to the negative image it produces of Thailand in the Western media, has largely been observed. Protestors can present themselves only as petitioners seeking the military's protection or the enactment of existing commitments, and strict limits on the number of people who may assemble in public to prevent such petitions from coalescing into more general strikes.

What distinguishes the protests of the last decade from those that preceded it, however, is the co-presence of opposed crowds, signified by the colours of their shirts: yellow for those who support the coup(s) in the name of monarchy, stability, and anti-corruption, and red for those who

---

17   Rosa Luxemburg, 'Mass Strike, Party and Trade Unions', in Dick Howard, ed., *Rosa Luxemburg: Selected Political Writings* (London/New York: Monthly Review, 1971).

support Thaksin and Yingluck, in the name of democratic proceduralism and the rights of the rural poor (mainly from the north and north-east). As late as 1992, the space of protest was polarized in a relatively dyadic manner: on one side were the protestors (at that time, mainly middle-class champions of electoral democracy); on the other were the state forces, the military and police representatives of its monopoly on violence. The new scene, which is precisely correlated with the rise of the Shinawatra family and media politics in the aftermath of the 1997 financial crisis, must be grasped as a triadic formation.[18] This triadic structure now also includes a social materialization of the force that the military and police would otherwise represent, albeit in the ironic form of violent immediacy. Where once the state's armed forces could exercise violence in the name of the citizenry (the people of the nation, *Chat Thai*) and thus preserve a rela- tively exclusive representational function in the very moment that they abrogated it, the official representatives of the Thai people no longer stand alone against those who compete for that status. The yellow-shirted presence in the streets is a kind of dangerous supplement to the military, calling it forth and exposing its lack of self-evident authority at the same time that it points out the vulnerability of the representative apparatus to its own negation.

The profundity of the transformation indicated by this newly triangu- lated confrontation, which nonetheless devolves into the primary dyad of pro- and contra-coup, cannot be overestimated. The protests against the government in favour of the state, or against the military in the name of bureaucratic proceduralism, make recourse to the same methods, but operate in different names. That they require these names, as guarantees of their authority and signifiers of their truth, tells us how tenuous is the

---

18   Thaksin's prime ministership was not the first time that a member of the family had held high office. Indeed, a recent study by the Siam Intelligence Unit has argued that the Shinawatra family should be recognized as comparable to the illustrious Ghandi-Nehru dynasty, on the basis that the family has collectively held three prime ministerships if one includes that of Somchai Wongsawat (a brother-in-law to both Thaksin and Yingluck, who was briefly in the prime-ministerial office in 2008, following the coup that ousted Thaksin). Two other members, including Thaksin's father, Lert, have been members of parliament representing Chiang Mai; one of these (Suraphan) having also served in the cabinet of Prime Minister Chatichai Choonhaven (1988–91) before it was deposed in a coup. Still another (Sujate) served as mayor of the northern capital city. Be that as it may, the basis of the Shinawatra family's power lies in its multi-sectoral economic power, which started with the capitali- zation of the silk industry in the early decades of the twentieth century, when the Chinese immigrant family also changed its Chinese clan name (they originally emigrated from Guangdong) to Shinawatra. Their empire later came to encompass retail (of both orchids and fuel), transport and telecommunica- tions. See Siam Intelligence Unit, 'The Shinawatra Family Tree', *New Mandala*, 8 August 2011, at asiapacific.anu.edu.au.

project of representative government in the current era, and how incapable it is of generating the discourse within which the facticity of the moment can be conceptualized, its truth attested.

The Class of 2014; Class in 2014

Analysts have repeatedly diagnosed the theatricalized, mass-mediatized confrontation between red and yellow shirts in terms of the class dynamics that they supposedly encode, with yellow shirts supported by the Bangkok middle classes, its intelligentsia, and the Siamese elite, and red shirts expressing the interests and aspirations of farmers, but also the elites of the northern and north-eastern provinces. The UDD describes its own membership in more classically proletarian terms, as follows: 'Most Red Shirts are ordinary working class Thais. They include unregistered laborers, farmers, the poor and those who don't qualify for any kind of welfare or pension. Red Shirts also include employees in industries and other services such as restaurant and hotel (*sic*).'[19] Nonetheless, and despite extreme poverty among some of Thailand's farmers, the agricultural sector of the north and north-east is one of significant and increasing internal stratification, a situation quite different from that which characterized the more feudal pattern of earlier decades, or even the era of initial capitalization, when so many were stranded between subsistence farming and tenancy based in landlessness. The last two decades have seen the emergence of a substantial stratum of middle-income farmers who are engaged in cash cropping, diversified investment strategies, and various kinds of small-scale entrepreneurialism. In many households, one or more members migrate for wage-labour either to Bangkok or other parts of South East Asia and the Gulf states, on both seasonal and longer-term bases. Those who move along the circuits of migrancy have acquired new forms of cultural literacy and cosmopolitan consumer aesthetics that they have now implanted in their home communities, where they compete with a more nostalgic, verily Georgic valorization of rural authenticity. Cash and credit flows have infused the rural areas with the media of accumulation, and large-scale infrastructural development projects have enabled middle-income farmers to reap the benefits of transnational capital networks – including the employment of more destitute migrant labour from neighbouring Cambodia and Laos.

19   'Who Are We?' – official blog of the United Front for Democracy against Dictatorship, available at thairedshirts.org.

The result has been a displacement of the axioms that previously oriented analyses of the rural–urban relation in Thailand. The red-shirt movement is, in this sense, one expression of the more general transformation of so-called peasant politics, such that the demand for inclusion and recognition now sounds louder than any call for an alternative to capitalist development. Indeed, it is against the backdrop of the middle-income farmers' emergence and in the shadow of their astute engagement with state authorities, particularly under Thaksin's policy of productive specialization ('one Tambon, one product'), that the murmur of protest and the call for more subsidies has assumed its current form.[20]

The subsidy programmes of the Shinawatra governments have actually been quite diverse, not only in the commodities covered but in the form of the subsidy. Rice is subsidized at the level of guaranteed prices, paid directly to farmers by a national body that then stockpiles and sells the grain on the world market. Since 2011, diesel fuel has been subsidized on the principle of maximum pump prices. Under Yingluck's government, the UDD solicited Pattaya's rubber farmers with a proposed strategy of government subsidies for production costs, rather than a guaranteed price per kilogram, on the grounds that the latter would by reaped by middlemen only. That protestors had demanded a guaranteed fixed price, and that the UDD had taken upon itself to organize a conference to persuade them otherwise indicates the degree to which the UDD has matured into an ideological apparatus tied to the state, albeit at the fringe of the party system.[21] But it also shows up the complexity of the rural world. The articulate volubility of those middle-income farmers, some of whom also operate wholesale businesses and thus function as middlemen, is directed at the pursuit of profits from exchange as much as support for production. Without irony, then, one may postulate that the emergence of the new class of middle-income farmers signals the end of the discourse of class, precisely because it interrupts the fantasy of class unity and its capacity for universalization at the spatialized periphery of the national economy.

In direct proportion to the class differentiation of the agricultural sector, the hyperbolization of national unity has gathered its force. This is

---

20   On the rise of this new class of middle-income farmers, see Andrew Walker, *Thailand's Political Peasants: Power in the Modern Rural Economy* (Madison, WI: University of Wisconsin Press, 2012).

21   Daeng, 'UDD Press Conference on September 4th, 2013', published on official blog of the UDD, at thairedshirts.org. In May 2014, rice farmers in Krabi Province, led by Boonsong Nabthong, head of the Krabi Rubber Farmers Association, nonetheless claimed that they had not yet been paid their subsidy and were petitioning the NCPO for its disbursement.

why protest is so vehemently carried out in the name of the people. This is also no doubt why the southern provinces feature so little in the current conflict. The ambivalence of the latter region and the relative absence of its four southernmost provinces from protest is significantly determined by the long-standing Islamic nationalist movement there, and the fact that Thaksin's government maintained previous regimes' Buddhist chauvinism (inscribed in the monarchy, defined as head of the Buddhist sangha) towards its populace, exercising extreme force against its insurgent groups, authorizing extrajudicial killing, and deploying emergency powers in a manner that enabled widespread abuse of police powers. Part of Thailand only by virtue of annexation in the early twentieth century, and historically marginal to the Siamese-centric category of Thainess, the southernmost provinces' struggle for sovereignty has also been transformed by Islamist internationalism and the War on Terror. But this does not mean that it lies beyond the populist dynamic that infuses the yellow- and red-shirt protests. An ironic confluence of circumstances and discourses organized by cultural (religious) axiomatics and new economic logics has, in fact, led to a resonant, if antithetical, set of populisms in both the north and the south.

In Thailand, both populism and the accusation of populism are modes of asserting (not necessarily constituting) an identity in the form of a people. The pivot between them is the name under which they gather, and the location of that name in the political field: it is either absolutely central or absolutely exterior. The concept of the people is, course, predicated on both a fantasy of identity and a postulation of antagonism. This antagonism is projected outward, precisely in order that another, prior and structuring antagonism internal to the society – that which in a previous era went unselfconsciously by the name of class – can be disavowed. This is true even when the claimants to the status of popular representativeness ground their petition in their marginality and in opposition to an elite, whose very elevation is read as evidence of a breach in the body politic. Since the defeat of communism in Thailand, anti-elitism has been relatively tempered, with the result that populism blends imperceptibly into nationalism. And given the structured function of the monarchy (see below), there is an absolute limit to the possibility that populism can become the basis for a more radically egalitarian political ambition. It is precisely in the gap between populism and egalitarianism that the nationalist vilification of ethnic others acquires its force.

The gesture by which red- or yellow-shirt protestors assert their status as

'real' Thais, or as the 'true' people, or, more likely, as the bearers of a specifically Thai moral truth, provides the rhetorical instanciation of this logic,
but it is most palpable in the activities of the yellow-shirted People's Alliance
for Democracy (PAD), who have coupled their opposition to Thaksin with
a vigorous agitation against Cambodian claims to the UNESCO-designated
world heritage site of Wat Prasat Preah Vihear (Cambodian)/Wat Phra
Wiharn (Thai). In the process, they have revived nationalist dreams of an
expanded Thai polity that dates back to the 1860s, though it has lain relatively dormant since the time of Sarit Thanarat's dictatorial reign (1957–63),
when the International Court of Justice recognized Cambodia as the legitimate authority.[22] Since the coup of May 2014, the NCPO's Committee on
Solving Migrant Problems has undertaken a stringent purging of so-called
illegal migrant labourers, instigating the largest mass migration in mainland
Southeast Asia since the end of the Vietnam wars. It is estimated that,
during the first four months following the coup, between 100,000 and
225,000 Cambodian migrants crossed back into their home country either
out of fear or by direct deportation, while uncounted numbers of Burmese
and Lao workers have similarly fled.[23] The particular plight of the
Cambodians, who do not constitute a majority of migrant labourers in
Thailand, is linked to the fact that Thaksin had strong ties to the Cambodian
president Hun Sen, so there is a degree to which anti-Cambodian xenopho-
bia collapses into opposition to Thaksin. Nonetheless, nationalist sentiment
suffuses the entire field of conflict, and is encoded in the protests of both
red and yellow shirts, both of whom claim to want to preserve a government of the people headed by the king – even when they do so with Thaksin
as their leader. The continued and merciless exclusion of the Rahingya
exiles from Burma, reveals the degree to which this nationalism exceeds the
question of Cambodia, or the negative identification of Thaksin with
Cambodian interests.

---

22   Puangthong R. Pawakapan, *State and Uncivil Society in Thailand at the Temple of Preah Vihear*
(Singapore: Institute of Southeast Asian Studies, 2013). The Cambodian acceptance of French
protectorship was undertaken partly in an effort to stave off encroachments from both the west
(Thailand) and the east (Vietnam). It was under the influence of French orientalism that the drive to
claim Khmer archaeological remnants of ancient imperial glory occurred, with Wat Preah Vihear and
Angkor Wat occupying the centre of that effort. During its period of alliance with Japan in World
War II, Thailand attempted to extend its control over the rural provinces on the border, and especially the temple, but with the transfer of alliance to the allies, and the demise of French colonial
authority in the region, Prince Sihanouk took the case of contested border territory to the International
Court of Justice, which found in Cambodia's favour in 1962.
23   Charlie Thame, 'Ominous Signs for Migrant Workers in Thailand', *New Mandala*, 15 June
2014, at asiapacific.anu.edu.au.

This insistence on the representational legitimacy of the sovereign acquires its importance partly because it marks the dividing line between populism and communism, but in a negative and indeed illusory manner. If communism divides, if its name marks a kind of rupture and scission in political history, then the disavowal of communism often takes the form of a claim to the popular and an accusation that the enemy has confused the two. The red-shirted UDD, for example, insists on its numerical representativeness, claiming a membership of several million and asserting a meagre few thousand among its yellow-shirted opponents. Its authority is grounded in a logic of the count. Nonetheless, the first of its six principles discloses the ambiguity of its aspiration to self-governance and popular sovereignty: 'To attain true democracy with sovereignty truly in the hands of the people of Thailand with the King as the head of state.'[24]

Opposing this logic of the count, but straining to sustain the claim to representativeness, the yellow-shirted PAD and its supporters accuse the Thaksin regime not only of republicanism (and hence *lèse-majesté*), but of parliamentary dictatorship. As Michael Connors so deftly argues, the concept of parliamentary dictatorship (*phetjakan ratthasupha*) emerged during the period when Thailand was transitioning from the severely 'despotic paternalism' that had characterized the dictatorship of Sarit to the kind of liberal military regime embodied in the National Peace-Keeping Council (NPKC), installed in 1991 by General Suchinda Khraprayoon.[25] The NPKC's reign was associated with the bloodiest suppression of oppositional protests since the massacre of student activists at Thammasat University in October 1976, but its discourse was that of peace-keeping rather than rule, of management rather than force. Commencing an entirely new era of military–monarchical alliance, the doctrine of parliamentary dictatorship, which arose in the 1980s and then authorized the NPKC's assumption of power, was predicated on a somewhat distorted reading of the Rousseauian doctrine of the social contract. Emphasizing a notion of the collective will as something irreducible to the sum of individual wills, the new doctrine claimed that the collective will could be represented equally well by elected or appointed representatives, and by the military itself.[26] Connors quotes a widely circulated

---

24   'The Six Principles', published on the official blog of the UDD, at thairedshirts.org.
25   Michael Kelly Connors, *Democracy and National Identity in Thailand* (London: RoutledgeCurzon, 2003).
26   Ibid., pp.187–8.

pedagogical text written for members of the military, which states the matter with tautological self-certainty: 'When the military is the people's it can do the people's duty because the military, which has power, can use that power in place of the people. This means the people's power is with the military itself.'[27]

Long before Yingluck Shinawatra would seem to have assumed the role of Antigone in the Siamese form of Hegelian tragedy, then, Connors discerned the rise of a neo-Hegelian political theory (he refers to it as *nearly* Hegelian) at the heart of the new Thai order – one that works by dissociating numerical representativeness from the moral representation of the otherwise secreted will of the people. In this scheme, parliamentary dictatorship is something like the political theory of vote-buying, which is itself the means by which the collective will is both divided and subverted. Under the new doctrine, the justification of military rule arises in the very moment when the problematic status of the people's will arises. Someone must determine what it is, and must arbitrate between the competing claims on its behalf – claims that are otherwise made via the institutional medium of the electoral party or some other organ of civil society. Precisely because they compete in a public sphere defined by that purpose, the claims fail to provide the guarantee of their own veracity. As a corollary, the Thai party system, largely modelled on the US system, though with more numerous electoral parties, is subjected to a permanent and radical scepticism.

Now, the response to the indeterminacy that such a predicament generates has recourse to one of two models. Either there is a postulation of a sacred centre around which the polity revolves, one that provides an absolute guarantee of the truth and authority of the ruling power's representativeness; or there is an ejection of that guarantee into a domain outside of the political altogether. That exteriority is variously conceived as an economic force or a secular truth. Connors, with most other scholars of Thai political history, avows the first hypothesis. He describes the pragmatic melding of Western political theory with 'Thai traditionalism' as a strategy for resolving the 'tension between rights and duties by conflating freedom with actions in accordance with the general will'. In doing so, he confirms Chalermkiat Phiu-nuan's thesis that the entire process is 'mediated at the deepest level by "unconscious" efforts to

---

27   Ibid., p. 108. Connors is citing, 'Ekkasan prakop kansuksa khrongkan 6601' ('Learning Material for Project 6601'), in *Chamlae naiyobai kongthap* ('Dissecting Military Policy'), n.d., pp. 142–56.

reproduce the stabilizing role of a sacred center at the heart of a chaotic whole, operationalized by the military and symbolized by the monarchy'.[28]

Before we consider the question of whether a sacral centring or a radical evacuation of the political is at stake, it is important to situate the new theory in relation to the history by which communism was displaced by and absorbed into a new kind of populist nationalism – a development linked to the fact that the end of the communist insurgency was not achieved militarily. The political education of the so-called democratic soldiers, to which Connors refers us, arose as part of an effort to redirect the counterintelligence programme of the Thai military through a strategy of national encompassment, supplanting earlier efforts to vilify CPT members as un-Thai, or indeed anti-Thai.[29] It was at this point that the Internal Security Operations Command (ISOC) began actively to promote poverty-amelioration programmes rather than the more narrow counterinsurgency efforts that had defined the conflict during the 1970s.[30] In other words, the military acknowledged the truth about inequality and rural poverty, and undertook to mitigate its most extreme forms in order to prevent the generalization of the communist hypothesis *tout cort*.

There is, therefore, an obscure continuity between the military strategy of poverty relief developed in the 1980s, and what has come to be written under the name of Thaksin-ism. But this continuity is also the source of conflict at the profoundest level of political logic. The military strategy included the enrolment of the king in various rural development projects, culminating in the elaboration of a doctrine promoting 'sufficiency economy'. Although entirely derivative (and barely concealing its origin in the anthropological rhetoric of subsistence economics and moral economies, though embedding it in developmentalism), the branding of this doctrine under the signature of Bhumipol Adulyadej effectively re-signifies the monarchy as an institution whose moral authority derives from its pure

---

28   Connors, *Democracy and National Identity in Thailand*, pp. 108–9. See also Chalermiat Phiu-nuan, *Khwaamkhit thangkanmeuang khong thahan thai 2519–2535* ('Political Thought of the Thai Military, 1976–1992') (Bangkok: Samnakphim phujatkan, 1992).

29   The vilification of communists as un-Thai defined counterinsurgency efforts in the 1960s and early '70s, and was institutionalized in ritualized cults like the Village Scouts movement, but also surreptitiously signified in the insistent refusal to translate 'communism' into Thai. The word is merely transliterated. See Katherine Bowie, *Rituals of National Loyalty: An Anthropology of the State and the Village Scout Movement in Thailand* (New York: Columbia University Press, 1997).

30   Chai-Anan Samudivanija, Kusuma Snitwongse and Suchit Bunbonkamet, *From Armed Suppression to Political Offensive: Attitudinal Transformation of Thai Military Officers since 1975* (Bangkok: Institute of Security and International Studies, Chulalongkorn University, 1990).

expression of the collective interest.[31] This is a significant reformulation of the principle of sacral kingship, which, far from being attenuated in the process of being subjected to representational logics, gathers additional force.[32]

The transformation of the monarch into a charitable functionary, which can be seen in places as distant as Britain and the Netherlands, has, in Thailand, been the mode of a ritual intensification. Instead of soliciting identification via the discourse of the 'common touch', it has underscored a fantastic exceptionalism whereby the king's capacity to reach across the threshold of his own sacrality becomes testimony to his uncommon genius. The same cannot be said for Thaksin, whose very exceptionality (his extraordinary wealth) has prompted his defenders to identify with him on the basis that he is as subject to military violence and government abuse as are they.[33] His commonness, which derives partly from the fact that he is the product of an economic logic – financial capital – that has no radical outside, also means that he cannot quite occupy the place of the monarch. The military nonetheless worries that this might occur. They have been able to contain the veritable cult of personality surrounding Thaksin largely by ensuring his exile. Nonetheless, Thaksin's image has acquired verily auratic power in Thailand. When, in July 2014, police broke up a Pheua Thai party event and demanded that celebrants of his birthday remove his images from the walls, they were specifically implying that they were being treated in the same fashion as royal images – images that are legally protected and mandated in all public spaces. The officials imply an aspiration to sacral centrality on Thaksin's part. However, the very fact that a contest can be perceived indicates the degree to which the country is now feeling the effect of that process described by Claude Lefort as the evacuation of the political centre in liberal democratic regimes.[34]

---

31   This has not stopped the United Nations Development Project from recognizing the 'Sufficiency Economy' as a gift, 'bestowed' on the Thai people by King Bhumiphol Adulyadej. See *Thailand Human Development Report: Sufficiency Economy and Human Development* (Bangkok: UNDP, 2007), p. iii. The term rendered in English as 'sufficiency' is *por piang* in Thai, which implies something more ambiguous. See Pornpimol Kanchanalak, 'His Majesty the King's Sufficiency Theory Goes Global', *Nation*, 3 October 2013, available at nationmultimedia.com.

32   Benedict Anderson long ago recognized the trajectory of the Thai monarchy during the twentieth century as one of resacralization, unlike almost every other monarchical tradition in the world. See his 'Studies of the Thai State: The State of Thai Studies', in Eliezer B. Ayal, ed., *The Study of Thailand: Analyses of Knowledge, Approaches, and Prospects in Anthropology, Art History, Economics, History and Political Science* (Athens, OH: Center for International Studies, 1978), pp. 193ff.

33   Morris, 'Intimacy and Corruption'.

34   Claude Lefort, 'The Permanence of the Theological–Political?' in *Democracy and Political Theory*, transl. David Macey (New York: Polity, 1991).

One can see the symptoms of that process most visibly in the dilemmas surrounding the translation of the famously regressive constitution of 2007, which replaced what had otherwise been construed as the most democratic constitution ever promulgated in Thailand. An initial translation into English led to the description of the Thai form of government as a 'constitutional monarchy'. Quickly realizing the consequence of this nomination, the government authorities issued a correction that makes visible something of the ambiguity in the Thai word for 'democracy', while implying that the monarchy is actually less central than exterior to the polity. The official name for the form of government in Thailand is 'democratic government with the King as Head of the State'. The word for democracy in Thai is *prachathipatai*, *pracha* referring to people as in *prachachon* and *thipatai*, meaning sovereign. Article 3 of the constitution states that 'the sovereign Power belongs to the Thai people. The King as the Head of the State shall exercise such power through the National Assembly, Council of Ministers, and the Courts.' In other words, the king exercises the power that belongs to the people; he exceeds them and encompasses them – not in order to be one with them, but in order that they be, for, as Article 1 states, 'Thailand is one and indivisible.' The king is not, technically speaking, subject to the constitution, and its principles are organized to prevent any contradiction between government and monarchical interest. This is why criticism of constitutionally mandated institutions and laws is vulnerable to the charge of *lèse-majesté*. It is therefore interesting to reflect upon the very history of the widely divergent idioms in which that accusation has attired itself during the long reign of the present monarch. These idioms comprise the rhetoric of Thai militarism, the particular dialects of coup-making.

The coup of 1951 legitimized itself on the grounds that revolutionaries working in the name of peace (and non-alignment) were threatening national unity and morals. By 1958, which saw the coup that established Thailand's most authoritarian regime under General Sarit, it was not the revolutionaries of peace but communism that provided the alibi for military intervention, this time through the adumbration of an identity between communism and anti-monarchism, as well as between communism and anti-tradition. The identification of the sovereignty of the sovereign with that of the people was initially accomplished by the military in this very move to expel communism, as the bearer of alterity, unconsciously recognizing its inventive potential. And, as we have seen, the end of that era coincided with the rise of the concept of parliamentary dictatorship. That rhetoric emerged with the fragmentation of previous alliances between particular parties and capital cliques, as the country emerged into new Tiger status. The hallmarks of that period were accelerating economic growth, the expansion of the manufacturing sector and the stock exchange, widespread real estate speculation, and the dramatic rise of import demand. In the 1980s, electoral office was a necessary means for accessing state resources, and increasing numbers of people who had formerly exercised local power via networks of immediate patron–clientship and economic monopolies entered the electoral process. As Benedict Anderson has noted, the importance of electoral office was signified by the very degree to which candidates for office were targeted for assassination.[35] But by 1991, under the guise of parliamentary dictatorship, a coup could appear as a mechanism to restrict government regulation of the economy, and as a means of restabilizing the power of big business, which otherwise might appear threatened by liberal-democratic proceduralism.[36] Needless to say, the decisive events in Germany and the Soviet Union played their part in enabling this entrenchment of capitalist interests in the governing body, under the banner of restitution. That restitution concealed itself in the discourse of cultural revival – and coincided precisely with the revivification of the silk industry, the resignification of tourism as a cultural encounter, and the investment in high-end artisanal production for export.

The coup of 1991 was undertaken with the king's explicit approval. The sovereign is now a decrepit old man in whom the two bodies of the king have already begun to dissociate, so that the image is becoming a mere corpse and the institution a hollow crown. He is often unable to address his people despite a rising tide of anxiety over his heir's possible incompetence. But this only intensifies the sense of the military's likely intervention – and the defensive nature of prosecution for *lèse-majesté*. If, as Claude Lefort has said, democracy functions on the basis of a vacancy at the heart of the political, the real evacuation that may occur upon the death of Bhumipol Adulyadej threatens to reveal the fact that the king's presence covers over a symbolic absence – even in (especially in) a democratic government with the king as head of state. The task that the military has assumed for itself is that of foreclosure – abolishing from the national consciousness the thought of the king's symbolic vacuity, and making it

---

35   Benedict Anderson, 'Murder and Progress in Modern Siam', in *The Specter of Comparisons: Nationalism, Southeast Asia and the World* (London/New York: Verso, 2000).
36   Hewison, 'Of Regimes, State and Pluralities'.

appear a real threat borne by others: first by communists, and then by populists headed by Thaksin Shinawatra and his sororal proxy – a threat in the Real, and thus in the order of the event, where something new might actually arise.

The Culture of Coups?

If the monarch cannot quite guarantee the unity of the nation or the truth of the state's claim to incarnate the will of the people, the promise of national culture promises to fill the gap. There are really two cultures here. One is the dominant culture of the Siamese, which, since the fifth reign (1868–1910), has been hegemonized through language laws, national education and other means. It was against this internally colonial culture that many ethno-nationalist groups (including Muslim separatist groups in the four southern provinces, and Lao nationalists in the northeast) initially arrayed themselves, in solidarity with the CPT; and it was in solidarity with Siamese nationalism that the Socialist Party of Thailand finally broke with the CPT in 1981, just four years after joining the armed struggle against the state. The other 'culture' is the principle that immunizes inequality against political critique. There is a relation between them.

To understand this, it is useful to revisit the moment when the culture concept became an alibi for recasting the question of debt and inequality as one of a legitimate patron–clientship, rather than a function of property ownership and the violence of what Marx rightly called capitalism's most fetishistic phenomenon: interest-bearing capital. In 1957, just before Sarit assumed full powers, Jit Poumisak published *Chomna Sakdina Thai* ('The Real Face of Thai Feudalism Today').[37] In it, he attempted to import a mode of analysis that he had learned from reading the redacted works of Russian and Chinese Marxists published largely in *Mahachon*, the magazine of the CPT. The party was legitimate throughout the late forties, as a result of a US-brokered agreement permitting the establishment of a Soviet cultural office in Bangkok – part of the early post-war efforts of the United States to mitigate British neo-colonial ambitions in the region, and the ground for its own imperial aspirations. The Soviets

---

37   Jit Poumisak, *Chomna Sakdina Thai* ('The Real Face of Thai Feudalism') (Bangkok: Dork Ya, 2000 [1957]). For an English translation with an excellent introduction, see Craig J. Reynolds, *Thai Radical Discourse: The Real Face of Thai Feudalism* (Ithaca, NY: Cornell Southeast Asian Programs, 1987).

had demanded recognition of the CPT, though the CPT would side with the Chinese following the Sino-Soviet split. Jit Poumisak's works were largely written under pen-names, and traversed a multiplicity of genres – poetry, historiography, ethnography, philology, and literary and arts criticism. Although he became a hero of student activists in the brief democratic experiment of 1973–76, he was dead by 1966 (at the hands of a reactionary village headman), and had by then spent six years in prison. In fact, he was only granted the status of party member posthumously. Moreover, his great work, arguing for the feudality of contemporary Thai society, was never taken up by the CPT, which endorsed instead the position of its secretary general, Udom Sisuwan, who argued for a semi-feudal, semi-colonial model as the framework for analyzing Thailand's modernity.

At the centre of the debates inaugurated by Jit is the concept of *sakдina/ saktina*, a term that originally referred to the ranks and gradations used in the Sukhothai period to denote landholdings, and extended by Jit and others to refer to a mode of power based in ownership of land. On one hand, Jit's use of the concept was intended to displace then dominant forms of historiography that were not only grounded in monarchical biography but grasped dependency in a personalistic idiom, as the gift of security from power; on the other, it was an effort to evade the ethnocentric implications of Marx's thesis on the Asiatic Mode of Production.

After the collapse of the democratic experiment in Thailand and the violent suppression of student activists at Thammasat University on 6 October 1976, Jit's thesis enjoyed increasing renown, if only as an effect of his signature: the thesis was not only that *sakдina* power originally lay in the ownership of land, but that the monopoly on land was the original cause of peasant indebtedness, because the usufructory allocations given to former slaves (when slavery was abolished) were too small to enable subsistence, and because the primary financers of loans were the 'masters of the land', in whom ownership and policing functions were united. The much-disputed centrality of slavery in Jit's account does not derive from the fact that he makes slavery the origin of the Siamese polity (it is not a question of rule and rights), but from the fact that it makes the ending of slavery the origin of capitalism. In Jit's account, the freeing of slaves was the basis of what Marx called *ursprüngliche Akkumulation*, or 'originary accumulation'. The freed peasants could borrow money to purchase food that their own production did not generate; but paying rates of 37.5 per cent per month, and with the right to mortgage their usufruct, they were quickly rendered landless and indebted, while the landlords accumulated liquid capital without having to relinquish their attachment to the land. At stake was the conversion of land into interest-bearing capital through the intervention of law, and the corollary of violent liberation into employ-ability, but not necessarily employment, of the rural population.

Although most scholars disavowed the place of slavery in Jit's analysis, his popularity lasted during the period of guerrilla warfare, when many students went into the jungle to join the armed struggle. During the 1980s, as many emerged to accept the military amnesty (offered in 1982), Jit's position came under increasing fire, and was then displaced by an argument that power in Thai history did not rest in control over land, but in control over persons, whose scarcity and capacity to flee in a relatively underpopulated space had given them a certain freedom. The figure of the slave came back in the watered-down image of lord and bondsman (*chaofa/phrai*) in a mutually sustaining dialectic of recognition. The combi-nation of relative freedom and culturally mediated but personally avowed dependency was implicitly assumed not only in nationalist ideology, which fetishistically remarked the meaning of *thai* (free) in the national moniker, but in the fluorescence of work on patron–client relationships as the basis of Thai society. This work found its most articulate incarnation in the writings of the Community Culture school of social sciences.[38] Former student activists and amnestied internal exiles, the scholars of this school claimed, as Chaiyan Vaddhanaphuti says, that their experience in the jungle had taught them that class analysis was itself violent, and that the admittedly hierarchical relations of rural communities were the source of a cultural meaningfulness that could not be disavowed. In place of class, they proffered community culture as the idiom for avowing inequal-ity as the ironic defence against more violent and more ostensibly antisocial forms of domination generated by neo-colonialism and global finance. In the process, of course, they embraced those very forms. By the end of the 1980s, Kasian Tejapira could write the history of Marxism in Thailand as itself a history of commodification.[39]

The well-intended culturalism of the Community Culture School had its truth, and it was the Thai form of a phenomenon that occurred

---

38   On the history of the community concept in Thai discourse, see Craig J. Reynolds, '*Chumchon/ Community*' in Carol Gluck and Anna Lowenhaupt Tsing, eds, *Words in Motion: Toward a Global Lexicon* (Durham, NC: Duke University Press, 2009).

39   Kasian Tejapira, *Commodifying Marxism: The Formation of Radical Thai Culture* (Singapore: Trans Pacific, 2001).

elsewhere in all those places where the violence of anti-colonial wars and of militant anti-capitalism had taken its toll, and then been ridiculed by the violence of the party-states. Nonetheless, the rise of the Community Culture School indexed the rapprochement between critical scholarship and military–monarchical ideology, the culmination of which can be seen in the participation of so many social and political theorists in the constitution-writing process undertaken during the post-1991 coup government of Anand Phanyarachun, and in the endorsement of the anti-Thaksin coups by so many in the academic sphere.

When some generals and more conservative members of the PAD initially accused Thaksin's supporters of communist sympathies, they were derided and rebuked by the professional middle classes for whom the fall of the Soviet Union had made such accusations anachronistic at best. But the communist/anti-communist dyad (both a period and an analytic) and its double displacement by the community culture model, on one hand, and the discourse of parliamentary dictatorship, on the other, bequeathed a powerful residual force with which to exercise the interests of both capital and military – namely, the revised concept of the sovereign as a being beyond the state, not so much an origin of legitimacy or a foundational force as a guarantee of its unity, and thus its truth.

The military–monarchical alliance, which once appeared isomorphic with the national interest, can now do so only as a contradictory ruse, insofar as Thailand's economy, like all economies, is thoroughly embedded in a globalized network of financial forces that operate far above the state level (where they are operated by institutions like the IMF, the World Economic Forum and the World Bank). To the extent that the military enacts the interests of big business, one might say, it is serving forces that exceed and contradict the nation. Like Hegel's Antigone, they are beholden to the very law they appear to oppose. So, too, is the populist Thaksin, whose apparent devotion to the men and women of the soil is enabled by his engagement with global financial capital.

The catastrophic financial crisis of 1997, which commenced a spiralling implosion of the South East Asian markets, is widely believed to have been precipitated, if not caused, by the currency speculations of George Soros and those who followed his lead in betting against the baht. Such speculation was only possible under the conditions of financial globalization. And it was in the aftermath of that crisis that Thaksin arose, initially creating the Thai Rak Thai Party, and running for election on a platform of rebuilding national capital. The fervent nationalism of that early moment in the Thaksin era quickly came under scrutiny precisely because he could not match his rhetoric with the practice of his own activities as a capitalist. His investments in global telecommunications systems – as well as his company's sale of shares to non-Thai investors – were frequently adduced as examples of a failure to sufficiently enact the national interest. Thaksin's turn to the rural periphery – and to his own base in the north – thus appears as a kind of counter-move in the strategic game of claiming the people.

One must also recognize here the degree to which the accusations against and defences of the Shinawatra governments collude to conceal the otherwise capital-friendly nature of what is, otherwise, a generally neoliberal orientation among the Phuea Thai. Proposals for tax-free special development zones on the rural periphery and other incentives to encourage foreign direct investment were significant parts of the Yingluck government's platform and were pursued by the military junta even after her overthrow. Consumer-friendly loan programmes targeting the middle and upper classes, which aimed to invigorate the Thai economy – even if that meant underwriting purchases of fifth cars – accompanied micro-credit for farmers. Critics who see in Thaksin's policies a modified version of Keynesianism recognize the combination of efforts to stimulate individual consumption with massive developmental schemes that enhance employment; but the economic development zones are a particular symptom of the capital mobility characteristic of a financialized world quite different than Keynes's.

In the end, perhaps, the phenomenon of Thaksinism must be read symptomatically – as an index of a set of contradictions whose resolution is no longer deemed possible but whose recognition cannot be avowed. The Thai polity is divided internally, by forces that exceed it without being exterior to it, in a globalized and financialized economy that knows no alternative. This is the essence of its tragedy, a contradictory totality in concrete existence, displaced and given its image in the melodrama of the Shinawatra family's repeated rise and fall from power. However, Thaksinism expresses an aspiration for transformations as much as it exhibits the tendency for recapture by older forces that promise to establish unity through recourse to a sacral centre and the projection of internal antagonisms onto ethnic others. The feared destitution of the monarchy and the rise of populism are the flipsides of each other – expressions of a drive for a unity that cannot but betray the violent difference that today characterizes Thai society, and all others. The history of communism – displaced by the discourse of community culture and by the political accusation of parliamentary dictatorship – is, of course, the history of an idea, and not of a form, and it therefore remains to be seen what techniques may yet be invented to realize that idea. Even the knotted lineage that links the military's turn to poverty amelioration and the recruitment of the king into charitable developmentalism with the Shinawatra family's pro-poor policies, contains a tacit recognition that there is some truth in the communist hypothesis. Not even the idea of the people can be sustained in its absence.

Acknowledgments

An early sketch of this paper was originally presented at the 'Žižek/Badiou event: 'The Idea of Communism in Asia', at Kyung Hee University, Seoul, South Korea. I owe an enormous debt of gratitude to the organizers of the conference, and especially to Alex Taek-Gwang Lee, for including me in the proceedings. I am similarly indebted to Alain Badiou and Slavoj Žižek for welcoming me into a community of thinkers whose concern with the divisive question of communism has been marked by such relentless commitment to our shared goal of radical equality. I learned much at the conference in Seoul, but am especially grateful to Alessandro Russo and Claudia Pozzana for their ongoing conversation and engagement on these issues.

11   No Way Out? Communism in the New Century

Slavoj Žižek

A recent scientific report indicated how future biotechnology could be used to trick a prisoner's mind into thinking they have served a 1,000-year sentence: drugs could be developed to distort prisoners' minds into thinking time was passing more slowly. According to Rebecca Roache,

> there are a number of psychoactive drugs that distort people's sense of time, so you could imagine developing a pill or a liquid that made someone feel like they were serving a 1,000-year sentence. A second scenario would be to upload human minds to computers to speed up the rate at which the mind works. If the speed-up were a factor of a million, a millennium of thinking would be accomplished in eight and a half hours. Uploading the mind of a convicted criminal and running it a million times faster than normal would enable the uploaded criminal to serve a 1,000 year sentence in eight-and-a-half hours. This would, obviously, be much cheaper for the taxpayer than extending criminals' lifespans to enable them to serve 1,000 years in real time.[1]

An ethical twist is then added to the argumentation:

> Is it really OK to lock someone up for the best part of the only life they will ever have, or might it be more humane to tinker with their brains and set them free? When we ask that question, the goal isn't simply to imagine a bunch of futuristic punishments – the goal is to look at today's punishments through the lens of the future.

But what about the opposite intervention, which would enable us to make love for ten minutes and experience it as thousands of years? And

---

1   See Rhiannon Williams, 'Prisoners "Could Serve 1,000 Year Sentence in Eight Hours"', *Daily Telegraph*, 14 March 2014.

what about a life whose temporality could be totally manipulated in both directions, so that one can also make someone experience a ten-year prison sentence as something that lasts only ten minutes? How would such temporarily manipulated life look? How would it be experienced? In short, does this imagining of the consequences of the manipulability of our perception of time only along the lines of how it could render serving a prison sentence more productive not provide an extreme example of the misery and limitations of our imagination of the future? This limitation is clearly perceptible even when we are dealing with critical dystopias: dystopias that abound in recent blockbuster movies and novels (*Elysium*, *Hunger Games* . . .), although apparently leftist (presenting a post-apocalyptic society of extreme class divisions), are non-imaginative, monotonous, and also politically wrong. In political and economic theory, this limitation is most palpable not in radical utopian visions but precisely in 'modest' realist proposals. The title of Joseph Stiglitz's comment 'Democracy in the Twenty-First Century' refers to Thomas Piketty's *Capital in the Twenty-First Century*, with an important twist, shifting the accent from capitalism to our liberal-democratic political system – here is its concluding line of argumentation:

> What we have been observing – wage stagnation and rising inequality, even as wealth increases – does not reflect the workings of a normal market economy, but of what I call 'ersatz capitalism.' The problem may not be with how markets should or do work, but with our political system, which has failed to ensure that markets are competitive, and has designed rules that sustain distorted markets in which corporations and the rich can (and unfortunately do) exploit everyone else . . . Markets, of course, do not exist in a vacuum. There have to be rules of the game, and these are established through political processes . . . Thus, Piketty's forecast of still higher levels of inequality does not reflect the inexorable laws of economics. Simple changes – including higher capital-gains and inheritance taxes, greater spending to broaden access to education, rigorous enforcement of anti-trust laws, corporate-governance reforms that circumscribe executive pay, and financial regulations that rein in banks' ability to exploit the rest of society – would reduce inequality and increase equality of opportunity markedly. If we get the rules of the game right, we might even be able to restore the rapid and shared economic growth that characterized the middle-class societies of the mid-twentieth century. The main question

confronting us today is not really about capital in the twenty-first century. It is about democracy in the twenty-first century.[2]

In some formal sense this is, of course, true: the organization of a market economy is effectively possible only within legal coordinates that are ultimately decided by a political process. Stiglitz is also fully justified in pointing out that, in order to change capitalism effectively, we would also have to change the functioning of our democracy. Here, however, problems arise: In what precise sense is democracy a problem? It seems that, for Stiglitz, it is simply a question of enforcing new rules (laws regulating economic life) within the existing democratic framework – we need an elected government which would pass some 'simple changes' like 'higher capital-gains and inheritance taxes, greater spending to broaden access to education, rigorous enforcement of anti-trust laws, corporate-governance reforms that circumscribe executive pay, and financial regulations that rein in banks' ability to exploit the rest of society'. But can we really imagine the transformation of society being achieved like this? Here Marx's key insight remains valid, perhaps more than ever: for Marx, the question of freedom should not be located primarily in the political sphere proper (Does a country have free elections? Are its judges independent? Is its press free from hidden pressures? Does it respect human rights?). Rather, the key to actual freedom resides in the 'apolitical' network of social relations, from the market to the family. Here the change required is not political reform but a transformation of the social relations of production – which entails precisely revolutionary class struggle rather than democratic elections or any other 'political' measure in the narrow sense of the term. We do not vote on who owns what, or about relations in the factory, and so on – such matters remain outside the sphere of the political, and it is illusory to expect that one will effectively change things by 'extending' democracy into the economic sphere (by, say, reorganizing the banks to place them under popular control). Radical changes in this domain need to be made outside the sphere of legal 'rights'. In 'democratic' procedures (which, of course, can have a positive role to play), no matter how radical our anti-capitalism, solutions are sought solely through those democratic mechanisms which themselves form part of the apparatuses of the 'bourgeois' state that guarantees the undisturbed reproduction of capital. In this precise sense, Badiou was right to claim that today the name of the

---

2   Quoted from Joseph E. Stiglitz, 'Democracy in the Twenty-First Century', 1 September 2014, at project-syndicate.org.

ultimate enemy is not capitalism, empire, exploitation, or anything similar, but democracy itself. It is the 'democratic illusion', the acceptance of democratic mechanisms as providing the only framework for all possible change, which prevents any radical transformation of society. In this precise sense, Badiou was right in his apparently weird claim: 'Today, the enemy is not called Empire or Capital. It's called Democracy.'[3] It is the 'democratic illusion', the acceptance of democratic mechanisms as the ultimate frame of every change, that prevents the radical transformation of capitalist relations.

The field of capitalist economy, of the organization of production, exchange and distribution, has its own inertia and immanent movement, and the democratic political frame is already accommodated to this capitalist structure. To really change the capitalist structure, one must also change this democratic political frame; one cannot do it by enforcing changes through democratic electoral procedures which remain the same as before. Here, we encounter Stiglitz's second, Keynesian, limitation: Does his designation of the present economic system as '*ersatz* capitalism' not imply that there is another, proper capitalism, in which markets are really and fairly competitive, not our 'distorted markets in which corporations and the rich can (and unfortunately do) exploit everyone else'? We can see Stiglitz's wager here: by way of democratically enforcing legal changes, we can replace *ersatz* capitalism with a more just and efficient one, thus combining the best of capitalism with the best of democracy. But what if this entire idea is *utopian* in the strict sense of the term? What if what Stiglitz calls '*ersatz* capitalism' is simply capitalism as such, capitalism that follows its immanent development, and not its secondary perversion? That is to say, although capitalist markets 'do not exist in a vacuum', the political process of democracy also does not exist in a vacuum but is always overdetermined by economic relations.

Radical leftists all around Europe complain how today no one dares to really disturb the neoliberal dogma. The problem is real, of course – the moment one violates this dogma, or, rather, the moment one is just perceived as a possible agent of such disturbance, tremendous forces are unleashed. Although these forces appear as objective economic forces, they are effectively forces of illusions, of ideology – but their material power is nonetheless utterly destructive. We are today under the tremendous pressure of what we should call enemy propaganda – let me quote

---

3   Alain Badiou, 'Prefazione all'edizione italiana', in *Metapolitica* (Naples: Cronopio, 2002), p. 14.

Alain Badiou: 'The goal of all enemy propaganda is not to annihilate an existing force (this function is generally left to police forces), but rather to annihilate an *unnoticed possibility of the situation*.'[4] In other words, they are trying to *kill hope*: the message of this propaganda is a resigned conviction that the world we live in, even if not the best of all possible worlds, is the least bad one, so that any radical change can only make it worse.

Is there any emancipatory potential in so-called *Ostalgie*, the nostalgia for the socialist past in some post-communist countries? Boris Buden perspicuously noted that the post-communist *Ostalgie* in some Eastern European countries is not the longing for the lost emancipatory potential that survived in socialist regimes, but is structured like nostalgia for a lost culture, a lost way of life. (We are, of course, dealing with the retroactively constructed memory of mythic times when life was modest but stable and safe.) This is why getting rid of *Ostalgie* is a *sine qua non* of a renewed emancipatory movement in these countries. The large public which has no sympathy or longing for communism perceive it (from the standpoint of the neoliberal universe) as some weird foreign culture, incomprehensible and irrational in its premises and rituals. What the two opposed stances share is the same ignorance of the radical emancipatory dimension of the communist project: in both cases, communism is treated as a particular culture.[5]

This status of communism as a lost culture is part of a more general de-politicization: a new state of things is emerging in which political differences reappear as cultural differences. What Khomeini wrote decades ago allows us to understand why an attack on *Charlie Hebdo* can be considered appropriate: 'We're not afraid of sanctions. We're not afraid of military invasion. What frightens us is the invasion of Western immorality.'[6] Is *Charlie Hebdo* not the epitome of 'Western immorality'? The fact that Khomeini talks about fear, about what a Muslim should fear most in the West, should be taken literally: Muslim fundamentalists do not have any problems with the brutality of economic and military struggles, their true enemy is not Western economic neo-colonialism and military aggressiveness but its 'immoral' culture. The same holds for Putin's Russia, where the conservative nationalists define their conflict with the West as cultural, in the last resort focused on sexual difference.

---

4   Alain Badiou, Seminar on Plato at the ENS, 13 February, 2008 (unpublished). Emphasis in original.

5   See Boris Buden, *Zone des Uebergangs* (Frankfurt: Suhrkamp, 2009).

6   Ruhollah Khomeini, 'Quotes', at goodreads.com.

Apropos of the victory of the Austrian drag queen at the Eurovision contest, Putin himself told a dinner in St Petersburg: 'The Bible talks about the two genders, man and woman, and the main purpose of union between them is to produce children.'[7] As usual, the rabid nationalist Zhirinovsky was more outspoken, and 'called this year's result "the end of Europe", saying: "There is no limit to our outrage . . . There are no more men or women in Europe, just *it*.' Vice premier Dmitry Rogozin tweeted that the Eurovision result 'showed supporters of European integration their European future – a bearded girl'.[8] There is a certain uncanny, quasi-poetic beauty in this image of the bearded lady (for a long time the standard feature of cheap circus freaks) as the symbol of a united Europe; no wonder Russia refused to transmit the Eurovision contest to its TV public, with calls for a renewed cultural Cold War. Note the same logic as in Khomeini: rather than the army or economy, the truly feared object is immoral depravity, the threat to sexual difference: Boko Haram just brought this logic to the end. (Incidentally, Lacan's point is that the true threat is not polymorphous perversion which destabilizes, sometimes even ignores, sexual difference, but this difference itself in its antagonistic dimension of a non-relationship. The key reference to stable and normalized sexual difference in conservative political movements bears witness to the political relevance of Lacan's formula: 'There is no sexual relationship.')

In his analysis of today's return of religion as a political force, Boris Buden[9] rejected the predominant interpretation which sees this phenomenon as a regression caused by the failure of modernization. For Buden, religion as a political force is an effect of the post-political disintegration of society, of the dissolution of traditional mechanisms that guaranteed stable communal links: fundamentalist religion is not only political, it is politics itself, i.e. it sustains the space for politics. Even more poignantly, it is no longer just a social phenomenon but the very texture of society, so that in a way society itself becomes a religious phenomenon. It is thus no longer possible to distinguish the purely spiritual aspect of religion from its politicization: in a post-political universe, religion is the predominant space within which antagonistic passions return. What happened recently

---

7   James Edgar, 'Putin Attacks Eurovision Drag Artist Conchita for Putting Her Lifestyle "Up for Show"', *Daily Telegraph*, 26 May 2014.
8   Claire Hodgson, 'Conchita Wurst's Eurovision Win Slammed by Russia as Politician Brands It "the End of Europe"', *Daily Mirror*, 11 May 2014.
9   See Buden, *Zone des Uebergangs*.

in the guise of religious fundamentalism is thus not the return of religion in politics, but simply *the return of politics as such*.

Why, then, is Islam the most politicized religion today? Judaism is the religion of genealogy, of the succession of generations. When, in Christianity, the Son dies on the Cross, this means that the Father also dies (as Hegel was fully aware) – the patriarchal genealogical order as such dies; the Holy Spirit does not fit the family series, but introduces a post-paternal/familial community. In contrast to both Judaism and Christianity, the two other religions of the book, Islam excludes God from the domain of paternal logic: Allah is not a father, not even a symbolic one – God is one, he is neither born nor does he give birth to creatures. *There is no place for a Holy Family in Islam*. This is why Islam emphasizes so much the fact that Muhammad himself was an orphan; this is why, in Islam, God intervenes precisely at the moments of the suspension, withdrawal, failure, 'blacking-out', of the paternal function (when the mother or the child is abandoned or ignored by the biological father). What this means is that God remains thoroughly in the domain of the impossible-Real: he is the impossible-Real outside father, so that there is a 'genealogical desert between man and God'.[10] This was the problem with Islam for Freud, since his entire theory of religion is based on the parallel of God with father. Even more importantly, this inscribes politics into the very heart of Islam, since the 'genealogical desert' renders impossible the grounding of a community in the structures of parenthood or other blood-links: 'the desert between God and Father is the place where the political institutes itself'.[11] With Islam, it is no longer possible to ground a community in the mode of *Totem and Taboo*, through the murder of the father and the ensuing guilt bringing brothers together – thence Islam's unexpected actuality. This problem is in the very heart of the (in)famous *umma*, the Muslim 'community of believers'; it accounts for the overlapping of the religious and the political (the community should be grounded directly in God's word), as well as for the fact that Islam is 'at its best' when it grounds the formation of a community 'out of nowhere', in the genealogical desert, as the egalitarian revolutionary fraternity. No wonder Islam succeeds when young men find themselves deprived of a traditional family safety network. This properly political dimension survives in Shia communities much more than in the Sunni majority – Khomeini stated clearly that Islam can not only ground a true politics, but that 'the foundation of Islam is in

---

10   Fethi Benslama, *La psychanalyse a l'epreuve de l'Islam* (Paris: Aubier, 2002), p. 320.
11   Ibid.

politics': 'The religion of Islam is a political religion; it is a religion in which everything is politics, including its acts of devotion and worship.' Here is his most succinct formulation: 'Islam is politics or it is nothing.'[12]

Buden quotes Živko Kastić, a Croat Catholic-nationalist priest who declared that Catholicism is 'a sign that you are not ready to renounce your national and cultural heritage – the integral, traditional Croat being'.[13] What this quote makes clear is that what is at stake is no longer the question of belief, of its authenticity, but of a politico-cultural project. Religion is here just an instrument and sign of our collective identity, of how much public space 'our' side controls, of asserting 'our' hegemony. That is why Kastić quotes approvingly an Italian communist who said 'Io sono cattolico ateizzato'; it is why Breivik, also an atheist, refers to the Christian legacy that grounds European identity – or, to quote Buden again: 'Belief appears now as culture, in its difference to another culture – either the culture of another confession or the culture of atheism in its modernist forms.'[14] One can see clearly how religious fundamentalists, who otherwise despise cultural relativism and historicism, already function within its horizon: 'The space of difference became now something exclusively cultural. In order for us to perceive political differences and divisions and to recognize them as such, they should first be translated into the language of culture and declare themselves as cultural identities ... Culture thus became the ultimate horizon of historical experience.'[15]

Does this mean that there is no way out of the global capitalist universe? The bleak picture of the total triumph of a global capitalism that immediately appropriates all attempts to subvert it is itself the product of ideological imagination. It makes us blind to the signs of the New which abound in the very heart of global capitalism. For example, in his *The Zero Marginal Cost Society*, Jeremy Rifkin elaborates how, with the emerging Internet of Things, we are entering the era of nearly free goods and services: the rise of a global Collaborative Commons entails the eclipse of capitalism. There is a paradox at the heart of capitalism that has propelled it to greatness but is now taking it to its death: the inherent entrepreneurial dynamism of competitive markets that drives productivity up and marginal costs down, enabling businesses to reduce the price of their

---

12   Khomeini, 'Quotes'.
13   Buden, *Zone des Uebergangs*, p. 134.
14   Ibid., p. 111.
15   Ibid., p. 59.

goods and services in order to win over consumers and market share. (Marginal cost is the cost of producing additional units of a good or service, if fixed costs are not counted.) While economists have always welcomed a reduction in marginal cost, they never anticipated the possibility of a technological revolution that might bring marginal costs to near zero, making goods and services priceless, nearly free, and abundant, and no longer subject to market forces.

Now, a formidable new technology infrastructure is emerging with the potential of pushing large segments of economic life to near-zero marginal cost in the years ahead. The Communication Internet is converging with a nascent Energy Internet and Logistics Internet to create a new technology platform that connects everything and everyone. Billions of sensors are being attached to natural resources, production lines, the electricity grid, logistics networks, recycling flows, and implanted in homes, offices, stores, vehicles and even human beings, feeding Big Data into a global neural network. People can connect to the network and use Big Data, analytics and algorithms to accelerate efficiency, dramatically increase productivity, and lower the marginal cost of producing and sharing a wide range of products and services to near zero, just as they now do with information goods. This plummeting of marginal costs is spawning a hybrid economy, part capitalist market and part Collaborative Commons: people are making and sharing their own information, entertainment, green energy and 3D-printed products at near-zero marginal cost; they are sharing cars, homes, clothes and other items via social media sites, rentals, redistribution clubs and cooperatives at low or near-zero marginal cost; students are enrolling in free open online courses that operate at near-zero marginal cost; entrepreneurs are bypassing the banking establishment and using 'crowdfunding' to finance startup businesses, as well as creating alternative currencies in the fledgling sharing economy. In this new world, social capital is as important as financial capital, access trumps ownership, sustainability supersedes consumerism, cooperation ousts competition, and 'exchange value' in the capitalist marketplace is increasingly replaced by 'sharable value' in the Collaborative Commons. Capitalism will remain, but primarily as an aggregator of network services and solutions – a powerful niche player in the coming world beyond markets where we are learning how to live together in an increasingly interdependent global Collaborative Commons (a term that sounds like a clumsy translation of 'communism').

Here, however, we encounter one of the great antagonisms of our digital age: this very feature that sustains utopian hopes also sustains new forms of alienation. The catch resides in the infinitesimal temporal gap between the pure synchronicity of the worldwide web (we appear to be all simultaneously connected, so that it doesn't matter where we are located in physical reality) and the minimal temporality that remains as a trace of the materiality of the worldwide web. This minimal gap is mobilized by the high-frequency traders (HFTs) to earn billions, as was exposed by Michael Lewis in *Flash Boys*.[16] Using fibre-optic cables that link superfast computers to brokers, HFTs intercept and buy orders, sell the shares back to the buyer at a higher price, and pocket the margin. Here, then, is how it works from the standpoint of a broker buying stocks: he sits in front of a screen, sees an offer he considers acceptable, presses the YES button, and the deal is instantly concluded, albeit at a minimally higher price. What he doesn't know is that, in the milliseconds between his pressing YES and the conclusion of the deal (which appeared to him instantaneous), the HFT's computer (operating on a special algorithm) detected his YES, bought itself the stock for the offered price, and then sold it back to him for a slightly higher price – in a gap of time so small that the whole operation goes unnoticed. This is why HFTs secretly built an 827-mile cable running through mountains and under rivers from Chicago to New Jersey: it reduces the journey-time of data from seventeen to thirteen milliseconds; there is also a transatlantic cable still under construction that will give a 5.2-millisecond advantage to those looking to profit from trade between New York and London.

After the book was launched, several regulatory agencies took action: the Justice Department, the FBI, the Securities and Exchange Commission and the Financial Industry Regulatory Authority had been investigating HFT firms and exchanges for violations of insider trading and other Wall Street rules. Why such an outcry, when receiving trading data a few milliseconds ahead of someone else – which is the *raison d'être* of HFT – is technically not illegal? The reason is obvious: what HFTs are doing is proof that the stock market is being rigged in favour of front-running traders, and that other players are being screwed for having slower connections, so that the all-important image of the stock market as open and transparent is ruined. But there is another reason. The HFT scandal is only the latest evidence that the stock market's clubby insiders

---

16   I rely here on Andrew Ross's review of *Flash Boys* in the *Guardian* (16 May 2014).

have always enjoyed the advantage of getting better and faster information. Yet the fiction of equal access is necessary to draw the punters into
the casino, and to ensure that the market escapes the fate of being heavily
regulated. Books like Matt Taibbi's *The Divide* attracted much less attention than Lewis's, although Taibbi fully details the record of bankers'
malfeasance and extortion: predatory lenders, crooked collection agents,
illegal foreclosures, PPI rip-offs and other swindles that are considered
business as usual by the finance industry – so that, as Andrew Ross put it
succinctly, the dupes in Lewis's story are the Wall Street brokers and
hedge-fund managers who were outrun by the flash boys. In Taibbi's
book, the victims are the rest of us. Focusing on HFTs thus brings forward
a marginal phenomenon that appears as a specific distortion, thereby
allowing us to adhere to the myth that the market is in itself a balanced
and open mechanism.

But there is yet a third, more fundamental – even 'metaphysical' –
reason. Franco Berardi located the origin of today's uneasiness and
impotence about the exploding speed of the functioning of the big Other
(the symbolic substance of our lives) and the slowness of human reactiv-
ity (due to culture, corporeality, disease, and so on): '[T]he long-lasting
neoliberal rule has eroded the cultural bases of social civilization, which
was the progressive core of modernity. And this is irreversible. We have
to face it.'[17] Are HFTs not an exemplary case of how our brains, our
mental abilities, are no longer synchronous with the functioning of the
social-symbolic system? What happens in those milliseconds is simply
beyond the scope of our normal perception. Agents don't know what goes
on, primarily not because of the immense complexity of the process, but
because what gets enacted there is a kind of minimal self-reflexivity: my
own act (my reaction to the offer, my pressing YES) is inscribed, taken
into account, in what I perceive as the state of things (the price I pay) – I
decide (to buy), and my decision changes the price of what I buy.
Furthermore, far from relying on some kind of mysterious synchronicity,
the HFTs' operation mobilizes precisely the minimal gap between the
virtual digital space and its material embodiment: our spontaneous illusion, while we surf on the web, is that we are in the domain of pure
synchronicity, where contact between all participants is direct – as the
saying goes, when I communicate on the web, it doesn't matter where I
am; my partner can sit in the next room or stand on some Himalayan

---

17   Franco Bifo Berardi, *After the Future* (Oakland, CA: AK, 2011), p. 177.

iceberg. The HFTs' operation demonstrates that it *does* matter where I am – it is a kind of revenge of materialism against the spontaneous idealist illusion that pertains to the digital space.

Effectively, there is a kind of twisted emancipatory potential in what HFTs are doing: to quote Marx, what happens in their operation is a minimal 'expropriation of the expropriators' (stock-market speculators, rich investors . . .) themselves, who are getting their comeuppance. Perhaps *this* is why *Flash Boys* created such a fuss. With HFTs, financial speculation reaches its meaningless pinnacle, bringing out the nonsense that sustains the entire edifice of financial speculations; in this sense, one can say that HFTs are too bright for their own good. The German weekly magazine *Der Spiegel* reported, among the greatest recorded stupidities and blunders of 1998, the case of a German robber who grabbed an old woman's purse while she was taking a photo of herself in an automatic photo booth at a railway station. However, unfortunately for him, one of the usual four photos was taken at exactly the moment he leaned in to snatch the purse, so that his face and hand were clearly discernible on the photo, delivering to the police the direct proof of the crime plus who committed it . . . Isn't it something similar that we encounter with HFTs? Do we not see there the direct proof of how the crime is committed?

But there is an even deeper and properly uncanny dimension in what HFTs are doing. The way they demonstrate how markets are rigged points towards a more fundamental ontological deadlock in which (what we experience as) *reality itself is 'rigged'*, in the sense that we don't perceive it 'objectively' since our act is already inscribed into what we perceive. It is thus as if HFTs do not simply operate in our reality, but intervene into the very mechanism of how we perceive/constitute (what we experience as) reality: the most spontaneous link between action and reaction (I press the YES button on a deal, the deal is immediately confirmed) is already manipulated. And does quantum physics not entertain the same 'riggedness' of reality itself? At its most daring, it seems to allow the momentary suspension, of 'forgetting', of the knowledge in the real. Imagine that you have to take a flight on day *x* to pick up a fortune the next day, but do not have the money to buy the ticket; but then you discover that the accounting system of the airline is such that if you wire the ticket payment within twenty-four hours of arrival at your destination, no one will ever know it was not paid prior to departure. In a homologous way, the energy a particle has can wildly fluctuate so long as this fluctuation is over a short enough time scale. So, just as the accounting system of the airline 'allows' you to 'borrow' the money for a plane ticket provided you pay it back quickly enough, quantum mechanics allows a particle to 'borrow' energy so long it can relinquish it within a time frame determined by Heisenberg's uncertainty principle ... But quantum mechanics forces us to take the analogy one important step further. Imagine someone who is a compulsive borrower and goes from friend to friend asking for money ... Borrow and return, borrow and return – over and over again with unflagging intensity he takes in money only to give it back in short order ... a similar frantic shifting back and forth of energy and momentum is occurring perpetually in the universe of microscopic distance and time intervals.[18]

This is how, even in an empty region of space, a particle emerges out of Nothing, 'borrowing' its energy from the future and paying for it (with its annihilation) before the system notices this borrowing. The whole network can function like this, in a rhythm of borrowing and annihilation, one borrowing from the other, displacing the debt onto the other, postponing the payment of the debt. It is really as if the subparticle domain is playing Wall Street games with futures. What this presupposes is a minimal gap between things in their immediate brute reality and the registration of this reality in some medium (of the big Other): one can cheat insofar as the second is delayed with regard to the first. So, as with HFTs, reality itself (the way we perceive it) is 'rigged' because of things taking place in the imperceptible interstices of time.

This 'riggedness' is not just an ideological blindness; it is grounded in the very material organization of production. Precarious work, which plays a more and more important role in our societies, deprives the worker of a whole series of rights which, until recently, were taken as self-evident in any country that perceived itself as a welfare state: workers have to take care themselves of their health insurance and retirement options; there is no paid leave; the future becomes much more uncertain; precarious work generates an antagonism within the working class between permanently employed and precarious workers (trade unions often tend to privilege permanent workers; it is very difficult for precarious workers even to organize themselves into a union, or establish any other form of

---

18   Brian Greene, *The Elegant Universe* (New York: Norton, 1999), pp. 116–19.

collective self-organization). One would have expected that this strength-ened exploitation would also strengthen workers' resistance, but it renders resistance even more difficult, and the main reason for this is ideological: precarious work is presented (and up to a point even effec-tively experienced) as a new form of freedom: I am no longer just a cog in a complex enterprise, but an entrepreneur-of-the-self; I am a boss of myself who freely manages his/her employment, free to choose new options, to explore different aspects of my creative potentials, to choose my priorities . . .

There is a clear homology between the precarious worker and today's typical consumer of TV and cultural programmes, where we are also as it were ordained to practise freedom of choice:[19] more and more, each of us is becoming the curator of his/her own TV and cultural life, subscribing to programmes we prefer (HBO, History Channel . . .), selecting movies on demand, and so on, according to our own taste, exposed to a freedom of choice for which we are not really qualified, since we are given no orientation, no criteria, and are thus left to the arbitrariness of our bad taste. The role of authorities, models, canons even, is essential here: even when we aim at violating and overturning them, they provide the basic coordinates (orientation points) in the messy landscape of endless choices. In such a totally non-transparent situation, the only way out is often a blind explosion of violence. *Rolling Stone* magazine recently drew the conclusion that imposes itself after the Ferguson incident:

> Nobody's willing to say it yet. But after Ferguson, and especially after the Eric Garner case that exploded in New York after yet another non-indictment following a minority death-in-custody, the police suddenly have a legitimacy problem in this country. Law-enforcement resources are now distributed so unevenly, and justice is being administered with such brazen inconsistency, that people everywhere are going to start questioning the basic political authority of law enforcement.[20]

In such a situation, when the police are no longer perceived as the agent of law, of the legal order, but as just another violent social agent, protests against the predominant social order also tend to take a different turn – that of exploding abstract negativity. When, in *Group Psychology*, Freud

---

19   I rely here on the work of Jela Krečič.
20   Matt Taibbi, 'The Police in America Are Becoming Illegitimate', *Rolling Stone*, 5 December 2014.

describes the 'negativity' of untying social ties (Thanatos as opposed to Eros, the force of the social link), he all too easily dismissed the manifestations of this untying as the fanaticism of the 'spontaneous' crowd (as opposed to artificial crowds: the Church and Army). Against Freud, we should retain the ambiguity of this movement of untying: it is a zero-level that opens up the space for political intervention. In other words, this untying is the pre-political condition of politics, and, with regard to it, every political intervention proper already goes 'one step too far', committing itself to a new project (or Master-Signifier). Today, this apparently abstract topic is relevant once again: the 'untying' energy is largely monopolized by the New Right (the Tea Party movement in the United States, where the Republican Party is increasingly split between Order and its Untying). However, here also, every fascism is a sign of failed revolution, and the only way to combat this rightist untying will be for the left to engage in its own untying – and there are already signs of it (the large demonstrations all around Europe in 2010, from Greece to France and the UK, where the student demonstrations against university fees unexpectedly turned violent). In asserting the threat of 'abstract negativity' to the existing order as a permanent feature that can never be *aufgehoben*, Hegel is here more materialist than Marx: in his theory of war (and of madness), he is aware of the repetitive return of the 'abstract negativity' which violently unbinds social links. Marx re-binds violence into the process out of which a New Order arises (violence as the 'midwife' of a new society), while in Hegel, the unbinding remains non-sublated.

One of the names of this 'abstract negativity' is the 'divine violence' about which Walter Benjamin wrote. In August 2014, violent protests exploded in Ferguson, a suburb of St Louis, Missouri, after a policeman shot to death an unarmed black teenager suspected of robbery: for days, police tried to disperse mostly black protesters. Although the details of the accident are murky, the poor black majority of the town took it as yet another proof of the systematic police violence against them. In the US slums and ghettos, the police effectively function more and more as a force of occupation – something akin to Israeli patrols entering the Palestinian territories on the West Bank. The media were surprised to discover that even their guns are increasingly those used by the US army. Even when police units try just to impose peace, distribute humanitarian help or organize medical measures, their modus operandi is that of controlling a foreign population. Are such 'irrational' violent demonstrations with no concrete programmatic demands, sustained by just a vague call for justice, not today's exemplary cases of divine violence? They are, as Benjamin put it, means without ends, not part of a long-term strategy.

The immediate counter-argument is this: But are such violent demonstrations not often unjust? Do they not hit the innocent? If we are to avoid the overstretched politically correct explanations according to which the victims of divine violence should humbly not resist it on account of their generic historical responsibility, the only solution is simply to accept the fact that divine violence *is* brutally unjust: it is often something terrifying, not a sublime intervention of divine goodness and justice.

A left-liberal friend from the University of Chicago told me of his sad experience. When his son reached high school age, he enrolled him into a school north of the campus, close to a black ghetto, with a majority of black kids. But his son then began returning home almost regularly with bruises or broken teeth – so what should he have done? Put his son into another school with the white majority, or let him stay? The point is that this dilemma is wrong: the dilemma cannot be solved at this level, since the very gap between private interest (safety of my son) and global justice bears witness to a situation which has to be overcome.

If it is to survive, the radical left should thus rethink the basic premises of its activity. We should dismiss not only the two main forms of twentieth-century state socialism (the social-democratic welfare state and the Stalinist party dictatorship) but also the very standard by means of which the radical left usually measures the failure of the first two: the libertarian vision of communism as association, multitude, councils, anti-representationist direct democracy based on citizens' permanent engagement. This perspective is unacceptable for our ordinary democratic stance. No wonder that, in a CUNY debate with Fredric Jameson, Stanley Aronowitz desperately tried to reduce Jameson's utopian idea of universal conscription back to the anti-representationist direct democracy in which people (soldiers) organize themselves in councils, as they do in rebellious people's armies. Such direct democracy is the extreme point of the politicization of the entire society, while Jameson repeatedly emphasizes that his idea of universal conscription aims at the disappearance of the political dimension as such: all that remains in Jameson's utopian society is a militarily (i.e. non-politically) organized economy with no need for the permanent engagement of the people, and the immense – also non-political – domain of cultural pleasures, from sex to art. (The truth we have to embrace is that, if we want to move away from representation towards direct democracy, this direct democracy has always to be supplemented with the non-representational higher power, say, of an 'authoritarian' leader – in Venezuela, Chavez's leadership was the necessary obverse of his attempts to mobilize direct democracy in the *favelas*.)

Berardi warns us against what he calls the Deleuzian 'gospel of hyper-dynamic deterritorialization'. For him, if we are not able to step outside the compulsion of the system, the gap between the frantic dynamics imposed by the system and our corporeal and cognitive limitations sooner or later brings about the fall into depression. Berardi makes this point apropos of Felix Guattari, his personal friend, who, in theory, preached the gospel of hyper-dynamic deterritorialization, while personally suffering long bouts of depression:

> Actually the problem of depression and of exhaustion is never elaborated in an explicit way by Guattari. I see here a crucial problem of the theory of desire: the denial of the problem of limits in the organic sphere . . . The notion of the 'body without organs' hints at the idea that the organism isn't something that you can define, that the organism is a process of exceeding, of going beyond a threshold, of 'becoming other.' This is a crucial point, but it's also a dangerous point . . . What body, what mind is going through transformation and becoming? Which invariant lies under the process of becoming other? If you want to answer this question you have to acknowledge death, finitude, and depression.[21]

Depression, finitude, exhaustion, and so on, are here not empirico-psychological categories, but indications of a basic ontological limitation. When Berardi talks of depression, it is with regard to interpellation proper – i.e. a reaction of the human animal to the Cause which addresses us, specifically with regard to late-capitalist interpellation, but *also* with regard to emancipatory mobilization. The critique of political representation as a passivizing alienation (instead of allowing others to speak for them, people should directly organize themselves into associations) here reaches its limit: the idea of organizing society in its entirety as a network of associations is a utopia that obfuscates a triple impossibility:[22]

1. There are numerous cases in which representing (speaking for) others is a necessity; it is cynical to say that victims of mass violence

---

21   Berardi, *After the Future*, pp. 177–8.
22   I rely here on Rowan Williams's 'On Representation', presented at the colloquium 'The Actuality of the Theologico-Political', Birkbeck School of Law, London, 24 May 2014.

from Auschwitz to Rwanda (and the mentally ill, children, and so on, not to mention suffering animals) should organize themselves and speak for themselves.

2. When we achieve a mass mobilization of hundreds of thousands of people self-organizing horizontally (Tahrir Square, Gezi Park . . .), we should never forget that they remain a minority, and that the silent majority remains outside, non-represented. (This is why, in Egypt, this silent majority defeated the Tahrir square crowd and elected the Muslim Brotherhood.)

3. Permanent political engagement has a limited time-span: after a couple of weeks or, rarely, months, the majority disengages, and the problem is to safeguard the results of the uprising at this moment, when things return to normal.

There is, of course, much to say against political representation. On 1 October 2014, David Cameron made a famous Freudian slip at the Conservative Party conference: enumerating the poor and dispossessed, he concluded with 'this is who we resent' (instead of 'represent'), thereby echoing the famous dialogue from *Citizen Kane* in which Kane is attacked by a rich banker for speaking for the poor in his media, and replies: 'Would you prefer the poor to speak for themselves?' So does the acceptance of representation imply a resigned surrender to the hegemonic power structure? No – there is nothing inherently 'conservative' in being tired of the usual radical leftist demands for permanent mobilization and active participation, demands that follow the superego logic – the more we obey them, the more we are guilty . . . The battle has to be won *here*, in the domain of citizens' passivity, when things return back to normal the morning after ecstatic revolts: it is (relatively) easy to have a big ecstatic spectacle of sublime unity, but how will ordinary people feel the difference in their ordinary daily lives? No wonder conservatives like to see from time to time sublime explosions – they remind people that nothing can really change, that the next day things return to normal.

Index